THE **SLOW FOOD** GUIDE TO
SAN FRANCISCO
AND THE BAY AREA

SLOW FOOD USA MISSION

Slow Food USA works to create a community of people who believe in a better food system. We take action by teaching the value of good food, preserving our endangered foods and traditions, and connecting people at all points along the food chain. Through our programs and with our members, we help Americans forge a deep relationship with the land and each other, laying the foundation for a global society that respects the diversity of the earth and those who cultivate it, providing good, clean, and fair food for all people.

OUR PROGRAMS

Ark of Taste & Presidia, dedicated to identifying and revitalizing foods, farmers, and traditions at risk of extinction.

Renewing America's Food Traditions (RAFT), a partnership of scientists, chefs, and cultural specialists that aims to preserve our country's food biodiversity through eater-based and market-driven approaches.

Slow Food in Schools, a unique program of garden-to-table projects in schools that cultivates the senses and teaches an ecological approach to food.

Terra Madre, an international network of 5,000 food producers from 130 countries, including over 500 producers from the United States, united by a common goal of global sustainability in food.

SLOW FOOD INTERNATIONAL MANIFESTO
Endorsed and approved in 1989 by delegates from 20 countries

Our century, which began and has developed under the insignia of industrial civilization, first invented the machine and then took it as its life model.

We are enslaved by speed and have all succumbed to the same insidious virus: Fast Life, which disrupts our habits, pervades the privacy of our homes and forces us to eat Fast Foods.

To be worthy of the name, *Homo sapiens* should rid himself of speed before it reduces him to a species in danger of extinction.

A firm defense of quiet material pleasure is the only way to oppose the universal folly of Fast Life.

May suitable doses of guaranteed sensual pleasure and slow, long-lasting enjoyment preserve us from the contagion of the multitude who mistake frenzy for efficiency.

Our defense should begin at the table with Slow Food. Let us rediscover the flavors and savors of regional cooking and banish the degrading effects of Fast Food.

In the name of productivity, Fast Life has changed our way of being and threatens our environment and our landscapes. So Slow Food is now the only truly progressive answer.

That is what real culture is all about: developing taste rather than demeaning it. And what better way to set about this than an international exchange of experiences, knowledge, projects?

Slow Food guarantees a better future. Slow Food is an idea that needs plenty of qualified supporters who can help turn this (slow) motion into an international movement, with the little snail as its symbol.

THE **SLOW FOOD** GUIDE TO

SAN FRANCISCO

AND THE BAY AREA

RESTAURANTS, MARKETS, BARS

SYLVAN BRACKETT, SUE MOORE, AND WENDY DOWNING WITH SLOW FOOD USA

CONTRIBUTING EDITORS
Bill Alber
Eleanor Bertino
Alice Cravens
Tatianna Graff
Cristina Salas-Porras
Lorenzo Scarpone
Carmen Tedesco
Jenny Wapner

SERIES EDITORS
Patrick Martins and Ben Watson

Chelsea Green Publishing
WHITE RIVER JUNCTION, VERMONT

Photographs by Aya Brackett, Penny Dedel, Andy Griffin, and Karen Steffen. Photographs copyright 2005.

Book design by Peter Holm, Sterling Hill Productions.

Printed in the United States on recycled paper.
First printing, December 2005.
10 9 8 7 6 5 4 3 2 1

Chelsea Green sees publishing as a tool for cultural change and ecological stewardship. We strive to align our book manufacturing practices with our editorial mission, and to reduce the impact of our business enterprise on the environment. We print our books and catalogs on chlorine-free recycled paper, using soy-based inks, whenever possible. Chelsea Green is a member of the Green Press Initiative (www.greenpressinitiative.org), a nonprofit coalition of publishers, manufacturers, and authors working to protect the world's endangered forests and conserve natural resources. *The Slow Food Guide to San Francisco and the Bay Area* was printed on New Life Opaque, a 30 percent post-consumer-waste recycled, old-growth-forest-free paper supplied by Quebecor.

Cataloging-in-Publication Data is available from the Library of Congress.
ISBN 1-931498-75-X

Chelsea Green Publishing
P.O. Box 428
White River Junction, VT 05001
(800) 639-4099
www.chelseagreen.com

THE SLOW FOOD GUIDE TO
SAN FRANCISCO AND THE BAY AREA

Sylvan Brackett, Wendy Downing, and Sue Moore

Contributing Editors

Bill Alber	Cristina Salas-Porras
Eleanor Bertino	Lorenzo Scarpone
Alice Cravens	Carmen Tedesco
Tatiana Graf	Jenny Wapner

Contributors

Wendella Abrahams	Meesha Halm	Norma & Edmund Ong
Bill Alber	Sarah Hamil	Vito Pasero
Katy Ansite	Allison Hopelain	Purvi Patel
Elizabeth Baker	Judee Humberg	Susan Patton-Fox
Roberto Ballabeni	Niloufer Ichaporia King	Michael Peternell
Jessica Benthien	Valerie Jackson	Tracy Potter
Eleanor Bertino	Kate Jessup	Claire Ptak
John Birdsall	Leslie Jonath	Robert Rich
Nicholas Boer	Carolyn Jung	Randy Robinson
Sylvan Brackett	Jonathan Kauffman	Karola Saekel
Meredith Brody	Phil & Peter Kaufman	Cristina Salas-Porras
Chelsea Chapman	Jason Kibbey	Lorenzo Scarpone
Miles Chen	Peggy Knickerbocker	Kim Severson
Young Whan Choi	David Knopp	Bill Staggs
Priscilla Coe	Michael Kunichika	Leith Steel
Bruce Cole	Chris Lakey	Barb Stuckey
Jane Connors	Robert Lauriston	Emily Su
Alice Cravens	Victoria Libin	Michael Sullivan
Laurie Dill	Hannah Love	Alan Tangren
Wendy Downing	Moyra Mauger	Carmen Tedesco
Mary Durbin	Tom McNamee	Lauren Travis
Philip Ferrato	Michele Meany	Brenda Tucker
Brigid Finley	Sue Moore	Jenny Wapner
Catherine Foo	Russell Moore	Jonathan Waters
Lynn Eve Fortin	Layne Mosler	Sarah Weiner
Michelle Fuerst	Jan Newberry	Frankie Whitman
Jon Gans	Samin Nosrat	Faye Yang
Tatiana Graf	Susan Odell	

Dedicated to the farmers of Northern California

KEY TO SYMBOLS USED IN THIS BOOK

Prices

$ = average entrée or main course costs less than $10
$$ = average entrée or main course costs between $10 and $20
$$$ = average entrée or main course costs between $20 and $30
$$$$ = average entrée or main course costs more than $30

All price symbols are approximations made for comparison's sake only.

Neighborhoods and Suburbs

Neighborhoods within the city limits of San Francisco appear in **bold-face** type, above the street address at the head of each listing. Names of other Bay Area cities and regions are set in ***boldface italics*** and appear below the street adress.

In this book we have designated with the icon of the snail (the Slow Food mascot) those establishments that go above and beyond in their support of the concepts of sustainability and biodiversity, from the producers they buy from through the foods they prepare and sell.

When appropriate, we have also included any special or unusual information in the entries (for instance, "Cash only," "BYOB," or "Closed Monday").

Finally, we have added a "Notable" section of brief listings at the end of most sections. Think of these places as honorable mentions—definitely worthy of inclusion, but perhaps not yet "slow" enough or familiar enough to our reviewers to warrant a full-length entry.

CONTENTS

Introduction / ix

PART FOUR • Outlying Areas

INTRODUCTION

A political and social bubble, birthplace of beatniks, hippies, and foodies, the San Francisco Bay Area is subject to ridicule and awe. It's the far edge of the country in more ways than one. It invites self-reinvention, serves as a refuge for nonconformists, and often suffers from parochial narcissism. It is also blessed with benevolent weather, one of the world's most beautiful natural settings, and an embarrassment of culinary riches from sea to vineyards to pastures and farms. If you are hungry, it is a very good place to be.

The region's first inhabitants were members of several different Native American tribes, loosely united under the common name *Ohlone.* Early explorers and settlers often dismissed the Ohlone as inferior because they were hunters and gatherers rather than farmers and herders. Today we recognize that they were simply wise enough to accept and honor the gifts so bountifully provided by nature. Acorns from the abundant oaks were their staple food, and oysters, abalone, deer, salmon, and waterfowl formed an essential part of their seasonal repasts. Sadly, European and American settlers decimated many native species and forever changed the landscape. Yet the area's rich soils and temperate climate have remained, and these attributes have attracted generations of farmers, ranchers, and fishermen, many of whom approach nature's gifts with a respect for quality, honest enjoyment, and sustainable cultivation and harvesting.

By the early 1970s two strains of food producers began to emerge in the Bay Area, both of them products of the counterculture sixties: back-to-the-land hippies, farming organically; and cooks, most notably Alice Waters, who wanted to recreate a Californian version of the fresh, ingredient-based, nonprocessed cuisines they had enjoyed in Europe. As both groups grew more sophisticated, they recognized their common interests and began to converge. Wormy organic apples gave way to beautiful organic produce; old seed strains were rediscovered and cultivated once more. Organic farmers and chefs forged direct business relationships, and farms were credited on menus beginning with Berkeley's Chez Panisse.

Today, the region is home to a wide range of artisanal cheese producers, organic pasture-based dairy farms, biodynamic and organic farmers of fruits and vegetables, winemakers, bakers of some of the world's best (and even organic) breads, and environmentally conscious fishermen and oyster farmers. Many of these producers sell at the area's extraordinarily popular farmers' markets, which are frequented by locals—home cooks and professional chefs alike—promising spectacular eating both in and out of restaurants. While these producers, with a few exceptions, have not yet received the homage paid to star chefs, they are increasingly acknowledged and thanked by those chefs.

A universal recognition of these producers took place in Turin, Italy, in 2004, at Slow Food's first Terra Madre gathering of "world food communities." There, Slow Food brought together 5,000 caretakers of the earth—small-scale, sustainable farmers, herders, gatherers, and artisans from 130 countries, some of whom had never before left their villages. More than fifty Bay Area delegates attended this historic event, and many are now involved in far-reaching networks launched at the gathering.

The international spirit of Terra Madre is happily echoed in the Bay Area, where immigrant populations continue to bring to this country the culinary traditions of their homelands. These incredibly diverse foods and traditions are showcased every day in the plethora of restaurants and ethnic and specialty food shops that call San Francisco home. This book highlights many of their delicious contributions to the local food community and applauds their "Slow" adherence to tradition, while at the same time encouraging them to reach even further to include more sustainably grown or harvested ingredients.

Sustainably raised foods from local family farms have many benefits. First, they have delicious flavor. Next, the farms themselves provide a greenbelt for urban areas. And, most importantly, they promote individual and environmental health. To paraphrase Michael Pollan, when you purchase food, you are purchasing a landscape. We hope you enjoy our landscape.

—Eleanor Bertino

THE SLOW FOOD GUIDE TO

SAN FRANCISCO

AND THE BAY AREA

PART ONE

CUISINES

AFGHAN

De Afghanan Kabob House

37405 Fremont Boulevard

Fremont   *EAST BAY*

(510) 745-9599

$

Although Fremont is home to the largest Afghan population in the United States, you must look carefully while driving down Fremont Avenue to realize you've entered "Little Kabul." The streets are wide, open, and decidedly suburban. But hidden away, next to a church-turned-movie-theater, De Afghanan Kabob House feels worlds away. A monstrous grill dominates the room at this bare-bones take-out restaurant. The menu is simple, and the kebabs (long metals skewers of chicken, lamb, beef, and a spicy mixture of ground beef called *chapli*) are put on the grill when you order. Due to the line out the door, a half hour might pass before your meat arrives, hot and slightly charred, accompanied by a sour chickpea salad, rice, and wonderful Afghan bread baked across the street at Pamir market. Be sure to order the *boulani*, a beautiful leek- or potato-stuffed turnover. For better or worse, word has spread about this place, so if your Farsi is up to snuff, you may want to call ahead to avoid the wait.

The Helmand

North Beach

430 Broadway, at Montgomery Street

(415) 362-0641

$$

Owned by the family of Afghanistan's head of state, Hamid Karzai, The Helmand is an ode to all things Afghan. Photos of Afghanistan and its people line the walls, and with its carpeted, white-tablecloth dining room, it couldn't feel farther away from the crowds on Broadway. It's the perfect place for a quiet conversation, and the waiters are gracious and the prices are more than reasonable.

Flat bread from an Afghan bakery in Fremont arrives at the table when you sit. Start with *aushak* (dumplings of melted leeks with garlic-yogurt and mint sauces) or the *kaddo chello* (pumpkin seasoned with sugar and served with ground-beef sauce). *Challow* (a traditional rice preparation seasoned with cumin) and *pallow* (a similar dish with the addition of cardamom, cinnamon, nutmeg, and black pepper) appear throughout the menu. You might also try the *seekh kabob*, leg of lamb marinated in pureed onion, cooked with eggplant, and served with *pallow*, or the *koufta challow*, with beef meatballs, sun-dried tomatoes, hot peppers, and peas. There are many vegetarian offerings, and wines are available both by the glass and by the bottle.

Kabul Afghan Restaurant

833 West El Camino Real
Sunnyvale   SOUTH BAY
(408) 245-4350
$–$$

Reputedly the first Afghan restaurateur in the country, Ali Taheri is a master at introducing his native cuisine to an American clientele. The walls are decorated with rugs and weavings sent from his family, photographs of Afghan tribesmen, and deep rose-colored carpeting. Soft Afghan music plays in the background.

Belying its name, the menu at Kabul offers an assortment of traditional Afghan foods from all over the country, not just the region surrounding the capital city. Favorite appetizers include *sambosa egoushti* (fried pastries filled with ground lamb and chickpeas) and *aushak* (leek dumplings with garlic-yogurt and mint sauces). Kebab dishes are well represented, and for your entrée you might choose skewered prawns, or cubes of tender marinated grilled chicken, beef, or lamb, served over a bed of *challow* or *pallow*. The lamb and beef stews with tomato, spinach, eggplant, peppers, and spices are delicious. You could also opt for a traditional vegetarian dish like the sautéed pumpkin with yogurt sauce.

And you can't leave without trying an Afghan sweet such as *goush e feel* (fried pastry in the shape of an elephant ear, dusted with cardamom, sugar, and pistachios) and *firnee* (a cardamom- and rose water–flavored milk pudding topped with pistachios).

Paradise Restaurant

1350 Grant Road, at Phyllis Street
Mountain View   SOUTH BAY
(650) 968-5949
$–$$

Once known for its fertile orchards and fields, Afghanistan and its neighboring regions are the native home of pistachios, almonds, apricots, and pomegranates. The owners, Afghan-born chef Nick Waziri and his wife, Faima, run this charming Afghan and Persian restaurant, improbably located in the Grand Plaza shopping center.

Dishes like the *fesenjon* (diced chicken breast cooked with walnuts in a pomegranate sauce) showcase the ingredients of the owners' native land, and the *gormeh sabzi* (marinated steak kebabs) and *chello kadu* (sautéed pumpkin topped with homemade yogurt) provide plenty to entice meat-and-potatoes lovers and vegetarians alike. Or you might try the *mourgh challow*, with chicken breast and yellow split peas in a glorious saffron tomato sauce with subtle Afghan spices, served over grain rice.

The "Persian iced tea" is indiscernible from regular iced tea. For something different opt for a *sharbat*, the Persian take on Italian soda, made with sour cherry or mint syrup.

AFRICAN

Asmara *(Ethiopian)*

5020 Telegraph Avenue
Oakland   *EAST BAY*
(510) 547-5100
Closed Monday
$

Okba Yohannes, a nationally recognized chef in Ethiopia, emigrated to California in the early 1980s and opened Asmara restaurant in Oakland's Temescal district in 1985 with her husband, Kesete. Although the interior is showing its age, Asmara is still a haven for the substantial Ethiopian and Eritrean community in the area.

Specialties at Asmara include *shiro,* or roasted and ground peas cooked in *berbere,* the thick red spice paste that is an essential element of Ethiopian cooking. Stew, or *wat,* comes with chicken, beef, lamb, or vegetables and can be made spicy or mild. *Doro wat,* a type of chicken stew, is another traditional dish done especially well at Asmara: lemon-marinated chicken is highly seasoned with *berbere* and then stewed until the meat is falling off the bone. While the chicken is fork-tender, some of the lamb and beef dishes can be a little tougher, since the traditional cuts of meat for most dishes made at Asmara are not as fatty as they are in Western cooking. If chewy meat is a problem, stick with the chicken and vegetables.

All dishes are served with *injera,* a sourdough flatbread made by fermenting a grain called *teff* and then cooking it like a pancake on a grill. The bread is used in lieu of utensils to scoop up meats and vegetables and soak up any extra juices. *Tej,* icy honey wine, is especially sweet and offers crisp relief to both those unaccustomed and familiar with the burning induced by the fiery *berbere.*

 Aziza *(Moroccan)*

Outer Richmond

5800 Geary Boulevard, at 22nd Avenue
(415) 752-2222
Closed Tuesday
$$

At his restaurant, Aziza, chef and owner Mourad Lahlou, a native of Marrakesh, combines time-honored Moroccan techniques with top-notch local, organic ingredients. The results of this happy marriage are dishes that are lighter and more vibrant than renditions found elsewhere. Witness Lahlou's chicken *bastilla,* made with minced Hoffman chicken, pine nuts, and sweet spices in phyllo dough. The dish is flaky, moist, and beautifully seasoned and made with the chicken that is arguably the best in the Bay Area. The lamb tagine might come with Watson Ranch lamb— meat that occasionally plays a starring role at Chez Panisse. The tender hand-rolled couscous is a revelation. The menu also strays from the classics, with dishes like California white sea bass with *charmoula* or Paine Farm squab with wild mushrooms and *ras el hanout,* a reduction-of-thyme. While dishes likes these are more Californian than Moroccan, Lahlou always references his native cuisine.

The restaurant has a full bar and an impressive list of house cocktails and beers. They serve a great range of wines that pair well with a traditionally nonalcoholic cuisine.

Cafe Colucci *(Ethiopian)*
6427 Telegraph Avenue
Oakland **EAST BAY**
(510) 601-7999
$$

The heart of Ethiopian cuisine is *injera,* the soft sourdough flatbread that serves triple duty as plate, starch, and eating utensil. And Cafe Colucci makes some of the best *injera* in the Bay Area, using teff (a type of millet) flour fermented with local wild yeast. Whatever you order, it's served family-style on a big *injera*-covered platter, with a basket of extra bread on the side.

The vegetable side of the menu includes lentil stew spiced with *berbere* (a spice mix akin to Indian *garam masala,* but spiked with hot pepper) and *bessobela* (an Ethiopian variety of basil); split peas cooked with fenugreek and basil; sautéed seasonal greens; lentil salad flavored with *senafitch* (Ethiopian mustard), jalapeños, and lemon juice; and *buticha* (fava bean powder mixed with a sort of spicy vinaigrette, resulting in a tofulike consistency).

The meat side of the menu includes a chicken leg or two sautéed in butter and *berbere* seasoning; bone-in chunks of chicken in a mild ginger-garlic sauce; a very spicy lamb stew; and beef simmered with ginger and turmeric. Adventurous eaters should try *kitfo,* the Ethiopian version of steak tartare, or *doulet,* a similar dish made with a combination of beef, lamb tripe, and lamb liver.

Before ordering a carafe of the house-made *tej,* or mead (Ethiopian honey wine), try a glass. The brew always has an intense honey flavor, but quality is variable: sometimes fresh and fruity, other times a bit funky, like real ale from the bottom of the keg.

The Lunch Box
(Ethiopian)

1876 San Carlos Street
San Jose **SOUTH BAY**
(408) 287-3511
Limited street parking
$

The Lunch Box is a tiny, low-key café that's almost invisible in a transitional neighborhood on busy San Carlos Street, a few blocks south of Bascom. Inside you'll find seven wooden tables, plastic booths, and metal chairs on a white linoleum floor. Ethiopian pop music percolates from a TV above the fridge. The service is slow here, so don't expect to drop in for a quick bite.

The customers are mostly Ethiopian, and a familiar community vibe pervades the room. Husband-and-wife owners Ferede Negash and Lielti Mesfin greet all comers warmly and serve them like family. Most dishes start with spiced clarified butter (called *nit'ir qibe* or *kibbeh*). Spices like turmeric, fenugreek, cardamom, cloves, and cumin are then added, along with ginger, onions, garlic, and other seasonings. The mixture simmers for fifteen minutes to fully integrate the flavors, and the resulting oil provides a deeply complex bed of flavors that guides the direction of every dish.

Beef is clearly the meat of choice, but it is the vegetarian dishes that really provide the foundation for most meals. Among the favorites is *gomen* (soft collard greens with minced garlic, onions, and sweet peppers), which has a delicious smoky fragrance. Staples include *miser kik* (a spicy red lentil sauce with strips of fresh hot peppers), *ater kik* (a similar dish using chickpeas), and *miten shiro,* made with roasted powdered chickpeas. *Alicha atkilt* is a mild savory blend of cabbage, carrots, potatoes, and onions.

With its authentic and expertly prepared food, The Lunch Box deserves a trek off the proverbial beaten path.

NOTABLE

Al Masri
(Egyptian)

Outer Sunset
4031 Balboa Street, at 41st Avenue
(415) 876-2300
Closed Monday to Wednesday
$$$$

On the outskirts of Balboa Avenue a colorful mirage rises from the stucco monotony of mid-sixties developments: Egyptian hieroglyphics and a bright cobalt blue awning beckon you to Al Masri. Open the door and enter a kitschy, handwrought ambience. Brightly painted murals adorn the walls; tablecloths with prints of sphinxes and pyramids drape the tables; flickering candles light the room; and pulsating Middle Eastern music entices you to stand up and join the belly dancers.

The food here is worthy of a pharaoh: *samak mahshi* (baked seasonal fish stuffed with sautéed onions and pine nuts, finished in a tamarind-ginger sauce), falafels made with fava bean, and *kufta* (tender lamb kebabs). The waitstaff and management are attentive and knowledgeable in every detail, from food to Egyptian culture. The Isis room, decorated with cushions and low tables, is a private party oasis that can accommodate up to fifteen people.

Axum Cafe   *(Ethiopian/Eritrean)*
Lower Haight
698 Haight Street
(415) 252-7912
$

This simply furnished café earns its reputation as one of the top places in San Francisco for Ethiopian fare with its *injera* and *tibsie,* and at a great price-to-quality ratio. While two people can feast sumptuously on their platter of all five vegetarian dishes, the delicious lamb *tibsie* (lamb sautéed with an earthy combination of jalapeño, garlic, tomato, and "authentic Ethiopian" spices) complements the meal nicely. *Tej* (Ethiopian honey wine) is offered by the glass, and there are several California beers on tap, as well as two bottled Ethiopian beers.

Other Location
1233 Polk Street; (415) 474-7743

AMERICAN

Acme Chophouse
SOMA

24 Willie Mays Plaza, adjacent to SBC Global Park
(415) 644-0240
Closed Monday, except for game days; dinner only, except for
  afternoon game days
$$$$

When star chef Traci Des Jardins came up to the plate as operator of a steak house at SBC Park, fans of both Des Jardins and the Giants had trepidations, but she hit one out of the park. Serving only carefully sourced, naturally raised meats, including grass-fed beef from Marin Sun Farms, she deliciously allayed the fears of carnivores who don't put their trust in the USDA, while perfectly cooked steaks, chops, and burgers won over ballpark traditionalists. Fresh local seafood—Dungeness crab, oysters, wild salmon—are seasonally on the menu, as are a variety of sides that are the best of their genre: macaroni and cheese, onion rings and fries, creamed spinach, scalloped potatoes.

While Acme and its lively bar are packed on game nights, it's more comfortably popular on nongame nights. On occasion, "Taste the Difference" dinners are featured to focus on hot-button food topics, including grass-fed beef; fishing, aquaculture, and ocean conservation; hog production; and the current state of organic farming. The evening's congenial format consists of a panel discussion by producers, scientists, and journalists accompanied by wine and hors d'oeuvres, followed by a dinner featuring the evening's discussed ingredients. Chef de Cuisine Thom Fox pulls out all the stops for these dinners, and the combination of knowledge, delicious food, and conviviality is a delightful embodiment of the principles of Slow Food.

Blue Plate
Mission

3218 Mission Street, at 29th Street
(415) 282-6777
Closed Sunday
$$–$$$

When did *soil* become *dirt*? My guess is that it happened about the same time that the "neighborhood" restaurant started serving sea bass from Chile, apples from China, and lamb from New Zealand. But Cory Obenour's Blue Plate has reclaimed the neighborhood with this lively

Outer Mission restaurant. Almost any night you can see one of Obenour's farmer friends coming in through the front door with a case of produce picked that morning, and you can be sure something from that case will appear on your plate.

Duck is on the menu almost every day, but the vegetables that tenderly support its breast will tip you off instantly to what season it is. In February sweet roasted turnips set off the succulent Liberty Farm legs cooked confit style. In late April the first favas glisten on the plate. And I can't wait for June, when peaches make their first blushing appearance in this dish. One thing's for certain: Rick Knoll's figs, perhaps the best in California, will be featured nightly as soon as their skins are bursting with ripe juices.

And speaking of Rick Knoll, Obenour recently spent a night sleeping on the *soil* of Knoll's farm to get a true sense of *terroir*. The crowd is young, the dining room loud, and on those rare warm nights, try for a table in the back garden.

Casa Orinda
20 Bryant Way, at Moraga Street
Orinda   *EAST BAY*
(925) 254-2981
$$

On first walking into Casa Orinda I braced myself for the fumes of long-spilled bourbon and old cigarette smoke that normally accompany genuine cowboy decor. However, upon further investigation I noticed that the moose head mounted on the wall was preternaturally free of dust and that the flower arrangements were more reminiscent of Chez Panisse than Dodge City.

The Casa, as it is locally known, has been in operation since 1932 and run for the last twenty-five years or so by John Goyak, a native of the environs, whose father bought it from the original owner. Like the decor, the menu is historic but fresh, utilizing free-range chicken, hormone-free beef, fresh fish, and a good deal of locally grown produce. The dishes range from old cowboy favorites, like large, juicy steaks and arguably the Bay Area's best fried chicken (with mashed potatoes, gravy, and biscuits), to Italian-American favorites of the 1950s and '60s, like chicken cacciatore, excellent cannelloni, veal cutlets, and veal piccata. Prices are reasonable, portions are more than generous, and the waitstaff is reassuringly seasoned, no-nonsense, and mostly female. One note of caution: This place is very popular, so reserve ahead.

Chow
Castro
215 Church Street, at Market Street
(415) 552-2469

Second Location
Park Chow
Inner Sunset
1240 9th Avenue, between Lincoln and Irving Streets
(415) 665-9912
$-$$

With its long wooden counter and comfortable tables, Chow feels like a small-town family restaurant. The town in this instance is San Francisco, so the place is reliably packed with couples from the Castro and pierced denizens of the Mission, some of whom come several times a week for an honest meal at an honest price. In fact, the genius of Chow is Chef Tony Gullisino's commitment to good ingredients and savvy in keeping tabs low.

The all-American Fulton Valley Chicken with Mashed Potatoes and Cranberry Sauce makes people feel instantly at home. The Meyer Ranch Short Ribs are meltingly tender—perfect comfort food that could easily serve two. You'll also find one-time foreign favorites, now American classics, like lasagna and Chinese chicken salad. And after the Ginger Cake with Pumpkin Ice Cream and Caramel Sauce you'll feel as if you've just finished Thanksgiving dinner.

Park Chow is also a great option while visiting Golden Gate Park.

Duarte's
202 Stage Road, at Pescadero Road
Pescadero   *SOUTH BAY*
(650) 879-0464
$$-$$$

It's not often that folks get misty-eyed over soup and pie, but they do when it's Duarte's fabled Cream of Green Chile Soup and its incomparable Olallieberry Pie. This restaurant is a rustic landmark, now run by the fourth generation of Duartes *(DOO-arts),* and it has more than stood the test of time. In 2003 it was even honored as an "American Classic" by the James Beard Foundation.

It all started in 1894 when Great-grandfather Frank Duarte opened a bar here with just one barrel of whiskey from Santa Cruz. One shot of whiskey was ten cents in those days; three were two bits (twenty-five cents). Business was good until Prohibition forced the bar to close.

In 1934 the second generation of Duartes reopened the bar and added a soda fountain, barbershop, and sandwich menu. That's when Grandma Duarte started baking the pies that would make the place famous. In the 1950s, with the third generation of Duartes at the helm, artichoke dishes were added to the lineup, as was crab cioppino, which became another house specialty. In the mid-1980s the fourth generation took over, revamping the restaurant's kitchen.

Of course, the seafood at this coastal café is always fresh, as are the vegetables, many of which are grown in the garden behind the restaurant. Look for deep-fried smelt, fresh local cracked Dungeness crab, sand dabs, octopus stew, and abalone sandwich with fries. For non–seafood lovers, there's also New York steak, linguiça sandwiches, and pork chops with fresh applesauce. Call one day in advance to order a whole pie, although the Duartes usually bake a few extra olallieberry each day. After all, they've known for a long time that folks just can't get enough.

Liberty Café
Bernal Heights

410 Cortland Avenue, between Bennington and Wool Streets
(415) 695-1223
Closed Monday
$$

Eating at Liberty Café is a little like going to an old friend's house for dinner. The comfortable dining room feels like the living room, and when the chicken pot pie arrives all puffed up and steaming, you'll wonder if you can move in.

Liberty doesn't take reservations, so it's best to arrive before 7:30 P.M. to avoid a wait. If you miss that window, go two doors down to the Wild Side West bar, shoot some pool, and someone will call when your table is ready. This teamwork reveals a bit of the spirit of the Bernal Heights neighborhood. Being somewhat isolated from the rest of the city, merchants and neighbors tend to stick together. If it's Thursday through Sunday, you can also pass time at the wine bar in the back, which doubles as a bakery and coffee bar by day.

The cuisine is classic American, by way of California: local and seasonal ingredients, treated with respect and lots of olive oil. The Caesar salad and the pot pie—both the chicken and vegetarian versions—are a constant, while the rest of the menu changes on the first Tuesday of every month.

Every meal starts with a bread basket filled with the day's bake, showing off owner-founder Cathie Guntli's affinity for the staff of life. A recent visit offered a plate of superthin *haricots vert* with cherry tomatoes and toasted bread crumbs, and pan-seared halibut with couscous and mint. The wine list is short and sweet, with enough good choices that it's hard to decide what to pick.

Sam's Grill & Seafood Restaurant
Financial District
374 Bush Street, between Kearny and Montgomery Streets
(415) 421-0594
Closed Saturday and Sunday
$$

At one point not long ago, Sam's Grill, Tadich Grill, and Jack's Bar & Grill made up the Holy Trinity of the Chapels of the Three-Martini Business Lunch. At Sam's, evensong began at 11:30 A.M., because Sam's wouldn't take reservations, and if you hoped to get a table you had better get there early. Services commenced with holy water—gin, not vodka. Having a martini before noon seems inconceivable today, but back then it was commonplace. But that was a different time, a time before the Internet, even before the fax machine. People didn't speed-date or work out at the gym. It was a time when people could and did conduct complicated business transactions while drinking a lot of hard liquor at lunch. Then they napped.

We're happy to report that things at Sam's are pretty much the same today. No one's drinking martinis at noontime, of course, and only a few have wine; most drink water. That was what Walter, our veteran waiter, told us recently with a sigh. But people do still have a nip at dinner. We did and can attest that the martinis are top-notch. The Caesar salad is excellent, the crab Louie with its homemade dressing still holds forth, and the sautéed sand dabs and petrale sole with homemade tartar are still tasty. The decor hasn't changed much, either. The dark wood paneling with the brass coat hooks has another layer of patina, the pictures of the trout and the hunting dogs are a bit more faded, and indiscretions still occur behind the curtains of the private booths.

It is and always has been a union shop; the owner comes in at 5:30 A.M. to take care of the books, and if it gets hectic at lunch, he's not above busing tables. It can take seven years to earn the title of waiter, and the waiters that serve the private booths have been there for thirty years (as have some of the dishwashers). So, if tradition means anything to you, a trip to Sam's is mandatory—quick, before anything changes.

Town Hall
SOMA
342 Howard Street
(415) 908-3900
$$$

Chef partners Mitch and Steven Rosenthal and famed mâitre d' Doug Washington have lit up an old South of Market brick warehouse and turned it into one of the liveliest dining and imbibing scenes in San Francisco. The menu is welcoming and combines a West Coast sensibility with East Coast ingredients prepared with a strong Southern flair. You'll see touches of the South in starters like Barbecued Shrimp with Worcestershire and Parsley Garlic Sauce, Tuna Tartar with Fried Green Tomatoes, and Warm Bakewell Cream Biscuits with Smithfield Ham and Pepper Jam. Hearty entrées include Sautéed Day-Boat Scallops with Smoked Andouille Sausage, jambalaya, and Cedar-Planked Wild King Salmon with Corn and Shrimp Hash and Hush Puppies.

The desserts are as comforting as they are sumptuous, particularly the butterscotch *pot de crème*, with its layers of rich, creamy butterscotch and chocolate. And the Best Hot Chocolate, made with thirteen types of chocolate, rich and puddinglike, lives up to its billing.

A varied and elegant wine list comprises both international and Californian wines, some of which are biodynamically grown, and a comprehensive list of beer and ale rounds out the dining experience at what is what is rapidly becoming a San Francisco institution.

NOTABLE

Chenery Park
Glen Park
683 Chenery Street, at Diamond Street
(415) 337-8537
$$–$$$

Bringing big-city savoir faire to the sleepy residential neighborhood of Glen Park, Chenery Park offers locals intelligent service and revved-up, yet reasonably priced renditions of all-American comfort food, just like mom used to make. That is, of course, if your mom trained under Boulevard's Nancy Oakes and New Orleans legend Paul Prudhomme, as Chef-Owners Richard Rosen and Gaines Dobbins did. In addition to classics such as macaroni and cheese, beef brisket with bourbon-braised cabbage, seafood gumbo, and other Southern-inspired specials, the restaurant also hosts

Tuesday Family Nights, when the top floor is reserved for budding Julia Childs who slurp root beer floats and Beef-a-Roni while their parents sip an expertly prepared Manhattan before tucking into the porcini pappa-radelle Bolognese.

The House of Chicken 'n' Waffles

444 Embarcadero West (Jack London Square)
Oakland   *EAST BAY*
(510) 836-4446
Open Sunday through Thursday 8:00 A.M. to midnight; Friday and
   Saturday to 4:00 A.M.
$–$$

The menu looks long here, with some three dozen numbered combination plates, all bearing a homey name (Mimi's Potluck, Billy's Best), and illustrated in a painted mural that looks like blown-up Polaroids of the dish's namesakes, holding their favorites in their hands. But careful reading reveals that most of them are slight variations on the two specialties here: fried chicken (excellent) and waffles (ask for them crisp; otherwise they come out a trifle pale) with the possible additions of eggs, grits, vegetables (black-eyed peas and collard greens, all cooked with smoked turkey instead of pork), or corn bread or biscuits. They also do chicken livers and giblets, fried or smothered in a thick, dark gravy. The room is an immaculate take on a 1950s coffee shop, with lavender-upholstered booths and colorful *Sputnik* light fixtures.

Lark Creek Inn

234 Magnolia Avenue
Larkspur   *MARIN*
(415) 924-7766
$$$

Located just thirty-five minutes north of San Francisco, the Lark Creek Inn is Bradley Ogden's first of five restaurants. This Bay Area favorite continues to prepare updated renditions of American favorites.

Located in a small grove of redwood trees, the converted old Victorian house is the perfect setting for Sunday brunch. It has a dressy but comfortable feel to it, with a great patio to enjoy Marin's fantastic weather. The staff is efficient yet personable, with many longtime employees. A wood-burning oven turns out excellent flat breads and other daily specials. The bar is lively and offers a great abbreviated menu.

Moose's

North Beach
1652 Stockton Street, at Filbert Street
(415) 989-7800
$$$

Home of Old Guard liberal politicos and journalists, Moose's has a boy's club ambience, great bartenders, and a beautiful view of Washington Square Park in North Beach. Legendary host Ed Moose, originally owner of Washington Square Bar & Grill, is around most nights. The food, contemporary American emphasizing seasonal ingredients, holds its own in the restaurant's comfortably elegant room. In a tip of the hat to its venerable history, a Moose Burger (made with Niman Ranch beef) is always available. There's also a piano jazz trio nightly and a great Sunday brunch.

Tadich Grill

Financial District
240 California Street, between Battery and Front Streets
(415) 391-1849
Closed Sunday
$$–$$$

Tadich Grill is the perfect place to go to drink your meal, especially if you're in the mood for martinis that are expertly made by the seasoned bar staff. There may not be better scenery in which to take a martini than sitting (or standing, as is often the case) at the bar at Tadich's. It's a last stand of old San Francisco—tiled floor, polished wooden bar, brass adornments, communal coatrack, and private dining booths. Oh, and curmudgeonly service. A highly refined curmudgeonliness, to be sure—slightly surly and detached, yet engaging—which seems to be an oral tradition handed down from generation to generation of Tadich waitstaff. It's only so you don't misbehave. After all, this place has a history dating back to Gold Rush days; someone had to impose law and order.

Some items on the menu have similarly passed the test of time, including the pan-fried sand dabs, the crab Louie, and the crab and avocado salad. You might come to Tadich Grill for a drink, for the atmosphere, or even for the attitude.

Tita's Hale Aina
Castro
3870 17th Street, between Noe and Sanchez Streets
(415) 626-2477
Closed Monday
$$

If you're in need of a little aloha spirit (and who isn't on a cold, foggy San Francisco summer night?), then Tita's Hale Aina is the place. A tropical fluorescent green light glows from the windows, bougainvillea crowns the doorway, and the aroma of their slow-roasted Kahlua pig lures you in. And this is some pig. First, it's seasoned with Hawaiian salt, then smoked, wrapped in banana leaves, and roasted for twelve hours. The meat is fall-apart tender and delicious, served with macaroni salad and boiled cabbage. They are open for weekend brunch, and on the last Friday of each month, there is live music and *lau laus* (ti tree leaf–wrapped meat and fish) are on the menu.

Washington Square Bar & Grill
North Beach
1707 Powell Street, at Union Street
(415) 982-8123
$$

The Washington Square Bar & Grill is more of a bar with a restaurant than a restaurant with a bar. A San Francisco institution and lunchtime meeting place for power brokers under original owner Ed Moose, the affectionately nicknamed "Washbag" still displays Moose's sports memorabilia and offers a great certified Angus hamburger as well as a delicious duck confit. The best seats are at the bar, for eating or drinking. The cocktails are strictly professional, and the bartenders are among the city's best.

CALIFORNIA

The term "California cuisine" has so many bad connotations that we were reluctant to use the designation at all in this guide. However, over the past thirty or so years it has become hard to deny that California cuisine, though certainly too immature to be considered a cuisine in the Slow world, does have some definite characteristics.

First, the very region where this cuisine was formed is blessed with unbelievably rich soil, moistened by the winds of the Pacific and sustained by much sun. The bounty produced in this Mediterranean climate is so diverse that the chefs of California are able to reproduce almost every cuisine on the planet, modifying the recipes with local and seasonal ingredients. A single California cuisine menu does not strictly adhere to any one culinary tradition, but it respects each tradition it utilizes. Not the wacky fusion food of the 1980s, not the oversauced Continental cuisine of earlier decades, the California style respects the integrity of techniques developed over centuries, be they Italian, French, Spanish, North African, Indian, Southeast Asian, or Japanese. Chefs here have created intimate and long-term relationships with the area's best organic family farms, and many chefs are regulars at the best farmers' markets—ensuring that what is grown in this spectacular climate is worthy of a spectacular dining experience.

The fact that San Francisco and the West Coast were the final steps on the westward march toward fulfilling this country's "manifest destiny" allowed chefs here a certain freedom to create their own culinary style. As a result you will find in San Francisco, more than in any other city, a cuisine that embraces the most sophisticated classical cooking techniques as well as home cooking served in a homegrown decor. Both styles share a dedication to freshness, a respect for the earth's bounty, and informed creativity in the kitchen.

 BayWolf
3853 Piedmont Avenue
Oakland   *EAST BAY*
(510) 655-6004
$$

At thirty-five, Michael Wild left his university teaching job to form a restaurant modeled after the Cheeseboard Collective in Berkeley, a decision he to this day calls "an existential leap." Still located in a renovated Oakland Victorian, though no longer a collective, BayWolf has a message that is pure and dependable. To Wild, his restaurant is a confirmation of Old World values, an idealized home that envisions socializing around the table with family and friends as a necessity of life. To three decades of loyal customers, however, BayWolf itself is one of life's necessities.

Wild often stands in the doorway between the outside veranda and the two artful dining rooms, greeting guests and taking them to their tables. Of course, you might also run into him at Monterey Market on Saturdays, and years ago you could see him driving away from Chinatown with a car-load of ducks—BayWolf's signature dish. These days the ducks are delivered, but they are still cooked to perfection.

Initiate yourself with the duck liver flan served with pickled onions and grilled bread. Sit outside for lunch with a glass of BayWolf Chardonnay and a salad of grilled wild salmon with saffron rice. The duck leg might be served with a reduced red wine–blackberry sauce, while the Provençal-style seafood stew will transport you to the mouth of some distant bay.

All around are signs of warmth. From the wine list to the gentle attention of the staff, BayWolf has long taken great care of its customers.

Boulette's Larder
See Ethnic & Specialty Markets, page 247.

Boulevard
Embarcadero

One Mission Street
(415) 543-6084
$$$$

When Golden Gaters want a big night out, they head to Boulevard. Voted most popular by *Zagat Survey* for seven consecutive years, Boulevard is a San Francisco institution.

Housed in the historic Audiffred Building along the Embarcadero, the restaurant is a collaboration between chef Nancy Oakes and famed designer Pat Kuleto, whose dazzling, some say dizzying, interior conjures up the Belle Epoque with hand-blown art nouveau glass light fixtures, pressed tin ceilings, steel girders, and artisan-made ironwork throughout. The dining room is divided into three intimate areas: a boisterous, see-and-be-seen front bar, the centrally located exhibition kitchen with counter seating, and an elevated back dining room with picture windows affording stunning views of the Bay Bridge.

Equally bold and artful are Oakes's large, lusty plates of seasonally driven, French-influenced cuisine. Although her food exhibits a passion for meat (she's married to nationally acclaimed sausage maker Bruce Aidells), Oakes's menu pays homage to the bounty of the Pacific and to Northern California's farms and ranches, and the accompanying sides and garnishes are as inventive and integral to the dish as what's on the center of the plate. On a recent menu sautéed Sonoma foie gras came with hazelnut pancakes and a blood orange salad, and wood oven–roasted heritage Berkshire pork chops were served with corn spoon bread and spicy pecans.

Rounding out the experience is a smooth-as-silk professional waitstaff; an awe-inspiring wine list, crammed with everything from cult California cabernets to lesser-known boutique producers; and gargantuan send-ups of American comfort desserts, such as Pineapple Upside-Down Babycake topped with Pineapple Sherbet and Vanilla Ice Cream Swirl. Of course, a meal at Boulevard doesn't come cheap, and reservations aren't easily made, but for the complete dining-out package (style, substance, and service) without all the pretense of other top-drawer spots, it's without rival.

Café Rouge
1782 Fourth Street, at Delaware Street
Berkeley   *EAST BAY*
(510) 525-1440
$$–$$$

Berkeleyites frequently refer to Café Rouge as the East Bay's answer to Zuni Café, and the comparison is apt: Chef Marsha McBride cooked at Zuni for nine years before crossing the bridge to start her own place. Like Zuni, Café Rouge has a hopping bar scene, a great raw bar, a cooking style focused on finding the best ingredients and maximizing their flavor, and customers filling the place with a happy buzz.

The butcher counter at the back (see Meat & Fish Markets, page 285.) sets the theme for the restaurant. The starters always include a sampler of the house-made charcuterie, and the entreés are dominated by birds and roasts from the rotisserie. You might also find a dry-aged Niman Ranch steak or two. If you're lucky there might be a two- or three-way combo on the menu, such as a pork plate of braised belly, barbecued ribs, and grilled sausage, or a lamb plate of sautéed chops, braised shoulder, and grilled *merguez* (sausage).

Despite the meaty focus, the most exciting food at Rouge could be the *tians,* ragouts, and other vegetable side dishes that accompany the meat entrées. A lamb *pot-au-feu* once came with a dumpling of morel spoon bread wrapped in a chard leaf and simmered in stock. The kitchen puts out some memorable fish too, such as a recent halibut *pithivier:* a fillet on a bed of greens, morels, and butter, baked in puff pastry, and served in a pool of beurre blanc. For dessert, the more classic and American, the better—think lemon meringue or banana cream pie, or seasonal fruit crisp.

Like a few other chefs in the Slow Food vanguard, McBride and her staff cure anchovies and olives, salt cod, preserve lemons, make limoncello, brandy fruit, and make jam in season. Café Rouge gets eggs, raw olives, and occasionally goat direct from McBride's cousin, Jeannie McCormack, who still owns four thousand acres in nearby Rio Vista, where their great-grandfather settled a century ago. Indirectly McCormack also provides the restaurant's lamb, as a supplier to Niman Ranch—whose pork, not coincidentally, comes from her Peace Corps buddy Paul Willis.

A tip: Café Rouge is frequented mostly by early-to-bed locals, so even on weekends the dinner rush starts to wind down around 8:30 P.M. Consequently you can usually call during the day and get a late reservation for that evening.

Canteen
Union Square
817 Sutter Street
(415) 928-8870
Dinner seatings at 6:00 P.M., 7:30 P.M. and 9:15 P.M.
Closed for dinner Sunday–Tuesday
$$

The first thing you see is the cheery green counter. Then you see the inviting banquettes. It's a diner, but not a diner upon closer inspection. No diner that I can recall kept bookshelves above the booths, let alone stocked with hardbacks like the *Collected Stories of Elizabeth Bowen* and *A Medieval Miscellany*. And no diner I know of starts you off with an amuse bouche of halibut ceviche in a swirl of bright red pepper sauce. Who is the short order cook here?

It's Dennis Leary, formerly of Rubicon, and due to space limitations—namely a kitchen the size of a walk-in closet and seating for just twenty—he keeps the menu small. There are four starters and four main courses—but it is anything but simple. The menu changes daily and highlights the season. Leary has a way with vegetables: one night his plate of spring offerings in a pea puree made even devout carnivores swoon; likewise his corn clafouti with wild mushrooms. But don't forego the *blanquette de veau*, the roasted chicken, or the pork belly.

Understandably the kitchen can get waylaid during prime times, and with one person waiting on everyone it's not surprising that misfires can occur. We didn't order the steak tartare, but we got it anyway and were glad we did. In fact, the only disappointment at Canteen is that with food this good, and a space this small, it will be virtually impossible to just drop in. Happily you can make a reservation. They are also open for lunch and breakfast.

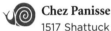 **Chez Panisse**
1517 Shattuck Avenue, at Cedar Street
Berkeley   *EAST BAY*
(510) 548-5525
$$$$

Forget for a moment that Chez Panisse is one of this country's most celebrated restaurants. Lodged in a former Berkeley house, which echoes the city's Craftsman architectural tradition, the restaurant's atmosphere is almost shocking in its lack of pretension or formality, as is the food. Everything here is completely natural and of the highest quality, from the painstakingly sourced local and organic ingredients to the carefully laid tables and the unobtrusive but unusually large number of naturalistic flower arrangements.

Downstairs at Chez Panisse is the main restaurant, serving a single prix fixe dinner every night except Sunday. For many people this is the quintessential Chez Panisse experience: the menu, which begins with a modest three courses on Monday and evolves into a more extravagant five to six courses on the weekend (with matching prices) is designed to give diners a perfectly orchestrated experience based on the best seasonal ingredients. It is like eating at the home of the best cook in the family, except in this case there is often one excellent cook attending to each course.

Upstairs is a more casual café that serves lunch and dinner. Here, the small but always satisfying a la carte menu offers seasonal salads and appetizers, pizzas from the wood-burning oven, pastas, main courses, and desserts.

The influence and effects of the Chez Panisse mission and its various initiatives are far-reaching. The restaurant has served not only as a model for New American cuisine but also as a launching pad for many creative young chefs. Yet in the end perhaps nothing conveys its contribution to American culture better than the simplicity of the fruit plate offered at the end of the meal or the absolutely perfect garden lettuces in the salad.

1550 Hyde Wine Bar & Café
Russian Hill

1550 Hyde Street, at Pacific Avenue
(415) 775-1550
Closed Monday
$$–$$$

At 1550 Hyde, the fifty-seat Russian Hill restaurant, top-notch purveyors populate the menu—Hoffman Gamebirds, for instance—affirming the footnoted declaration, "We use local producers that practice environmentally sustainable agriculture." The restaurant is owner operated: Mâitre d' and Sommelier Kent Liggett graciously handles the front-of-house duties, while partner Peter Erickson runs the kitchen. The menu is simple, seasonal, and sensible, and the roughly seven starters and seven main courses offer something to please patrons of almost every dietary persuasion. You might enjoy grilled California Wild King Salmon with Fresh Garbanzo Beans and Pea Shoots, while vegetarians will feel welcomed by Garganelli with Tomato Sauce, Fresh Ricotta, and Pesto.

Liggett has put together an ample yet tightly edited wine list that covers the keystone varietals. Lots of bottles fall within the twenty- to thirty-dollar range, yet in every category there is a delightful and more indulgent option, should you feel the urge to splurge. Wines that are organically grown are marked with an asterisk. If you can't make up your mind, opt for the wine flight—three half-glasses organized along a varietal theme. The pours are generous, and it is a fun and affordable way to sample the list.

A small candlelit bar in the center of the restaurant invites spur-of-the-moment singles and couples, and it is house policy to set aside a number of tables for drop-ins. 1550 Hyde is a standout neighborhood restaurant that happens to be well worth a trip across town. But a word of caution: Parking is daunting. It is probably best to take public transport—the Hyde/Beach Street cable car will drop you off right in front.

Flea Street Café
3607 Alameda de Las Pulgas
Menlo Park   *SOUTH BAY*
(650) 854-1226
Dinner only; Sunday brunch; closed Monday
$$–$$$

Flea Street Café takes it name from the busy Spanish-named street, the Alameda de las Pulgas, where it's located. The café has been offering a California bistro-style menu for more than twenty-two years, and Chef-Owner Jesse Cool has been a leader in promoting small-scale organic farming and ranching. Accordingly, the menu changes with the seasons to take advantage of the best of what's available in Northern California.

From your first friendly greeting, the service is thoughtful and unhurried yet attentive. The à la carte menu offers choices for "little plates from the bar," and starters such as the delicious Beet, Arugula, and Pistachio-Crusted Goat Cheese Salad; Wild Salmon and Smoked Trout Cake; or seasonal soups. Main courses can include the Portobello Mushroom and Goat Cheese Wellington, Niman Ranch Pork Osso Buco, locally harvested seafood, and Pan-Seared Rosie Chicken. The wine list offers excellent choices in all categories, as well as several organic labels. And an outdoor deck area shaded by trees and market umbrellas gives you an option of eating al fresco.

Foreign Cinema
Mission
2534 Mission Street, at 21st Street
(415) 648-7600
www.foreigncinema.com
Open for brunch on weekends
$$–$$$

Wall-to-wall troupes of Prada-clad dot-comers occupied newly opened Foreign Cinema in 1999, but they couldn't stop the invasion of outside forces. Foreign Cinema has always been as attractive to eighty-three-year-old food doyenne Marion Cunningham as to any overpaid twenty-something. In Cunningham's words, "The minute you walk in the door you feel a sense of community." The door is actually two swinging doors with portholes, opening off a down-at-the-heels block of Mission Street. Once inside, a long corridor leads to parallel spaces: an outdoor patio with long family-style tables where films are screened nightly against the far wall (sound provided by tableside drive-in movie sound boxes), and an adjacent indoor dining room with floor-to-ceiling windows and a striking fireplace. Located in an abandoned department store, Foreign Cinema is original, stylish, and comfortable.

Bringing it all together is the truly great food made by husband-and-wife team Gayle Pirie and John Clark, formerly of Zuni Café and Chez Panisse. They adhere to the local, seasonal, organic mantras of their alma maters, but add their own edgy sensibilities to the mix: Moroccan spices, Andalusian touches, and pristine platters of fruit de mer. For a "premiere" you might try Grilled Monterey calamari with aioli, and for your "feature" you might try a mixed grill of Moroccan duck breast, quail, and chicken sausage, with roasted grapes and liver toast. Dinner is served nightly, but don't forget weekend lunch and brunch, with lovely egg dishes and legendary margaritas. Both at night and on weekend days, the outdoor patio—set in the sunny Mission District—is the best off-the-street street party in town.

For a film schedule visit their Web site, listed above.

 ### Greens
Fort Mason

Building A, Fort Mason (enter across Marina Boulevard from
  Safeway)
(415) 771-6222
$$

When Greens opened in 1979 under the auspices of the San Francisco Zen Center, it quickly became one of the most popular dining spots in the Bay Area. Founding Chef Deborah Madison, who had a stint at Chez Panisse, and the Zen Center were at the forefront of the organic, sustainable movement. Produce and bread from the Zen Center's Green Gulch Farm and Tassajara Bakery (now defunct) was brought in daily. Chef Madison brought refinement and a newfound respect to vegetarian cuisine—which up until that time had been mostly limited to notions of beans and brown rice.

Today diners are still drawn to Greens' imaginative vegetarian menu and the dramatic dining room, with a sweeping view of the San Francisco Bay. Chef Annie Sommerville's repertoire takes inspiration and flavors from many cuisines, and she uses the finest organic ingredients in her cooking—still, like her predecessors, she sources produce from the Zen Center's Green Gulch Farm in Marin County.

Special dishes include mushroom soup with Asiago cheese and tarragon; phyllo layered with artichokes, crimini mushrooms, leeks, and Parmesan cheese; fresh pea ravioli that combines snap, snow, and English peas with saffron butter; and pizza with wilted escarole, red onions, lemon, and Asiago.

The wine list features both local and imported selections, and the extensive beverage menu offers ales, organic teas, lemonades, and espresso

drinks. The adjacent Greens to Go—just off the main dining room—sells homemade breads, sandwiches, soups, salads, and pastries.

Insalata's
120 Sir Francis Drake Boulevard
San Anselmo   *MARIN*
(415) 457-7700
$$–$$$

The trip across the Golden Gate to San Anselmo can be a trek in bad traffic, but Insalata's is worth the trip. It is often packed for lunch and dinner with relaxed, happy diners savoring Chef Heidi Krahling's heartfelt Mediterranean cuisine. The ingredients are consistently top quality, from the house-made bread to the produce, meat, and fish. Dishes are pulled from around the Mediterranean, and you might find *fattoush,* the classic Syrian bread salad with feta, red onions, mint, cucumbers, olives, and pita; or Portuguese *catapalana* with Manila clams, tomato, chorizo, and garlic with rouille; or Moroccan braised-chicken tagine with preserved lemons and harissa over couscous.

The warm and pleasant staff is an added bonus, as is the large deli with an extensive take-out menu and the fantastic theme dinners.

 Jardiniere
Hayes Valley
300 Grove Street, at Franklin Street
(415) 861-5555
Dinner only
$$$

Traci Des Jardins's Jardiniere is very popular among San Francisco swells
who frequent the adjacent symphony, opera, and ballet—but don't let that
put you off. By 8:00 P.M. (curtain time), one of the sexiest restaurants in
San Francisco returns to earth. And earth is essential to Traci Des Jardins.
A native of Fresno in California's Central Valley, Des Jardins combines her
brilliant, classically trained approach to food with a thorough respect both
for the earth that provides our best ingredients and for the people who
grow, pick, cook, and serve them. While making the most of luxe ingredi-
ents for perennial favorites like Maine Diver Scallops with Pommes Purée
and Black Truffle Nage, Des Jardins also turns her brilliance to the most

traditionally humble ingredients, like local sardines, transforming them into truly delectable dishes.

While Des Jardins is never far from the kitchen, Chef de Cuisine Robbie Lewis has run the day-to-day operations for the past few years, and his influence is felt in a more generally Mediterranean than strictly French approach. The excellence of the kitchen is matched by superb service and a superior wine list.

With its interior space resembling nothing so much as an inverted champagne glass, Jardiniere is a great spot for a romantic dinner at a ringside table on the second-floor mezzanine, or a drink at the bar with a plate of fabulous house-cured charcuterie (don't miss the mortadella). Everything about this restaurant exudes professionalism, and while it's among San Francisco's more expensive restaurants, it's well worth it.

Rivoli Restaurant
1539 Solano Avenue
Berkeley   EAST BAY
(510) 526-2542
$$–$$$

What was conceived ten years ago as a small neighborhood restaurant has evolved into a destination for diners from all over the Bay Area. Thankfully, the personal, friendly attitude of owners and staff has not changed.

Chef-Owner Wendy Brucker, an alumna of Square One, among others, has mastered the art of combining simplicity and sophistication. Her menu changes every three weeks to reflect the best of what's local and seasonal. Her husband and partner, Roscoe Skipper, matches the food with a thoughtful, compact selection of Californian, French, and Italian wines.

Brucker is a discerning shopper, frequently visiting nearby Monterey Market to scope out the best produce. While she keeps some flexibility, she favors organically grown fruit and vegetables, with all salad greens coming from local organic farms. Rivoli relies on such suppliers as Acme Baking and Niman Ranch and Monterey Fish; farmed Atlantic salmon is never allowed to cross the threshold.

Though the menus change, there are a few items Brucker can't leave off. Regulars might stage a diners' strike if she didn't serve her signature Portobello Mushroom Fritters with Arugula and Parmesan, drizzled with sherry vinaigrette and finished with assertive aioli.

The intimate dining room of the restaurant, located in an old North Berkeley house with a wall of windows affording a view of a charming backyard, offers an added attraction for animal lovers. Neighborhood feral cats, raccoons, and other wildlife from nearby Berkeley creeks drop by nightly for the pet food Brucker puts out for them.

The Village Pub
2967 Woodside Road

Woodside   *SOUTH BAY*

(650) 851-9888

$$$–$$$$

This landmark seventy-eight-year-old building, revamped but with its original bar kept intact, is no pub in the usual sense of the word. Sure, you can always sidle up to the bar for the popular pub burger and fries. But you can also take a seat in the plush dining room with its deep burgundy banquettes and roaring stone fireplace, which makes every visitor feel a bit more genteel.

Executive Chef Mark Sullivan, named by *Food & Wine* as one of the Best New Chefs of 2002, serves contemporary American food with a strong emphasis on local ingredients. So strong, in fact, that the Village Pub has its own fifteen-acre organic farm just west of Woodside, where Sullivan grows Easter egg radishes, Toscano kale, Armenian cucumbers, German butterball potatoes, and French red pumpkins.

Indulge in the king of beef: a dry-aged rib-eye steak for two served with marrow butter. Or try the Truffled Ricotta Agnolotti with Foraged Mushrooms; Proscuitto-Wrapped Monkfish with French Lentils; house-cured charcuterie; or, if it's on the menu, the Olive Oil–Poached Wild Salmon, a signature fish dish that's beyond succulent. Finish with a chocolate soufflé for two, with a Grand Marnier sauce.

Zuni Café
Hayes Valley

1658 Market Street, between Franklin and Gough Streets

(415) 552-2522

Closed Monday

$$–$$$

With all the restaurants to choose from in and around San Francisco, it may be surprising to learn how many people here have a long-term, quasi-monogamous relationship with Zuni Café. While we might stray to the new thing in town, in the end we always come home.

And we usually stick to the classics. At the top of the list is Chef Judy Rogers's Chicken for Two. Somehow after all these years, that plate of roast chicken and bread salad still manages to thrill. We start with the house-cured anchovies and shaved celery, or the *piccolo fritto,* or both. We usually order the ricotta gnocchi and often finish with the *pot de crème.*

We go to Zuni to celebrate engagements, promotions, and Sunday afternoons. We visit before the parade and after the march. We go to Zuni because we're starving and we want a late-night, post-performance hamburger (with ground Niman Ranch beef on focaccia) and a pile of shoe-string potatoes, or because we're craving the Caesar salad or a margarita. We take our friends, our relatives, and out-of-town guests. We have our favorite seat in the bar, our favorite table (not upstairs), our favorite variety of oyster from the bustling oyster bar. The smell of the wood oven calms us, and we're comforted by the wedge of Acme Bakery's *levain* and cold butter that arrives while we decide what to order and what we're doing with our lives.

Indeed, Zuni is what you want in a partner: exciting, dependable, ready to listen, and waiting to please. Oh, except it's closed on Mondays. Well, we all need a little space in our relationships.

NOTABLE

Chez Nous
Fillmore
1911 Fillmore Street, between Bush and Pine Streets
(415) 441-8044
$$$$

Petite Chez Nous, with its Mediterranean small-plate menu, fits its Fillmore Street location like a glove. The lamb chops with lavender salt and the French fries with *harissa* aioli are particular favorites. And the domestic Kobe beef burger fits in nicely for lunch. For dessert try the *canales*: this confection from Bordeaux is divine. Small tables and the noise level can be problematic, but they now accept reservations, so if you call ahead you may not have to wait.

Citizen Cake
Hayes Valley
399 Grove Street, at Gough Street
(415) 861-2228
Closed Monday
$$$

Executive Chef Elizabeth Falkner can make Citizen Cake almost anything you want it to be. Stop by this Hayes Valley patisserie-*cum*-restaurant for a quick pastry or an ice cream, a dazzling birthday cake, or delicious rose-infused crème brûlée. Meet friends for a weekend brunch of fried egg and bacon sandwiches, have a *croque monsieur* for lunch, or come before the ballet for a house-brined Niman Ranch pork chop with celery root *spaetzle*. A full range of fun, fruity cocktails and a serious wine list complete the lineup.

Firefly
Noe Valley
4288 24th Street, at Douglass Street
(415) 821-7652
$$

The kitchen at Firefly is so small that there is no room for a walk-in refrigerator; as a result meats and vegetables are ordered daily, and Chef-Owner Brad Levy can frequently be seen flitting around town, picking up last-minute items. Since opening in 1993, Firefly has attracted regulars from all over town to this rather remote, residential corner of Noe Valley.

The dining room enchants patrons with its small, inviting bar and canopied ceiling. And the menu, which borrows from several continents, includes Butter Lettuce Salad with Beets, Avocado, and Creamy Curry Dressing; and Five-Spice Blackened Yellowtail with Shiitake Rice and Seaweed Cucumber Vinaigrette. The reasonably priced wine list includes about fifty choices from California, Italy, Spain, and all the regions of France.

 ## Globe
Jackson Square
290 Pacific Avenue, between Battery and Front Streets
(415) 391-4132
Open to 1:00 A.M.
$$

Open late (for this city), Globe has long been an after-hours hangout for those in the restaurant biz. Local organic ingredients, often picked up from the nearby Ferry Plaza Farmers' Market, form the basis for earthy dishes. The lunch menu is a little simpler than the dinner menu, but both offer hearty, rustic food. With architectural elements like exposed brick (revealing the building's former life as a livery stable), Globe's cutting-edge yet comfortable interior befits the surrounding streets of historic Jackson Square.

 ### Grégoire   *(Café/Takeout)*
2109 Cedar Street
Berkeley   *EAST BAY*
(510) 883-1893
www.gregoirerestaurant.com
$$

Within a stone fruit's throw of the Cheese Board and Chez Panisse, a tiny takeout has opened that offers a meal on par with what you would find at a fine restaurant. Although there are a few stools at the counter and a couple of tables outside, most people stop in here to pick up lunch or dinner to go. Grégoire posts its menu online, making it easy to call ahead for pickup.

Owner Grégoire Jacquet grew up in Normandy, eating fruits and vegetables straight from the family garden and meats from the farm next door. His keen sense of seasonality is apparent in the menu, which changes every few weeks and features naturally raised meats and organically grown ingredients.

Hawthorne Lane
SOMA
22 Hawthorne Street, between Folsom and Howard Streets
(415) 777-9779
$$$

Hawthorne Lane is the place to go for quiet, sophisticated dining. Carefully appointed without feeling stuffy, it achieves that difficult balance between elegant and comfortable. Many people never get beyond the cushy bar where you can order a pile of tempura-style green beans and several orders of the Duck Buns. But the full menu is best enjoyed at a table in the dining room. Prints from Crown Point Press, the legendary fine art print house and publisher that happens to be located in the space above, hang on the walls. Chef Bridget Batson's cooking is Californian with an Asian tilt. Try the Trio of Bluefin Toro Sashimi with Shiso and Sesame Soy Dipping Sauce. There's a formidable wine list, with many selections available by the glass. Be advised that it is possible to run up quite a tab, but the experience makes it well worth the price.

The House
North Beach
1230 Grant Avenue, at Columbus Avenue
(415) 986-8612
Closed Sunday
$$

Owners Angela and Larry Tse have created their own brand of Asian fusion cuisine at their intimate North Beach restaurant. Every day the menu features terrific specials, such as succulent sea scallops with a ponzu sauce, delicious tempura green beans, and salmon rolls. Larry gets so excited when his suppliers bring in freshly caught fish that he'll sometimes pull out his camera to take photographs of the beautiful creatures.

Among The House favorites are the chicken salad with julienned vegetables and juicy grilled chicken, and their superb version of short ribs. Angela is famous for her delicious apple and key lime pies.

 Lalime's
1329 Gilman Street
Berkeley   *EAST BAY*
(510) 527-9838
$$$

Lalime's has been a fixture in Berkeley's Westbrae neighborhood for fifteen years. The owners, Cindy and Haig Lalime-Krikorian, reinforce their connection to the community through a newsletter about their travels, local winemakers, local farmers, and seasonal events, such as the beginning of wild mushroom season. One can easily enjoy a glass of wine and a light dinner at the bar or dine in the more formal and lovely dining room. The menu, which always features a vegetarian entrée, may have grass-fed rib-eye steak or local wild salmon. The desserts complement the seasonal menu with options. The food is simply but beautifully presented and delicious.

Lavanda
185 University Avenue
Palo Alto   *SOUTH BAY*
(650) 321-3514
$$$

Food and wine get equal billing at this Mediterranean restaurant and wine bar. Step up to the granite bar, a showcase for wines from all over the world, including both hard-to-find small producers and famed vintners who need no introduction. You'll find about twenty-five wines available by the glass each day. With your taste buds whetted, take a seat in the dining room to enjoy robust cuisine made with great ingredients, including Niman Ranch meats and specialty peppers from Happy Quail Farms across the highway in East Palo Alto.

Luna Park
Mission
694 Valencia Street, at 18th Street
(415) 553-8584
$$

Expertly positioned to capture Valencia Street revelers, Luna Park packs them in with the irresistible combination of great value and great cock-tails. The mojitos are arguably the best in the city, and the Pot on Fire — Luna Park's translation of *pot au feu*—with ample portions of braised Niman Ranch brisket, thick carrots, melting leeks, and broth was an unbe-lievable bargain for less than $17. Start your meal with a voluptuous Tuna Poke—diced sashimi tuna with lime, chiles, chives, and avocado. Accompanied by fried wontons, this is almost a meal in itself. The satay stars three skewers of pork, basted in a gingery curry with hints of turmeric and lemongrass and partnered with a cilantro-and-fish-sauce-seasoned coleslaw. The salads, like the Cobb, feature fresh, bright mixed greens. You can round out your meal with a number of à la carte sides, like braised broccoli rabe or grilled asparagus. For those not in the mood to party, you can order out from Luna Park. We have ordered all the above-mentioned items to go (except for the mojito). The items trav-eled spectacularly well, the tab amounted to $58 and change, and it was plenty satisfying for four people.

PlumpJack Café
Marina/Cow Hollow
3127 Fillmore Street
(415) 563-4755
$$$

PlumpJack Café, formerly part of San Francisco Mayor Gavin Newsom's small food and beverage empire, is where the city's power people love to dine. Chef James Ormsby's food is multifaceted, sensual, and delicious. He understands ingredients and cooks seasonally. During crab season, try the sparkling Dungeness Crab and Endive Salad with Roasted Celery, Slivered Mango, and Red Onions, which is transformed by a cognac and herb dressing. Sonoma Liberty Duck is thoroughly celebrated in a dish containing Thigh and Leg Confit and Pan-Seared Sliced Breast. Broccolini, Yukon Gold mashed potatoes, and a wild huckleberry sauce round out the plate. And don't forget dessert. Ormsby is an accomplished pastry chef and takes his desserts seriously. You should, too, especially if his devil's food cake is on the menu.

PlumpJack has the most price-friendly wine programs in town. All the wines on their broad list (including those made at their winery) are sold at the same price you'll find at their retail store around the corner. For more about PlumpJack Wines, see Wine Retailers, page 297.

RNM
Lower Haight
598 Haight Street, at Steiner Street
(415) 551-7900
Closed Monday
$$-$$$

Walking through the evanescent, chartreuse curtain into the main dining room of RNM is like walking into another dimension. A plasma screen silently beams images of the Buddha while backlit diners sip glowing, fuchsia-colored cocktails at the bar. Opaque window treatments mute the familiar street scene outside. Gone is the grit of the Lower Haight.

The California menu helps you find your bearings, though it's the French-inspired entries that really please. The house-made duck *rillettes*, part of the charcuterie plate, alone are worth a trip. Thank goodness eating protein and fat is now considered part of a diet strategy.

Prices are reasonable and the wine list is user-friendly. You'll find plenty of choices in the $30 range, with lots of Italian and Rhône-style territory to explore. RNM's chef-owner, Justine Miner, takes you on a different kind of trip in the Haight, a transcontinental meditation on California fare without any of the jet lag.

Slow Club
Mission/Potrero Hill

2501 Mariposa Street, at Hampshire Street
(415) 241-9390
Closed Sunday for dinner
$$

Slow Club is hidden away in what was a no-man's land fifteen years ago, and what is still a somewhat offbeat corner of the Mission/Potrero Hill neighborhood. Slow Club does not take reservations, so you may have to spend time in the bar, sipping cocktails with the crowd. Once you have tried chef Sante Salvoni's food, you'll see why it is so crowded. I'd come back for the Halibut with Potato Gnocchi or the hefty Lamb Shoulder Chop and Farro Salad with Feta and Mint. The Peach Upside-Down Cake with Berry Compote and Whipped Cream is perfect. This is also a great place for weekend brunch (see Breakfast & Brunch, page 185).

Universal Café
Mission

2814 19th Street, between Bryant and Harrison Streets
(415) 821-4608
Dinner Tuesday through Sunday; weekend brunch
$$

Tucked away in the semi-industrial flatlands of the Mission, Universal Café is a local favorite. The award-winning decor, with its floor-to-ceiling blackboard wine lists and locally forged metalwork, successfully bridges that fine line between urban chic and comfortable café. Chef Leslie Carlos Avolos grew up on a farm in the Hudson Valley, and this connection to the soil shines through in her food. The menu, with such offerings as Grilled Chicken Livers with Blackberries and Lettuces and Brined Pork Chop with Wild Juniper Butter, highlights Willis Ranch and local Lagier Ranch. Weekend brunch is extremely popular.

Woodward's Garden
Mission

1700 Mission Street, at Duboce Street
(415) 621-7122
Closed Sunday
$$

For years under the shadow of the Fell Street on-ramp, and now caught in the middle of a major thoroughfare construction zone, Woodward's Garden simply carries on, as it has always done. A last stand of civility between the tough edge of the Mission district and Zuni Café, Woodward's Garden serves up earnest, upright, yet politely edgy food. Studious pairings like Penne with Sautéed Chicken Livers, Bacon, Shallots, Dates, Arugula, and Port Sauce are not something you see on many menus around town. And Chef-Owner Dana Tommasino really knows her fish. Some of her dishes include Smoked Trout Brochette, Slow-Roasted Wild Pacific King Salmon, and a delectable Dungeness Crab-Citrus-Watercress Salad. Her partner, Margie Conrad, looks after the front of the house with as much care and grace as Tommasino imparts to her food.

CHINESE

DIM SUM

Good Luck Dim Sum
Richmond
736 Clement Street, between 8th and 9th Avenues
(415) 386-3388
Cash only
$

Whether you're in the mood for a snack or a full meal, follow the crowd to Good Luck Dim Sum. Be prepared on the weekend to encounter a line of neighborhood mothers, who are here to pick up boxes of dumplings and buns for family lunch.

You can order staples like the *har gao* pork or *sui mai*, or you can be adventurous and try the crystal dumpling—a small, light, meatball seasoned with cilantro and wrapped in a rice-flour skin. Other options include the chive dumpling, stir-fried with a touch of shrimp, steamed in a rice wrapper, and then pan-fried again to give it extra flavor; or the *wu gok* (deep-fried taro root), a puffy pillow of mashed taro seasoned with stir-fried pork and bits of water chestnut and green onion deep fried until it is light and golden.

Finally, for dessert, sample a Sweet Rice Puff—steamed rice flour snowballs dusted with coconut and wrapped around a chopped peanut and sugary coconut filling. After a meal like this, you will feel lucky you went to Good Luck Dim Sum and unlucky when you have to go without it. Make up your mind before you order; the ladies behind the counter are impatient, and he who hesitates is ignored.

Harbor Village
Embarcadero
4 Embarcadero Center
(415) 781-8833
$$$$

Located on the mezzanine level of Embarcadero Four, one of the large towers within walking distance of the Ferry Building, Harbor Village is a popular stop on the dim sum circuit. Its dark carpeting, cherrywood furnishings, and Chinese artifacts give it an upscale feel and make Harbor Village a good choice for a business lunch. The trouble is that the food is so tasty it makes it hard to conduct any business. Try to lobby for a table in the glassed-in atrium for a pleasant, tree-filtered view of Justin Herman Plaza and the Embarcadero beyond. There are also six banquet rooms to accommodate large groups.

Uniformed waitstaff glide around the busy restaurant with dim sum carts that are filled with various temptations. While a plate of Peking duck, some sautéed pea greens, and several rounds of steamed dumplings make a satisfying lunch for two, the trick with dim sum is to know when to pass and when to play. The full dinner menu is also available at lunch to further complicate your choices.

Hong Kong East Ocean
3199 Powell Street
Emeryville   *EAST BAY*
(510) 655-3388
$$

Few places in the Bay Area offer great dim sum and sweeping views of the Bay. Hong Kong East Ocean sits at the tip of the landfill jetty that juts out from the Emeryville shoreline. Beware that on the weekend, long lines of Chinese families wait for their number to be called. You might have to queue up on weekdays as well, but it's worth the wait.

Instead of rolling carts of food by your table, HKEO gives you a paper menu and a pencil to mark the dishes you want. While this may not be as straightforward as snagging appealing dishes from the passing parade, it does help you learn the names of your favorites for future visits.

The eclectic, eighty-plus-item menu draws from several regions of China as well as Japan. Familiar standards such as the sticky rice in lotus leaf and *bao* (steamed pork buns) are great, but don't forget to try the more unusual dishes like tripe in ginger sauce, a canonical pan-fried daikon cake, and a deep-fried pear stuffed with scallops. Shanghai appetizers include dishes such as fish in honey sauce, spicy beef shank with jellyfish, and Shanghai dumplings *(xiao long bao)*. To balance the rich food, order a dish of Japanese-influenced cucumber in ginger sauce or "pickled spicy vegetable" (napa cabbage and red chile strips in rice wine vinegar).

If you're feeling adventurous, end your meal with one of the more exotic of the fifteen desserts, such as "tortoise plasma with herbal jelly." Or play it safe and get a fried banana or custard tart. In order to remember your favorite dishes for your next visit, hang on to the bill—it includes an itemized list, in English, of everything you ordered.

Ton Kiang
Richmond
5821 Geary Boulevard, between 22nd and 23rd Avenues
(415) 387-8273
$$

Located across the street from the landmark onion-domed Russian Orthodox church on Geary, Ton Kiang is absolutely packed on the weekends. No surprise: the restaurant serves some of the best dim sum in the city. Their steamed dumplings, from the classic shrimp *har gao* to the fresh pea shoot and scallop version, are more carefully made than any others you'll find. The lotus-wrapped sticky rice and *char siu bao* are equally refined. Non–dim sum items are prepared with the same care, featuring dishes from the Hakka region of China, such as chicken baked in salt.

It's best to come with a group and, rather than crowding into a booth downstairs, take a seat at one of round tables upstairs in the larger dining room.

Yank Sing
Embarcardero
One Rincon Center
101 Spear Street, at Mission Street
(415) 957-9300
$

Eating dim sum is like playing a shell game: thrilling, especially when you're starving. Anticipation builds as the cart approaches. What morsel will be revealed when the top of the bamboo steamer is lifted? And at Yank Sing there are many delicious reveals. I like to warm up with the shrimp and snow pea dumplings and a round of the pot stickers—fairly tame choices, I admit, but feel free to jump in blind; at Yank Sing there is a high risk/reward quotient. Also rewarding is an order of their Peking duck, served on gloriously puffy white rice buns slathered with plum sauce and several sprigs of scallion. You will definitely see it coming, riding like a homecoming queen on top of the cart to which it is singularly devoted. An order of Chinese broccoli or other seasonal green is advised. And a glass of sake, served cold, marries well with the food. Note: You are allowed to request a half-portion of most offerings.

NOTABLE

DIM SUM

City View Restaurant
Financial District
662 Commercial Street
(415) 398-2838
Open every day of the year; lunch only
$

Tucked away down an alley in the Financial District, just on the outskirts of Chinatown, City View is one of the best-kept secrets for delicious, hassle-free dim sum on the weekends. While better-known places will have lines spilling out onto the street for Sunday brunch, there is no wait at City View. Weekdays are a different story: The lunchtime crush is intense, so getting there before 11:00 A.M. is recommended.

City View has a great variety of dim sum, and the flavors are fresh and distinct. The restaurant is clean, modern, and even stylish, with tropical plants throughout and a beautiful mural of Quai Ling adorning the east wall.

Dol Ho
Chinatown
808 Pacific Avenue
(415) 392-2828
Cash only
$

Duck into Dol Ho when you need a break from the frenzied shopping scene on Stockton Street. You will be joined here by many others seeking the same refuge. The place is absolutely plain, but the dim sum is tasty. Speaking some Cantonese will help you get what you want, but patience and pointing go a long way. The steamed dumplings are a great bet; shrimp dishes are good too.

Ocean Seafood

See Chinese, page 51.

Old Shanghai Restaurant   *(Shanghai)*
Chinatown
5145 Geary Boulevard, at 16th Avenue
(415) 752-0120
$$

Old Shanghai is an institution that introduced some of the finest steamed dumplings and pan-fried pork buns to the Bay Area. Most items on the "Dim Sum" and "Cold Plate" portions of the menu are standouts that highlight the distinctiveness of Shanghai cuisine. Other highlights include Tan Tan noodles and rice cake.

BANQUET & SEAFOOD

Daimo   *(Hong Kong Noodles)*
Pacific East Shopping Mall
3288A Pierce Street
Richmond   ***EAST BAY***
(510) 527-3888
Open to 3:00 A.M.
$-$$

The extreme usefulness of Daimo to Bay Area eaters can best be experienced after midnight, when it is one of the only restaurants open. In fact, Daimo, the first U.S. branch of a Hong Kong noodle house that has six branches in its home region and two in Vancouver, is only closed for six hours out of twenty-four. Between midnight and 3:00 A.M., it amounts to a private club for those in the know, tucking into fresh crab sautéed with scallions and ginger and stir-fried frogs' legs with lily flowers and Chinese celery. At any hour you'll find lots of people enjoying its freshly prepared Cantonese cooking, which ranges from inexpensive bowls of noodle soup and *congee* to elaborate but still reasonably priced preparations of whole fish and crab and lobster snagged from the tanks lined up against one wall of the brightly lit, comfortable, large dining room.

The menu offers more than five hundred dishes: Its scope is considerable, from the expected (hot-and-sour soup, Peking duck) to the unusual (duck tongues, served cold or fried; pork stomach with pickled mustard greens), and its standards are high. Specialties include a wide range of cold and hot barbecued meats.

Daimo is a free-standing restaurant in the parking lot of the Pacific East Mall, a warren of small Asian restaurants and the nicely stocked Ranch 99 market (see Ethnic & Specialty Markets, page 253).

Jai Yun Restaurant   *(Nanjing)*
Chinatown
923 Pacific Avenue, at Powell Street
(415) 981-7438
Dinner only, 6:30 to 9:30 P.M.; closed Thursday
Prix fixe, cash only
$$$$

A tiny nondescript restaurant on the edge of Chinatown, Jai Yun serves dinner by reservation only, and there is no menu. After you've arrived, you'll be asked how much you want to spend. The levels seem to vary, but usually start at $35 and go to over $100 per person. The number of dishes you receive will depend on the price level and the number of people in your party.

Once you are seated, cold appetizers will appear in rapid succession, such as a delicate, very lightly dressed dish of jellyfish, a plate of smoked fish, and a stack of pickled cucumbers. After a pause, the main dishes will begin to arrive. The selection varies with the season, but it may include crispy eggplant, tender winter melon, crunchy orange-spiced chicken, and *foo yung* abalone. Before the bill arrives, Chef-Owner Chia-Ji Nei will come out to greet each table, often to a round of applause. The quality of the food at Jai Yun is unmistakable. The only way to get more authentic Chinese food would be to travel to China yourself.

Everything else—the service, the presentation, the quantity—is highly variable and depends not only on how much you spend, but also on how much the other parties that night decide to spend. If your table is paying $35 per person and the neighboring table is paying $100, expect to receive less attention and, more significantly, less food.

Koi Palace   *(Hong Kong/Seafood)*
365 Gellert Boulevard
Daly City   **SOUTH BAY**
(650) 992-9000
$$

Koi Palace is reminiscent of the large, bustling operations that you'll find in Hong Kong. As soon as you walk in the front door, you are struck by the wall of tanks filled with a variety of live seafood—crab, lobster, fish, clam, and an occasional eel.

Take the opportunity to handpick your own seafood with your waiter. Try the rock cod or sea bass steamed with ginger, scallion, and soy sauce. The "swimming shrimp" are poached for a few seconds in boiling water, then brought to the table with a soy dipping sauce. Both of these dishes showcase the freshness of the seafood.

Every dish is characterized by its distinctive taste and the great care taken in its preparation. For instance, try their version of pork and beans—the crisp skin of a roasted piglet sits on a bed of small cooked beans. You'll need to arrive early to ensure the availability of this dish. It actually comprises three courses: roast skin as the first course, sautéed pork and vegetables as the second course, and a broth made from the bones as the third course.

Little Sichuan   (*Szechaun*)

168 East Fourth Avenue, at Ellsworth Street
San Mateo   ***SOUTH BAY***
(650) 345-9168
Closed Monday
$$

Directly across from Draeger's in downtown San Mateo, Little Sichuan's unique yellow oval sign adorned with chiles and garlic is a beacon to fans

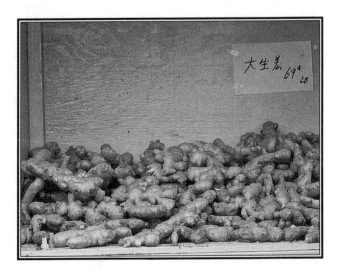

of Szechuan cuisine. This low-key, comfortable space gets packed with a mostly Chinese and Indian clientele during peak dining hours.

Along with tea, the first things that come to your table are a dish of fiery pickled vegetables and some cold boiled peanuts to snack on as you peruse the lengthy menu. The key to ordering properly—a lesson not better learned the hard way—is to order a combination of both spicy and cool dishes and to focus on the Szechuan part of the menu. Start with the Hot Spicy Dumplings, to get the endorphins geared up, and continue with the Spicy Szechuan Cold Noodles and Cumin Lamb. Chinese Salty String Beans combine minced green beans and pork with various peppers, giving it an irresistible texture and a slightly pickled taste. These spicier choices balance nicely with the Tea-Smoked Duck and Dong Poa Side Pork with Spicy Ginger Sauce. (In this case, spice refers to star anise and other aromatic, not hot, spices.)

If you are feeling a need to boost your immune system, the delicious Chinese Herbal Chicken Soup, steaming with Chinese medicinal herbs and ginger root, is designed to do just that. Since one of the owners is from Beijing, Little Sichuan offers special dishes from northern China as well, like a stellar Beijing-Style Sweet and Sour Pork, which bears little resemblance to the technicolor mass one normally gets at other Chinese restaurants. For the more adventurous, try one of the many authentic small plates most may bypass on the menu, like the beef tripe, jellyfish, or pork ears and tongues.

R&G Lounge *(Cantonese Seafood)*
Chinatown

631 Kearny Street, between Clay and Sacramento Streets
(415) 982-7877
$$

Chinese pickles, geoduck clam sashimi-style served with seaweed salad, steamed clam and egg, winter melon or other seasonal soup, Peking duck, a whole fish, sauteed pea greens, and what a friend affectionately refers to as "run-over" chicken (an entire bird stuffed with a delicious sticky fried rice and then deep-fried) generally end up on the table when we go to R&G Lounge.

Despite its cozy name, R&G is a big, bustling place with a big, exhaustive menu, and it is generally packed with enthusiastic fans of its Southern Chinese cuisine. It's a great place to go with a big group to celebrate almost any occasion. Slow Food's president and founder Carlo Petrini does whenever he can. You should, too. They have a full bar here, but you're also welcome to bring your own wine.

NOTABLE

BANQUET & SEAFOOD

China Village Restaurant   *(Szechuan)*
1335 Solano Avenue
Albany   **EAST BAY**
(510) 525-2285
$

Some claim that China Village serves some of the best Szechuan food
around, but to ensure that you experience what it really has to offer, make
sure you receive the correct menu. There are two versions, and the one you
want is smaller with blue print on the cover.

The Spicy Beef Tendon and the Cucumber with Garlic Sauce are both
cold dishes and are refreshing ways to begin. I particularly recommended
the West Style Spicy Fish soup. When the lid is lifted from the tureen, a
deep layer of dry red chiles is revealed floating on top; these peppers add
a smoky flavor and a little heat. They are removed before the soup is eaten.
Instead of ordering rice to accompany your dishes, try the traditional
Szechuan leavened sesame flat bread, studded with green onions.

Go Go Café   *(Shanghai/Hong Kong)*
Inner Sunset
1830 Irving Street, at 19th Avenue
(415) 661-4289
$

Go Go Café has much to offer the lover of Chinese food. Here you will
find delicious Shanghai dim sum items for the day and tasty Hong
Kong–style live seafood for dinner.

The live seafood served Cantonese style makes Go Go Café stand out,
because you would never expect a noodle, dumpling, and porridge shop
to serve such fare. Poached geoduck, salt-and-pepper Dungeness crabs,
and steamed spot prawns are all whisked from the tanks only moments
before they arrive on your table. Besides the great food, you also have to
love the price—usually less than $7.

Great Eastern   *(Cantonese Seafood)*
Chinatown
649 Jackson Street
(415) 986-2500
$$

This is Cantonese seafood of the highest quality. Ignore the tourist fare (sweet-and-sour pork and the like) and insist that you want real Chinese food and will eat anything. Try the duck tongues. Also excellent: jellyfish salad, beef shank (a sort of pressed pâté), salt-baked squid (actually deep-fried), fried squab, frogs with Smithfield ham, and steamed shrimp unadorned but for ginger and soy sauce.

Mayflower *(Hong Kong)*
Richmond
6255 Geary Boulevard, at 27th Avenue
(415) 387-8338
$-$$

Mayflower is a neighborhood venue that reflects many of the characteristics of a Hong Kong restaurant with overly bright lighting and *re-nao* ambience, which literally means "hot-noisy" and indicates a certain festive bustle. Every square inch is used for restaurant seating, and the waiting space is outside on the sidewalk. The focus is on good ingredients, with a particular concentration on live seafood, which can be seen in the tanks next to the front door. Recommendations include sautéed snow pea vines, clams with black bean sauce, and any preparation of seafood from the tanks. If you're coming with a large party consider ordering a whole roast piglet prepared three ways twenty-four hours in advance. The waitstaff is generally very helpful and has, on occasion, even indicated when they believe that you have overordered. To avoid being rushed into completing your meal, go during the week rather than on the weekend.

Ocean Seafood *(Seafood)*
Richmond
726 Clement Street
(415) 788-3608
BYOB
$

You won't find Ocean Seafood listed in the *Zagat Survey* (not yet, anyway). It may look unpromising from the street, but it's a highly refined restaurant, presided over by an attentive and charming owner. There is neither wine nor beer, but you may bring your own, and there's no corkage fee—the prices here are unbelievably low. The soul-food specialty of the house is sea cucumber, a gelatinous creature not always a favorite of Westerners; fortunately, there are lots of more congenial and still utterly delicious seafood dishes available. For instance, there are usually several varieties of live fish in the tanks, including catfish, which Ocean serves in two courses (soup and meat), as well as prawns and Dungeness crab. The weekend dim sum is highly regarded.

Old Mandarin Islamic   *(Chinese Muslim)*
Outer Sunset
3132 Vicente Street, at 42nd Avenue
(415) 564-9588
$$

Old Mandarin Islamic is a rare restaurant in San Francisco. All the meat is from a halal butcher, and no pork or alcohol is served. A couple of meat starters give a good sense of the flavors of Islamic Chinese food: Fried Lamb Skewer and the Boiled Chicken De Zhou Style. Or try the unique cold tofu salads.

The warm pot soups are perfect for those frequent foggy evenings at Ocean Beach. Every item on the chef's specials menu is distinctly Islamic Chinese. Some classic dishes include Lamb with Green Onion, Spicy Bean Curd Beef, Egg-Surfaced Lamb, and Steamed Sliced Fish.

Old Mandarin Islamic is more fun to experience with a group of friends or family, though if you come by yourself, you'll find one of the best bowls of spicy beef noodle soup in the city.

Saigon Seafood Harbor Restaurant   *(Seafood)*
3150 Pierce Street
Richmond   **EAST BAY**
(510) 559-9388
$$-$$$

Saigon Seafood Harbor is not a Vietnamese restaurant. *Sai-kung* is the Cantonese term for a seafood harbor market. Once you've found your table, walk over to the fish tanks with your waiter to appraise the daily catch. Plan your meal around the live seafood and browse the menu for different preparations. Check out what's hanging in the deli window. If you need a hint to start, the Chiu Chow Cold Crab may be the best first course to any meal on this side of the Pacific.

Spices! II, Szechuan Trenz   *(Chinese Fusion)*
Richmond
291 6th Avenue, at Clement Street
(415) 752-8885
$

Spices! II is just two blocks from its sister restaurant, Spices! I (294 8th Avenue at Clement Street; [415] 752-8884; cash only). Both serve a fusion of Taiwanese and Szechuan cuisines with a healthy dose of spice. The second restaurant is the hipper, louder of the two but shares an owner and chef with the first. You'll often have to wait for a table, and pop music fills the dining room. Hot dishes are denoted with one to three dots, but there is a range in the type of spiciness. Some dishes, such as the Sauteed Fish Fillet, are drenched in a numbing bright-red chile oil. Others come with dried chile peppers or Szechuan peppercorns. The snacks portion of the menu offers traditional cold dishes, ranging from various pickled vegetables to more adventurous thinly sliced pig's ears. If the heat becomes overwhelming, you can round out your meal with a variety of cold tropical juices.

Taiwan Point Restaurant *(Taiwanese)*
Inner Sunset
1920 Irving Street
(415) 665-9879
$

Taiwan Point offers one of the most diverse Taiwanese menus in the Bay Area. The menu is organized into categories that indicate the dining experience rather than the ingredients, such as Street Food, Rice and Noodles, or House Special Combos, which are meant to be family meals. An item described as Chicken in Special Sauce is actually a very famous Chinese dish cooked with soy, sesame oil, wine, and basil. Some highlights from the combo menu are Taiwanese Roast Pork, On Choy with Garlic Sauce, and Anchovy with Bean Cake.

BARBECUE, NOODLES & CONGEE

Cheung Hing *(Hong Kong–Style Barbecue/Takeout)*
Outer Sunset
2339 Noriega Street, at 30th Avenue
(415) 665-3271
$

"I don't know what it's called, but it's out on Noriega across from the Safeway, and there'll be a line out in front. You can't miss it. Get the fermented bean chicken." Those were the instructions of an in-the-know friend on where to find some of the tastiest Hong Kong–style barbecue in town. Sure enough, at about 32nd Avenue, I spotted the Safeway and then I spotted the line. Though there are four or five inviting tables at Cheung Hing, few people seem to use them; everyone gets takeout. Rows of ducks and chickens hang on hooks in the window. An entire roast pig, cut in half and wearing a thick coat of crispy fat, hangs behind the counter.

Patrons wait quietly in line until it's their turn to order. Then it gets hot.

Rapid-fire banter and emphatic gesticulations ensure that the customers get the exact cuts of roast pork they want (my informant's mother-in-law only gets the fatty section under the front arm) or just the right slice of *cha siu* (barbequed pork loin). With the important decisions out of the way, the chopping begins; most everything at Cheung Hing gets lopped into easy-to-eat chunks. It's best to stand back from the counter to avoid getting hit with the shrapnel. In about two minutes' time it's over, and you're out the door, carrying home a pink plastic bag full of barbecued bounty.

Lam Hoa Thuan   *(Chinese Barbecue/ Noodles)*
Inner Sunset
2337 Irving Street
(415) 661-1688
$

Sometimes referred to as the "NEW New Hai Ky" because the former staff of New Hai Ky opened this restaurant just down the street, Lam Hoa Thuan is similar to its predecessor. It boasts a large assortment of barbecue and roasted meats hanging in the window. When dining at the restaurant, be prepared to sit next to another party of eager patrons at one of the long tables parked next to each other, bench style.

Order a barbecue rice plate with your choice of meats. Loyal fans of both New Hai Ky and Lam Hoa Thuan will argue the merits of one over the other—too sweet or too salty, too lean or too dry. We may have our individual preferences, but both are top rate. Or try a bowl of soup noodles, flat or thin, with your choice of barbecue on top. Lam Hoa Thuan also offers an extended menu of traditional Vietnamese grilled rice plates and *pho* dishes. A must-have for your main entrée is the grilled boneless chicken over rice.

For your beverage, treat yourself to a *café sua*—strong Vietnamese coffee with sweetened condensed milk—served either hot or iced.

New Hai Ky   *(Chinese Barbecue/Noodles)*
Outer Sunset
2191 Irving Street
(415) 731-9948
$

A mainstay on Irving Street, New Hai Ky, from all appearances, looks like just another combination Chinese barbecue and takeout/sit-down noodle shop. Roast ducks, soy sauce–marinated chickens, spareribs, strips of *cha siu* (barbecued pork marinated and fire-roasted, then covered with a sweet coating of honey), and a whole roast pig hang in the window. Local takeout customers cluster around the front barbecue counter, eagerly eyeing which choice cuts they want. Behind the Plexiglas enclosure the *see fu* (literally "master," as the chef is called) looks up from behind a massive wooden chopping block, its surface grooved from thousands of cuts expertly made, and is ready to take your order. The steady thunk of his cleaver skillfully chopping your selection into uniformly bite-size pieces in less than a minute is the mastery that has earned him this honorific title.

And of course, if there is barbecue, there must be noodles, so try the Combination Noodle *(mein)* and ask for the noodles pan-fried—thin and crispy—and topped with bean sprouts, roast pork, squid, fish cake, shrimp, and scallops in a light sauce. Or for something warm and satisfying on a cold, foggy day, order Beef Stew Soup with braised noodles. It's hearty fare with chunks of beef, daikon, and tendon in a rich, flavorful broth laced with anise and topped with cilantro. The Preserved Orange Skin Duck with egg noodle soup (get the flat noodle) is also a satisfying choice.

San Tung   *(Noodles)*
Inner Sunset
1031 Irving Street, between 11th and 12th Avenues
(415) 242-0828
Closed Wednesday
$

San Tung is named after the Shandong province where its cuisine originated. Like many other Shandongese restaurants, the food is Korean-
influenced (due to the proximity of Shandong to Korea) and the specialty
is noodles. When you sit down, you'll receive a complimentary plate of
cabbage kimchee. Almost every table will order either dumplings (plates
of twelve available in shrimp and leek or pork and vegetable) or dry-fried
chicken wings, coated with a sweet and savory sauce.

Follow up with the jellyfish salad—crunchy strips of jellyfish and
cucumbers tossed in a bright, hot mustardy dressing. If it's cold out, which
it often is, the seaweed soup is a recommended antidote. And, vegetarian
or not, everyone will love the dried sautéed green beans.

Now to the noodles. They are "hand-pulled," a process of stretching and
twisting the dough into ever-thinner strands until the desired thickness
and texture is achieved. At San Tung they are served fourteen different
ways. My favorite is the Three Deluxe Spicy Sauce Noodles with calamari,
shrimp, and scallops. This pièce de résistance could easily feed two, maybe
more. For years the noodles were pulled by hand, but Frank, whose parents opened the original San Tung fifteen years ago and who has been
working the floor every time I have ever been there, told me they are now
pulled by machine. They are still wonderful.

Other Location

A stripped-down version of the San Tung menu is available at its
sister establishment, So Noodle House, 2240 Irving Street, near
24th Avenue, San Francisco (Sunset); (415) 731-3143. So occupies
the site that housed the original San Tung. Dishes are served in
raku-inspired earthenware.

Shanghai Dumpling Shop   (*Dumplings/Shanghai*)
Outer Richmond
3319 Balboa Street, at 34th Avenue
(415) 387-2088
$

Dumplings are the main course at this bustling neighborhood noodle and
dumpling shop. They are close to those you will find in China, and, in fact,
some consider them to be the best in the Bay Area; the bun/dumpling section of the menu should be appreciated all by itself.

The Boiled Chive Dumplings are beyond compare and are consumed
by the dozens. For variety, the assorted steamed dumplings and pan-fried
pork buns or wontons are all equally good choices, as is the Green Onion
Cake and the Crispy Salt Pan Cake.

Other specialties of the shop include the Shanghai-style noodles (Tan
Tan Noodles) and the Fried Rice Cakes. Cold appetizers, hallmarks of

Shanghai cuisine, like the classic Preserved Egg with Tofu plate, are also offered here. The Cucumber Salad and the Spicy Bok Choy are both refreshing. For something more unusual, try the Spicy Tendon and the Cow Stomach, the most popular appetizers on the menu.

NOTABLE

BARBECUE, NOODLES & CONGEE

Hai Ky Mi Gia *(Noodles)*
Tenderloin
707 Ellis Street, at Larkin Street
(415) 771-2577
Closes at 6:00 P.M.; closed Wednesday
Cash only
$

Everybody seems happy at Hai Kai My Gia. It must be something in the noodle soup. Parties of five and six gather here to gleefully sup and chitchat. The cheerful pink Formica tables and pink trim match the mood of the diners—and belie its location on the gritty corner of Larkin and Ellis. The free-range chicken noodle soup is particularly soothing on a cold, damp, foggy day.

Hing Lung *(Jook)*
Chinatown
674 Broadway, near Stockton Street
(415) 398-8838
$

This well-known Chinatown restaurant deserves its fame for having some of the best *jook* (rice porridge) with fried dough and shrimp dumplings in soup in San Francisco. The interior is functional, and service borders on rude. However, it is a good dining choice in Chinatown, as long as you focus on their specialties.

Fatima Restaurant *(Chinese Muslim)*
1132A South De Anza Boulevard
Cupertino *SOUTH BAY*
(408) 257-3893
$

Like any typical Chinese Muslim restaurant, Fatima's dishes do not include pork. Instead their menu offers a variety of lamb, beef, seafood, and tofu selections. Groups of four or more often order a Warm Pot (large bowls filled with soup, vermicelli noodles, vegetables, and other delights, such as lamb or oxtail), which can be enjoyed with the thick, crispy, oven-baked Sesame Green Onion Bread. If you run out of the soup but still have plenty of filling left in your Warm Pot, just ask for more broth. The waiters will gladly oblige.

Try one of the many noodle soups, particularly the Three-Flavor Noodle Soup, a spicy yet flavorful dish full of seafood, slices of beef, and shredded vegetables. Fatima makes their own rough-cut, dough-sliced noodles by holding a large ball of dough and rapidly slicing small ribbons directly into a pot of simmering water or flavorful broth. The result is a chewy but hearty pasta.

Shan Dong *(Dumplings/Northern Chinese)*
328 10th Street
Oakland *EAST BAY*
(510) 839-2299
$

The dumpling makers pulling, folding, and steaming away at the entrance to Shan Dong Restaurant signal the restaurant's strength. One of a few restaurants in the East Bay to specialize in Northern Chinese fare, as opposed to Cantonese, Shan Dong excels in noodles, homey dumplings, and buns. But the restaurant hides its treasures amid pages of sweet-and-

======= **TOUR OF CHINESE BUNS** =======

When you first arrive at the Lung Fung Bakery (1823 Clement Street) on a foggy weekday morning in San Francisco's Richmond District, trying to find parking might distract you. Cars and pickups double-parked or blocking nearby driveways are your first hint that this nondescript shop is a popular destination.

Outside the entrance old men sit and chat, construction workers mill about, and even the occasional office worker can be seen carrying out pink boxes filled with buns. Inside the small seating area is loud and crowded.

Approach the counter, and if you're a regular you get a nod of recognition. Order a pineapple bun *(bolo bao)*, named for its sweet, stippled, pineapple-colored topping, and prepare to sink your teeth into a warm, soft, yeasty roll; the topping crumbles as you eat it. Or sample a cocktail bun, shaped like an éclair but with a buttery filling of coconut and sugar. Feel like something savory? Try a *cha siu bao,* stuffed with warm, glazed barbecued pork seasoned with a hint of wine. True comfort food. And whatever you do, don't throw away your takeout bag, because more than likely there's some topping from your pineapple bun left behind, and as you enjoy the last sweet morsels, the fog is probably beginning to lift, and a beautiful day is starting to take shape.

Want more? Go to the Red A Bakery No. 2 (634 Clement Street). Try a Denmark bun, a twisted braid of briochelike bread filled with raisins. Farther down the street at 503 Clement is the Wing Lee Bakery. Order a *dai bao,* a large steamed bun filled with chicken, Chinese sausage, hard-boiled egg, and shiitake mushroom—a meal in itself. And for the comforting richness of golden custard nestled in a crisp, flaky crust get a *don tat* from the Golden Gate Bakery (1029 Grant Avenue) in Chinatown. Whether as a breakfast treat, an afternoon coffee companion, or an after-dinner dessert, this is the pastry people line up for.

—*Mary Durbin*

sour pork menu listings. Your best bet is to have the waiters translate the signs on the wall, or just turn to the back page of the menu. There you'll find a marvelous Terrine of Slivered Pig's Ears, at once crunchy and gelatinous; Fish Fillet in Rice Wine Sauce; or, best of all, square, chewy hand-cut noodles, stir-fried with your choice of meats or vegetables.

Weekend mornings, the tables are filled with people ordering Mandarin-style breakfast: Shandong-style boiled dumplings as big as golf balls, bowls of sweet soy milk with fried crullers or twisted steamed buns for dipping, and wontons coated in an aromatic chile oil.

BARBER COURT

Barber Court in Milpitas is as close to San Francisco's Chinatown as you can get in the South Bay, a more modern and authentic version of Chinatown for the twenty-first century. Built in the late 1990s, Milpitas Square is the flagship 99 Ranch Market Plaza Shopping Mall in Northern California and features some of the most distinctive Chinese restaurants in the Bay Area.

Darda Seafood Restaurant
296 Barber Court
Milpitas
(408) 433-5199
$
Chinese Muslim; no alcohol or pork served. Specialties include knife-cut homemade noodles, sesame bread with green onions, lamb soups and hot pots, and live seafood.

Lu Lai Garden
210 Barber Court
Milpitas
(408) 526-9888
Cash only
$
Chinese vegetarian cuisine, featuring mock-meat dishes made with soy, gluten, vegetables, or fungi. Specialties include clay pot or sizzling platter dishes, as well as a number of vegetarian dim sum offerings on the appetizer section of the menu.

Mayflower
428 Barber Court
Milpitas
(408) 922-2700
$
Cantonese and live seafood. Specialties include Peking duck, seafood with bamboo pith soup, sautéed beef with XO sauce, and Chinese roast chicken or squab.

Tainan Restaurant

218 Barber Court

Milpitas

(408) 434-6888

$

Taiwanese street-food café. Specialties include Tainan meatball and squid potage soup, simmered pig's feet, boiled or fried chitterlings, rice cake with pork blood, and deep-fried "stinky" tofu.

FRENCH

FINE DINING

Aqua
Financial District
252 California Street, between Front and Battery Streets
(415) 956-9662
$$$$

Even after almost fifteen years in business, Aqua remains one of the most beautiful restaurants in the city, with its mirrored walls and larger-than-life floral arrangements. Occasionally a restaurant is so good that it assumes a reputation in the national arena. Aqua has achieved this status partially because of excellent service and a fine wine list, but mainly thanks to a succession of three brilliant San Francisco chefs: George Morrone, Michael Mina, and since 2003, Laurent Manrique, who has brought a Gallic sensibility to the restaurant's seafood dishes.

Aqua caters to Financial District swells, and the food is creative and elegant. Sample dishes like sweet corn bisque laden with oyster, *hamachi* tartare, and *uni* or Maine skate with butter lettuce, pancetta, and herb vinaigrette. A native of Gascony, Manrique weaves foie gras into the menu, and it can be found served with corn blini, chanterelles, and fig vinegar jus, or integrated into a seafood dish as it is with his Lobster Salad with Sharlyn Melon and Pistachio Oil. The wine list is top-notch thanks to Sommelier Sean Crowley. The bar at Aqua is a great place to slip in for a less formal occasion.

In an age of fast food and quick fixes, it is nice to know there are still places that serve food with pomp and circumstance, and Aqua is here to remind you that everyone deserves to be pampered once in a while.

Campton Place
Union Square
In the Campton Place Hotel
340 Stockton Street, at Sutter Street
(415) 955-5555
$$$$

Campton Place, a small, elegant hotel on Union Square (and a favorite spot of Carlo Petrini, founder of Slow Food) is home to a formal, if a bit sedate restaurant of the same name. Since its opening under the young, then-unknown chef Bradley Ogden, this dining room has been the starting gate for several of California's finest chefs, including Jan Birnbaum and Laurent Manrique.

Today you will find Swiss Chef Daniel Humm at the helm. After two years in the Bay Area, Humm's cooking has been influenced by local ingredients with a nod to Provence and Italy. One of his finest creations is a Wild Mediterranean Branzino, baked in a fish-shaped crust that is broken to release aromatic juices and served table-side. As in other restaurants of this caliber and price range, Humm offers all the luxury ingredients and the newest haute cooking methods (like *sous vide*), but his cooking style is definitely his own. Following in the footsteps of his predecessors, he has received local and national acclaim and was recently named one of America's Ten Best New Chefs by *Food & Wine* magazine.

As befits the quality of food and atmosphere, Campton Place service is formal and seamless, the seating luxurious and comfortable. It is quiet enough for easy conversation and a great choice when your rich, elegant aunt comes to town, ready to reveal all the family secrets *sotto voce.*

A less formal dining option is the intimate Campton Place Bar adjacent to the dining room. Caviar and foie gras are both on the menu, but a local favorite is the excellent cheeseburger with fries.

 ### The Dining Room at the Ritz-Carlton
Nob Hill

In the Ritz-Carlton Hotel
600 Stockton Street, at California Street
(415) 773-6168
Closed Sunday and Monday
Prix fixe
$$$$

To call this tiny Nob Hill restaurant a dining room is a bit of understatement, as what you experience at the Ritz-Carlton Hotel's flagship restaurant is nothing short of, well, ritzy. Night after night, a dressed-to-the-nines clientele sits on cushy upholstered chairs at well-spaced tables while supping on haute cuisine and sipping first-growth Bordeaux from Riedel decanters.

For years The Dining Room was a bastion of New French fare, but now, under the tutelage of new Executive Chef Ron Siegel (formerly of the famed Masa's), an undercurrent of Japanese influence resonates throughout the menu, where daring creations such as Uni Gelée and Sashimi of Kampachi share the menu with more traditional offerings such as Sweetbread Medallions or Rib Eye with Bone Marrow and Bordelaise Sauce.

One thing that hasn't changed at The Dining Room, however, is the staff's dedication to the art of fine service, overseen by Mâitre d' Mario Nocifera and Master Sommelier Stephane Lacroix. This is, after all, the only hotel in the nation to capture Mobil's Five Stars and AAA's Five

Diamonds for the hotel and the restaurant. And while diners select from a choice of four prix fixe menus, the presentation gives new meaning to à la carte, as the staff rolls around an endless parade of carts—from the champagne cart intended to start you off in a festive mood to the candy and cheese carts that declare a decadent denouement to the meal.

Fifth Floor
Union Square

In the Hotel Palomar
12 Fourth Street, at Market Street
(415) 348-1555
Dinner only; closed Sunday
$$$$

When it originally opened with George Morrone as chef, Fifth Floor immediately ascended to the top rung of the San Francisco fine dining scene. Located in the Hotel Palomar, the sexy dining room and extensive wine list featuring exceptional Burgundies were a perfect fit for Morrone's playful, sensual masterpieces. When he departed, no one could imagine a proper replacement, but enter Laurent Gras, who had headed Alain Ducasse's kitchens in Nice and Paris. When he introduced his exacting, perfectionist, and exquisitely delicious dishes, he was considered by many to have raised the bar even higher for French cooking in San Francisco.

Current chef Melissa Perello is younger than her predecessors and more a product of her environment. Her menu faithfully draws from the area's best seasonal fruits and vegetables, and her cooking style is clean, allowing the natural flavors of excellent ingredients to shine. One of the best dishes is a perfectly balanced crab salad wherein the essence of beautiful fresh crab is subtly enhanced but never masked. While elegant, her food is more modest, less showy than that of Morrone and Gras. Dishes may be ordered à la carte, or in a five course "Seasonal" or "Garden" menu, with the first including meat and fish and the second strictly vegetarian.

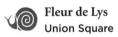

Fleur de Lys
Union Square

777 Sutter Street, between Jones and Taylor Streets
(415) 673-7779
Dinner only; closed Sunday
$$$$

My husband and I took our daughter to Fleur de Lys for her eighteenth birthday, and the restaurant easily met our expectations. We arrived for the early seating at 6:15 P.M. and were promptly seated in the recently redone dining room with lots of rich fabric cascading from the center of a square room.

The freshly baked breads arrived, followed by the *amuse bouche* of Chilled Tomato Pudding with a Crème Frâiche Quenelle and Chive. The sommelier stopped by to assist us with the extensive wine book. We steered clear of the 1976 Chateau Margaux magnum at $2,300, instead selecting a tried-and-true white Bordeaux.

The Foie Gras Prepared Two Ways and the Lobster in Artichoke Cream Sauce were delicious, as was the first course I ordered, a slightly spicy Tuna Tartare with Tarragon and Truffle Coulis. Piled next to the tuna was a stack of French-fried chickpea sticks and a small ramekin of tartar sauce. The emphasis at Fleur de Lys is clearly on technique, which certainly causes one to take note of every food arrangement, but superior presentation is only possible with quality ingredients, and here they are top-notch, mostly organic, and often local.

For an entrée my husband went for the veal, simply roasted tournedos with a foamy lobster bisque finished with a reduction of veal stock. Lauren tried squab—a culinary first for her—an exquisitely prepared breast filled with foie gras with hints of summer truffles in the mix. Alongside were tiny raviolis with duck confit tucked inside, sitting in a pool of ginger sauce. I chose the lightest entrée on the menu, the local halibut. I could not have been happier with the sweet, moist fillet accented with a refreshing blood orange jus and shiitake mushroom mixture. For dessert a three-tiered plate, each level with an assortment of petit fours, truffles, and miniature cookies, held the bar just as high as the first courses. We could get used to this—and so will you!

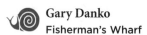

Gary Danko
Fisherman's Wharf
800 North Point Street, at Hyde Street
(415) 749-2060
$$$$

Sometimes we go out to eat at restaurants that project a cozy familiarity; sometimes, it's to places that are nothing like home, unless home happens to be a luxurious, well-staffed place where the food is extravagant, challenging, playful. and always delicious. Restaurant Gary Danko is one of those places. Without being at all stuffy or over-decorated, Danko is dressy enough to encourage a sense of heightened expectation. We don't go there nearly often enough, but when we do we always leave feeling welcomed, well-fed, and happy, just as we did during Gary Danko's time at the Ritz-Carlton. Now, as then, he conveys a sense of occasion in both the setting and the menu, which offers the choice of eating with restraint or total indulgence. Apart from a tasting menu with wines to match, you choose from several categories from appetizers all the way through dessert. This flexible format allows you to be as whimsical as you like.

Gary Danko was one of the first of San Francisco's grand restaurants to have an exciting artisanal cheese cart—well chosen and carefully sourced like everything else he handles. The wine list is full of good surprises, and for those who need to chat about the wine, there's friendly guidance. In case you haven't been pampered enough, dessert is followed by an entrancing plate of doodads, which puts you in a good mood for the bill.

You need to plan ahead for reservations, but every now and then, a last-minute phone call gets you in, and you can always get a nibble at the bar. The restaurant's Web site allows you to look at the current menu, and, since this changes with the season, there's little point in carrying on about specific dishes here. Suffice it to say, it's all good.

La Folie
Russian Hill

2316 Polk Street, between Green and Union Streets
(415) 776-5577
Closed Sunday
$$$$

One of the most beloved French restaurants in San Francisco, La Folie is a small family-run operation with Chef-Owner Roland Passot, a native of Lyon, France, at the helm. Passot began his career as a teenage apprentice to some legendary French chefs, including Jean-Paul Lacombe of Leon de Lyon and Pierre Orsi at his Michelin-star restaurant in the same city.

Diners can order either à la carte or the four-course prix fixe menu. Chef Passot's early training shines in dishes like the Snail Soup with Garlic; the Seared Foie Gras; the Lobster with Veal Sweetbreads, Leeks, and Seasonal Mushrooms; and the Roti of Squab and Quail Stuffed with Mushrooms and Wrapped in Crisp Potatoes. Passot has developed a skilled hand with vegetables as well, one that is highlighted in his vegetarian tasting menu.

Passot's brother, Georges, is in charge of the wine program at La Folie. He has compiled an extensive list, consisting mostly of wines from Burgundy, Bordeaux, and the Rhône. Service here is excellent and achieves the perfect blend of attentiveness and unobtrusiveness. The dining room has recently been remodeled with Moabi wood paneling and red banquettes that give the place an amber glow. The overall experience comes together beautifully, making La Folie a superb choice for a celebratory dinner.

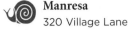

Manresa
320 Village Lane
Los Gatos   *SOUTH BAY*
(408) 354-4330
Dinner only; closed Monday and Tuesday
$$$$

Manresa's David Kinch is one of the Bay Area's most avant-garde chefs, having taken inspiration from French and modern Catalan cuisine, and from such revolutionaries as Chef Ferran Adria of El Bulli. Before working at New York's renowned Quilted Giraffe, Kinch honed his skills cooking in Europe. He opened his first restaurant, Sent Sovi, in Saratoga, California, before opening Manresa in 2002. The restaurant takes its name from the medieval town in the Catalonia region of northern Spain, famous for its Gothic basilica and monastery, as well as from a stretch of beach south of Santa Cruz, which the Jesuits of early California named Manresa.

Create your own three-, four-, or five-course meal ($58, $68, and $78, respectively) from such selections as Japanese Fluke Sashimi Style with Olive Oil and Chives; Roast Planked Sea Bream with Orzo and Basil Pesto; Braised Veal Cheeks with Cider Vinegar Caramel; and Red Wine–Braised Fig Shortcake with Buttermilk Panna Cotta and Fig Sorbet. Or put yourself in Kinch's hands by ordering the $94 "Seasonal and Spontaneous" chef's tasting menu.

How good is it? New York's four-star superchef Eric Ripert, of Le Bernardin, unexpectedly wandered into Manresa for dinner one night and was so captivated by the food that he invited Kinch to New York to cook at his restaurant for a bevy of city food press. You're sure to leave equally impressed.

Masa's
Nob Hill

In the Hotel Vintage Court
648 Bush Street, between Powell and Stockton Streets
(415) 989-7154
$$$$

Greg Short has some tall shoes to fill. After seven years under the tutelage of Thomas Keller at the French Laundry, he's recently taken over the helm at Masa's, one of the juggernauts of the San Francisco fine dining scene. Named for opening chef Masataka Kobayashi, many powerhouse chefs have been in charge here after Masa, including Julian Serrano and Ron Siegel.

The dining room has also recently been updated by Orlando Diaz-Azcuy, trading dark heavy velvet hues for a lighter feel—an elegant, yet modern look with a shimmery white draped entryway, rich chocolate brown walls, and deep red shirred lamp shades suspended from overhead. The room is refined, tasteful, and, well, swanky. The Sean Connery James Bond would have had his own private table here.

You can choose from a variety of prix fixe tasting menus—three-course, six-course vegetarian, nine-course, and a chef's choice. On a recent outing we had the three-course: chilled Maine crab to start, served with favas, red shiso, ponzu and a hit of chile oil. It was great. Next came steelhead trout with potato puree and fennel nage, followed by milk-fed poularde with black truffle jus. And with a cellar of more than seven thousand bottles, we chose to have Sommelier Alan Murray decide what would complement our meal. Desserts are sure to leave you feeling pampered and indulged; a Minaret cart with little candies, chocolates, and petit fours sends you off sweetly.

 **Michael Mina**
Union Square

In the Westin St. Francis Hotel
335 Powell Street, at Geary Street
(415) 397-9222
Dinner only
$$$$

More than a decade after he made seafood the star at the city's Aqua Restaurant, and on the heels of splashy and successful restaurants in Las Vegas, Chef Michael Mina has returned to open his eponymous restaurant in the Westin St. Francis Hotel.

The restaurant, in a subdued palette of gray, green, and cream, exudes calm and simplicity, in direct opposition to the complexity and drama of the cuisine. Subtle artwork decorates the high-ceilinged space, while the more dramatic art is on the plates. There's little about the food that is simple or understated.

The chef and his crew have a mastery of delicate flavors, alone and in combination, but despite its languorous pace, enjoying a meal chez Mina is not necessarily a relaxed affair. Mina's plates are actually plates on plates, in most cases three variations on a single ingredient, with three accompanying "tastes." The visual effect is dramatic, all color and shape on broad white plates dotted with smaller plates and cups and bowls. For instance, a tasting of Dutch Valley veal is prepared three ways: a scaloppine with egg fettuccine and lemon-caper brown butter; a pancetta-crusted loin with polenta, tortellini, and sage mascarpone; and braised short ribs with cauliflower gnocchi and vin jaune. Desserts are also served in triplicate. But for those seeking a more straightforward meal, order from the "Classics" menu and finish with Mina's famous root beer float—made with house-made root beer.

Michael Mina is an experience as much as a meal, much in the fashion of the French Laundry. Perusing the menu and comprehending the plates requires time and attention, but the sensory rewards are sublime.

NOTABLE

FINE DINING

Chez TJ
938 Villa Street
Mountain View   *SOUTH BAY*
(650) 964-7466
Closed Sunday and Monday
Prix fixe
$$$$

When Chez TJ opened its doors in November 1982, it stood alone as Mountain View's only high-end restaurant. Cofounder Thomas J. McCombie (the T. J. of Chez TJ) studied French cooking with Julia Child and Simone Beck. And TJ's tradition of exceptionally fine cooking lives on, with a lineage of talented chefs who have maintained consistent high quality, with current Chef Joshua Skenes at the helm.

Skenes has introduced Pacific Rim influences, combining fresh local produce and artisanal ingredients in innovative yet logical fusions. One recent menu included such delicacies as Steamed Egg with Uni, Chives, Lime Foam, and Caviar; Diver Scallops with Yellow Corn Sauce and Lemon Verbena; and Lamb Tenderloin with Fresh Peas and Cardamom.

BISTROS & BRASSERIES

Brigitte's Restaurant
351 Saratoga Avenue
Santa Clara   *SOUTH BAY*
(408) 404-7043
Closed Sunday and Monday
$$

Look closely as you drive along Santa Clara's busy Saratoga Avenue, past the 7-Eleven, and you will spot it. Tucked just off the street is this charming, contemporary French-Mediterranean bistro, where the food is authentic, simple, moderate in price, and utterly satisfying.

Inside the small brasserie, with its pale yellow walls and colorful French posters, you'll be greeted by founder Brigitte Benquet, a native of Paris. Lunch may include sandwiches such as Paris ham on a buttered French baguette or tuna with a dollop of saffron aioli. Dinner selections sometimes feature a plate of charcuterie; classic onion soup topped with gooey

Gruyère; or rabbit slowly cooked in white wine, sage, and rabbit stock. The prix fixe lunch includes soup and salad, and the prix fixe dinner offers a starter, main course, cheese plate, and dessert. Benquet's wine list has eighty selections, most from France, with a smattering from California, Argentina, and Portugal.

Brigitte's also hosts special events—wine tastings and cooking classes on everything from braising to simple sauces.

Café Jacqueline
North Beach
1454 Grant Avenue, at Union Street
(415) 981-5565
Dinner only; closed Monday and Tuesday
$$$-$$$$

For more than two decades, French-born Madame Jacqueline Margulis, with copper egg bowls as big as her smile, has single-handedly overseen this Lilliputian lovers' destination that specializes in nothing but heavenly soufflés for two. With cute lace curtains framing the windows and long-stemmed roses and candles on each table, the room is ripe for a romance-filled evening.

The selection of savory and sweet soufflés—perfectly poufy with a dark brown crust outside, light and creamy inside—changes daily. Some standards, such as lobster or salmon and asparagus are found year-round, but seasonal variations include a decadent black truffle in the winter and a fresh white peach rendition in the summer.

A limited selection of starters, such as a simple Watercress Salad with Mustard Vinaigrette or rich onion soup round out the limited menu and tide you over while you wait. And wait you will—most soufflés take more than thirty minutes to prepare! Even though you'll be tempted to while away the long lulls munching on crusty baguettes, don't; the pricey dinner soufflés, which run between $25 and $50, go down light but fill you up. Desserts are also in soufflé form at Chez Jacqueline, so be prepared for something special to end your meal. Just be sure you reserve in advance: Given the small size and slow pace of the restaurant, walk-ins cannot always be accommodated.

Chez Papa
Potrero Hill
1401 18th Street, at Missouri Street
(415) 824-8210
Closed for lunch on Sunday
$$

Walking into Chez Papa on Potrero Hill on a Friday night is a bit like walking into a restaurant in Marseilles. The atmosphere is warm, boisterous, and chic, and you are likely to hear French, rather than English, spoken by the waitstaff.

The food is simply prepared and unpretentious—hallmarks of a good French bistro. The menu is made up of *petites assiettes* and *grandes assiettes;* while both are good, you might want go with the petite option so that you can try numerous specialties, including the potato, asparagus, and artichoke salad with shaved parmesan and bacon or the pastis-marinated prawns with fennel, tomato, and artichokes.

If you still have an appetite, the chefs make a Provençal bouillabaisse with halibut, mussels, scallops, and potatoes and a good roasted half-chicken with olives, lemon, garlic, and Swiss chard. Traditional desserts include *mousse au chocolat* and crème brûlée subtly laced with lavender. The wine list, the final and perhaps most important element of a good French bistro, is good too.

Jojo
3859 Piedmont Avenue, at Rio Vista
Oakland   *EAST BAY*
(510) 985-3003
Closed Sunday and Monday
$$-$$$

This small, delightful, country-French dinner house on a pleasant shopping street in the East Bay has a short but thoughtful menu that changes with the seasons. While you'll find expected French bistro fare to be perfectly executed, you'll also discover unexpected touches that add a new take to the simplest dishes: a fresh tomato bisque boasts a truffled crouton; mussels are steamed with rose wine; smoked salmon comes with tomatoes stuffed with goat cheese. Jojo's chef-owners (Mary Jo Thoresen, who cooked with pastry chef Lindsay Shere at Chez Panisse, and Curt Clingman) prepare every dish themselves, from their pâté to their apricot sorbet served with fresh ginger cake. Signature dishes include the Trio of Little Salads (a starter) and a Savory Bread Pudding with Vegetable Ragout. There is something beautiful about simple dishes being prepared perfectly, since there is no margin for error. At Jojo you will be wowed by dishes you might eat on a weekly basis, and for that we say to Mary Jo and Curt, *merci beaucoup!*

South Park Café
SOMA
108 South Park Street
(415) 495-7275
Dinner only; closed Sunday
$$

The clock on the wall of this French bistro stopped at 10:30 and has been that way ever since this beloved South of Market café opened back in 1985. Hidden in a tiny, lovely green park full of plane trees, with a few outdoor tables under a red awning, you'd swear that you had landed near Les Jardins du Luxembourg. A zinc bar and a long dining room with banquettes add to the Parisian feeling, as, of course, does the food: classic French, selectively accented with California flavors.

On the concise and well-balanced menu you'll find classic bistro fare such as grilled flatiron steak with red wine sauce and French fries; sautéed rabbit with rosemary and carrots; and roast chicken with Yukon Gold potatoes, salad greens, and walnut oil. With its warm, professional service and its charming location, South Park offers a little taste and feel of Paris (with a soupçon of California), set in the heart of San Francisco.

NOTABLE

BISTROS & BRASSERIES

Bistro Aix
Marina
3340 Steiner Street, between Chestnut and Lombard Streets
(415) 202-0100
$$

Bistro Aix is a sure bet when dining with less adventurous friends, relatives, or a finicky date. Sometimes all you want in a meal is reliable French fare, which will seldom lead you astray: steak *frites,* roasted half-chicken with mashed potatoes, and ratatouille. At Bistro Aix these constants are done well and for prices that you can manage. Service is attentive, and the tented back patio is a very pleasant place to dine.

Chapeau!
Richmond
1408 Clement Street, at 15th Avenue
(415) 750-9787
Dinner only; closed Monday
$$

It's always reassuring when the owners of a restaurant are there all the time to oversee each diner's meal. Chapeau!'s owners, Phillipe and Ellen Gardelle, do it just about as well as anyone. Chapeau!'s menu is a mixture of bistro classics, including one of the best cassoulets in town: It's well balanced between lingot beans that are perfectly cooked (creamy yet still holding their shape), garlic sausage, and duck confit.

The restaurant serves a three-course prix fixe menu that represents one of the best values around. The excellent wine list is chock-full of bargains from Southern France, the Loire, Alsace, and the Rhône.

Chouchou Patisserie Artisanale & Bistro
Forest Hills
400 Dewey Street, at Laguna Honda
(415) 242-0960
$$

With large plate-glass windows overlooking the stately grounds around Laguna Honda Hospital, Chouchou is a lively and charming French bistro in an unlikely location. Chouchou's dinner specialty is country stew baked in an earthenware cassoulet dish with a pastry shell lid, but the chefs also make a mean *daube Provençal*, a dark and rich lamb stew with mushrooms. Pastry chef and owner Samie Didda, of the famed Parisian pastry shop Les Petits Mitrons on Rue Lepic in the eighteenth arrondissement, has brought his trademark recipes with him and creates sensational tarts with a variety of seasonal fruits. These can be eaten on the premises or ordered to go, along with a loaf of bread or one of their many cakes.

Clementine
Richmond
126 Clement Street, between 2nd and 3rd Avenues
(415) 387-0408
Dinner only; closed Sunday
$$

Although the neighborhood bistro is a dying breed in France, it's alive and well here in San Francisco. Clementine, a charming restaurant, seems almost out of place tucked into the end of Clement Street, crowded next to Chinese markets and restaurants. With a three-course early bird special priced at $23, it's no wonder so many regulars keep coming back for more steak *frites*, escargots, and *boeuf bourguignonne*. The wine list relies heavily on French vintages, with a smattering of California vineyards for those who like to eat internationally but drink locally.

Fringale
SOMA
570 Fourth Street, near Brannan Street
(415) 543-0573
Closed Sunday
$$

Chef Thierry Clement serves up Basque- and Gascon-inspired bistro fare at this stylish South of Market eatery. The white linens and wood finishes give the room a warm glow that the food happily reinforces. Service is impeccable—helpful yet unobtrusive. The thoughtful wine list offers interesting choices from France and the United States that pair well with the food. Consummate the evening with a snifter of Armagnac and a slice of the *gâteau Basque.*

Jeanty at Jack's
Financial District
615 Sacramento Street, between Montgomery and Kearny Streets
(415) 693-0941
$$$

Jack's was the quintessential power spot of San Francisco in days gone by, ornately decorated in the whorehouse/palace style of the Gilded Age. Philippe Jeanty rescued it from desuetude, and it is once again one of the city's most beautiful restaurants, with three floors of Victorian gilt and wrought iron. Jack's offers a menu of hearty bistro classics: rabbit terrine, duck *rillettes, quenelles de brochet,* coq au vin, cassoulet—all prepared perhaps not brilliantly but *correctement,* which is just what you want from this kind of food.

Le Charm French Bistro
SOMA
315 Fifth Street, between Folsom and Shipley Streets
(415) 546-6128
Closed for dinner Monday
$$$

In the middle of the chaos that is the South of Market neighborhood sits Le Charm, a chef-owned restaurant calmly offering unadulterated French bistro classics without a trace of fuss. The space is serene and spare, making a dinner at Le Charm more about the food than the decoration. The chicken liver salad is both inspiring and grounding in its simple honesty. The house-made sausage with mashed potatoes is so comforting you'll become a regular. Definitely opt for a side of the bitter greens. And don't worry about the bill's arrival, as prices here are remarkably modest.

Le Petit Robert
Russian Hill
2300 Polk Street, at Green Street
(415) 922-8100
$$

Located on a sunny corner of Polk Street in Russian Hill, Le Petit Robert bears restaurateur Pascal Rigo's trademark Parisian panache. Like his Boulangerie du Polk next door, the decor, the menu, and the service are all thoroughly French. Niçoise salad, mussels *mariniere,* and the roasted chicken are favorites. Indeed Le Petit Robert excels in all the simple French dishes that are best when prepared without much fuss. This is definitely a neighborhood darling in an area known as Rue de Polk.

Marche aux Fleurs

23 Ross Common, off Lagunitas Road

Ross   *MARIN*

(415) 925-9200

Closed Sunday and Monday

$$$

Marche aux Fleurs offers a Provençal neighborhood experience, with menus following the seasonal offerings in the nearby farmers' markets. Devotees point to the excellent wine list, which features small, local producers. In warm weather, you can enjoy dining outside on the patio. Call ahead to get an upcoming calendar of the restaurant's famous wine dinners, each of which is hosted by a different well-known vintner or food producer.

INDIAN AND PAKISTANI

Ajanta   *(Indian)*
1888 Solano Avenue
Berkeley   **EAST BAY**
(510) 526-4373
$$

Lachu Moorjani's dissatisfaction with the curries at local Indian restaurants ultimately led him to open his own establishment. And while the curries at Ajanta are exceptional, it would be unfair not to consider his menu as a whole—reflecting the chef's tireless pursuit of the vast spectrum of regional fare from all over India.

Moorjani's menu contains some twenty-three entrées, each detailing ingredients right down to the spices used and specific region of origin. A typical monthly special might be a Goa-style lamb curry made with Niman Ranch lamb, cubed and simmered in a sauce made with tomatoes, ginger, coconut milk, and spices including coriander, cumin, and chiles.

If the menu doesn't impress you with the wide range of options, then surely the gastronomic high of filling up on vegetable *pakoras,* Kandahari chicken, and a bowl of cardamom ice cream will have you plotting the shortest distance between wherever you are and a table at Ajanta.

Amber India   *(Indian)*
2290 El Camino Real, No. 9, in the Olive Tree Shopping Center
Mountain View   **SOUTH BAY**
(650) 968-7511
$$–$$$

Since 1994 Amber India has been the top choice of Indian-food lovers. While Amber does offer the ubiquitous Indian lunch buffet, this quiet oasis, tucked just off congested El Camino Real, also offers an array of Northern, Moghlai, and tandoori specialties, all served with grace and panache.

Butter chicken is legendary here, a heavenly mix of shredded tandoori chicken simmered with tomato, fenugreek sauce, and, of course, lots of butter. Julia Child would have approved. You'll even find the likes of tandoori lobster, its tail marinated in lemon juice and spices.

In 2003 owner Vijay Bist, who went to culinary school in India, then trained in Europe, opened a second Amber India in San Jose. It was a smart move. The always-crowded San Jose locale is a hit. Be sure to have the duck crepe appetizer, an unforgettable masala crepe rolled around tender, star anise–flavored duck leg meat. Order the assorted bread basket to soak up every drop of sauce on every plate.

Even the buffet is not standard here—it's pricier than most ($13.95) and features fifteen to twenty dishes daily. You won't find naan sitting on the steam table, turning limp and lifeless. Instead it is brought fresh and hot to your table.

Other Location
377 Santana Row, San Jose; (408) 248-5400

The Empress of India *(Indian)*
3426 El Camino Real, at Flora Vista Avenue
Santa Clara **SOUTH BAY**
(408) 296-0717
Lunch Tuesday through Friday; dinner Saturday; group
   reservations other days
$$

One would never expect to find such a treasure tucked in back of an old El Camino strip mall near Lawrence Expressway, yet Empress of India attracts a following of passionate food lovers. People come from all over to taste Jeanne Bonk's cooking and to be greeted by her husband, Robert; together they run one of the best Indian restaurants in the South Bay. Jeanne grew up in Allahabad in Northern India. Although her parents were Scottish and Armenian, she learned Hindi in school and learned how to cook from the locals.

Empress of India has no printed menu, and the selection changes daily. Robert shops each morning for fresh ingredients, which Jeanne then weaves into the daily menu, improvising on whatever he finds. The results are sublime. The fried vegetable *pakoras* showed no hint of grease. Crisp breading of garbanzo flour, redolent of coriander, wrapped strips of onion and fresh spinach leaves. We dipped these into a fresh, spicy green chutney made of cilantro, mint, jalapeño, lemon juice, and salt. The *dal* (lentils) featured crumbs of toasted garlic, whose nutty, soft bitterness offset cumin and fresh ginger. The *palak paneer* used fresh house-made cottage cheese *(paneer)* combined with spinach, browned onions, fresh tomatoes, cumin, turmeric, ginger, garlic, and chiles. Jeanne's meat curries have occasionally astonished me with their balance between subtlety and intensity.

Little Deli *(Indian/Pakistani)*
Tenderloin
552 Jones Street, near O'Farrell Street
(415) 409-3354
Closed Monday
$

Of late, there has been an explosion of no-frills Indo-Pak eateries in the "Tandoorloin," but the most overlooked is Little Deli. Getting there may

feel a bit like crossing the River Styx: The area swims with hustlers, hookers, hookers, dealers, and, lately, hipsters snaking a line into the overrated joint next door. But enter Little Deli and you'll find an oasis of made-to-order food at bargain prices. The proprietress smiles, takes your order, efficiently chops vegetables, and bosses her frazzled husband around. He, sweating from the heat, cooks several dishes at once while shooing away the would-be hoodwinkers outside. Watch him handle with his tongs a great blistery puffed round of naan—the best in the 'Loin—extracted from a hot clay-encased well.

Start with tangy *papri chat,* a chickpea-potato concoction over a pastry crisp, smothered with cilantro and chutneys. The lamb curry is tooth-some; the lamb *biryani* (slow-cooked rice, meat, and whole spices) is true comfort food; and the *sag paneer,* packed with spinach and cheese cubes, is as good as it gets.

Unless you've called ahead, be prepared to wait. The Muslim proprietors kindly allow you to bring in cold beer, but please dispose of your empties outside the establishment!

Lovely Sweets & Snacks *(Indian)*
41031 Fremont Boulevard
Fremont   *EAST BAY*
(510) 657-1412
$

A nondescript minimall off the Fremont thoroughfare is home to Lovely Sweets and Snacks, a *chaat* house in downtown Fremont. It's the perfect place for a quick dinner before heading over to the Naz 8 Theater for a Bollywood movie. There are only a handful of tables here, and the tone is set by Indian families dropping by to pick up boxes of confections. Westerners will feel as if they're traveling to a foreign land, with all the sense of confusion and discovery that implies.

Order the *thali* dinner with a half-dozen vegetarian items that always seems to include *cholle* (chickpea stew). In fact, chickpeas are so prevalent—whatever we order, they seem to appear on the table—the place could be called Lovely Chickpeas. The appetizers are also delicious, especially the samosas and fried stuffed chiles.

Lovely Sweets is, of course, also a sweet shop, and there is a large glass case filled with beautiful Indian desserts. Try *rasmalai* (a dessert made of fresh curd in a sweet milky sauce), *ladoo* (corn flour fritters soaked in corn syrup), or one of the nut-based desserts decorated with gold leaf. Don't forget to wash it all down with a mango *lassi* or chai—you'll need the caffeine for the three-hour movie later on.

Other Location
Lovely Sweets, 932 East El Camino Real, Sunnyvale (South Bay); (408) 245-7012

Maharani Magic Cuisine of India *(Indian)*
Tenderloin
1122 Post Street, at Polk Street
(415) 775-1988
$$

You might guess that the hardest reservation in town for Valentine's Day would be Michael Mina or Gary Danko, but my guess would be one of the six alcoves in the fantasy room at the Maharani. Shoes come off as you slip into the booth, beaded curtains are released, closing off each table from the room, and the dimmer switch to the right of the *Kama Sutra* painting is in your control. Rose water–scented warm towels ready you for the feast.

There are four feasts to choose from: Fantasy Feast No. 1 is vegetarian, while Fantasy Feast No. 4 is the *Kama Sutra* Love Banquet and includes aphrodisiacs like a Hot-and-Sour Ginger Oyster Soup and Lobster

Maharani, complete with a Mystical Love Couplet signed by the author, who just happens to be the restaurant's owner. On certain evenings live music and dancing further enhance the mood. Wine pairings range from the new Indian winery, Sula, to Dom Perignon. The flavors are great, and the ingredients, though not organic, are fresh and local.

For everyday dining the same fabulous flavors and a whole lot more are available à la carte. The samosas and *pakoras* are some of the best in town, and in addition to tandoori specialties, there are special regional dishes like a traditional Goa-style fish curry, lamb Madras, and a Kashmiri pilaf. The menu changes with the zodiac and the vegetables with the seasons.

Mela India Restaurant   *(Indian)*
Union Square
417 O'Farrell Street, between Jones and Taylor Streets
(415) 447-4041
BYOB
$

Until recently Mela was known as the "fancy" Shalimar, to distinguish it from its hole-in-the-wall cousin around the corner on Jones Street. Now under new ownership, it is even fancier, with ceramic plates, an expanded menu, and a remodeled dining room with low tables and cushions. (Taller people, especially those who are not yoga-inclined, may want to opt for the tables and chairs.) Many things have remained the same, though, like the worn red carpeting on the stairs, winding down into a foyer with a gurgling fountain. Indian music, colorful tapestries, and lots of hand-crafted flourishes add to the festive ambience of the dining room.

The food at Mela is better than ever. The only problem is that by the time I order what I cannot live without (Seekh Kebab, chicken *tikka* kebab, onion *kulcha,* rice, *chana masala,* and *palak paneer*), I don't have enough room for the new items on the expanded menu. Mela is one of the few Indian restaurants in the area that serve beer and wine.

Punjab Kebab House   *(Indian/Pakistani)*
Tenderloin
101 Eddy Street, at Mason Street
(415) 447-7499
$

When I first ate at Punjab Kebab House, located on a sunny corner not far from Union Square, it immediately became my absolute favorite tandoori restaurant. The spicy food sparkled, the vegetable curries were fresh and delicious, the tandoori chicken was moist and perfectly spiced, and Bollywood videos entertained throughout the meal. Then tragically, just months later, they suddenly closed for what they thought would be several months, as the building needed an earthquake retrofit.

My friends and I were heartbroken. I would call to check on them, but there was never any answer, and I even detoured through the gritty Tenderloin to monitor the progress in person. Finally, twenty-two months later they reopened again. The whole restaurant has been fully remodeled, but the same friendly owner oversees the kitchen, and the food is better than ever. There are now quite a few good, inexpensive tandoori restaurants in San Francisco, but Punjab Kebab House still ranks as one of the best.

Udupi Palace   *(Southern Indian)*
1901 University Avenue
Berkeley   **EAST BAY**
(510) 843-6600
$

Named for a temple in India, Udupi Palace in Berkeley is full of Indians looking not just nostalgic but also gleefully happy. Clearly, you've come to the right place for South Indian vegetarian food that is cooked and served with convincing integrity. Rice-and-lentil-based regional standards like the shatteringly crisp *dosas,* airy *idlis,* and *medu vadas* are served with a robust, comforting *sambhar* (soupy *dal* with vegetables) and a pair of house-made chutneys—one tomatoey and the other made with fresh coconut. The *thali,* a circular tray bearing several vegetable and lentil dishes accompanied by rice, *pappadam,* and *poori* or *chapati,* is exceptional for the changing variety of featured vegetables. To drink there's the usual offering of *lassis,* sweet and salty, but my favorites are the appetite-sparking spiced buttermilk, served before or with the meal, and the South Indian filter coffee (hot milk and superstrong drip coffee mixed in inverse ratio—much heavier on the milk). Be sure not to pass up one of the tasty and unusual desserts. The carrot *halwa* is especially good, with shredded carrots baked with ground cashews, butter, and sugar, served warm.

Udupi Palace is housed in a simple storefront, with big windows that face the street and warm the dining room with afternoon sun. The decor is minimal, the atmosphere cheerful, the service kind, and the prices clement.

Other Location
976 East El Camino Real, Sunnyvale (South Bay);
   (408) 830-9600

Vik's Chaat Corner   *(Indian)*

726 Allston Way
Berkeley   **EAST BAY**
(510) 644-4412
$

Vinod Chopra's family was stunned when he announced plans to serve *chaat* out of a corner of his Indian import shop (Hindi for "lick," *chaat* encompasses a vast repertoire of roadside dishes sold across India). After all, Bombay-born Chopra was a respected businessman and owner of Vik Distributors, the largest distributor of Indian beer, rice, *dal,* and spices in Northern California—a far stretch from the street vendors whose livelihood depends on a single burner and a cooking pan. Plus *chaat* was all but unknown in this country. He did it anyway and never looked back.

Located in a warehouse space where you order at the counter, Vik's is foremost about the food. A favorite is the *bhatura cholle,* a fermented wheat dough that is rolled to order and deep-fried, in a venerable cast-iron pot, into a puff the size of a soccer ball; it comes with chickpea curry and mango pickle. Grandmotherly women, elegantly dressed in saris, are stationed at the griddles, turning out breathtakingly beautiful *masala dosa*—newspaper-sized rice-and-lentil crepes stuffed with spiced potatoes. They also turn out *idli sambar,* steamed cakes of the same rice-and-lentil batter that are served in lentil soup, with cilantro and coconut chutney. Characteristic of Hindu food, most items are vegetarian, but specials include chicken *biryani,* a dish of layered chicken, rice, and spiced and slightly sweet yogurt *raita.*

Drinks include Indian sodas, chai, mango *lassi,* and coconut water straight from young coconuts. A pastry case by the register is stocked with colorful, nut-based Indian confections. The *gajar halwa* (a house-made carrot and milk dessert) or the *rasmalai* (fresh milk curd cake with saffron milk) are particularly delicious.

NOTABLE

Dasaprakash *(Southern Indian/Vegetarian)*
2636 Homestead Road
Santa Clara *SOUTH BAY*
(408) 246-8292
$

Dasaprakash, an American outpost of a popular chain of vegetarian hotels and restaurants in Southern India, is headed by the "Hotel King of South India," Shri Seetharama Rao. It's a casual, peaceful place and specializes in crisp *masala dosai* (lentil-flour crepe). At $4, the mango *lassi* drink seems expensive compared with the average $8 entrée, but it's not. Comprised of house-made yogurt and sweet fresh mango, it's the perfect cool complement to the spicy dishes.

Rotee *(Indian/Pakistani)*
Lower Haight
400 Haight Street, at Webster Street
(415) 552-8309
$

While Rotee offers many of the same menu items as other tandoori restaurants, it is also clean and stylish, even verging on hip. Much of the food is prepared in the tandoor and *karahi* (a woklike pan) in an open kitchen separated from the rest of the room by a tall, sage-green, tile counter. Feel free to bring your own alcoholic libation.

Shalimar *(Indian/Pakistani)*
Tenderloin
532 Jones Street, at Geary Street
(415) 928-0333
BYOB
$

When Shalimar first opened on Jones Street in the Tenderloin, it was the first restaurant of its kind, and it whetted San Franciscans' appetite for the food of Pakistan and Northern India.

The folks behind Shalimar hail from Lahore, the capital city of Punjab province, near the Indian border. Music and tourist posters from home provide color in this otherwise nondescript restaurant, but the real decor is the scene in the kitchen. A gaggle of men scoot back and forth, shouting at each other while dishing up bowls of *dal paneer* and plates of saffron-flecked rice. Shalimar is semi-self-service, so the first thing to do is grab a table and a menu, then go to the front counter to place your order, which will be delivered to your table. The *kabli channa* (stewed chickpeas seasoned with garam masala and tamarind) are a favorite, as is the *bengen bhujia* (eggplant slow-cooked with onion and tomato). Alcohol is not served here, but you can bring your own. If you forget, there are liquor stores on nearly every nearby corner.

Other Location

1409 Polk Street, at Pine Street, San Francisco; (415) 776-4642

Sue's Indian Cuisine *(Indian)*

216 Castro Street
Mountain View *SOUTH BAY*
(650) 969-1112
$

Subhadra (a.k.a Sue) Sista had a mission: to open a restaurant that would showcase the rich cuisine of all of India. She began with her mother's and grandmothers' recipes from Telugu Desam and ground and mixed all of her own spices for each dish. Today both of her restaurants are run by other members of the Sista family. Skip the lunch buffet and instead go for dinner, where the cuisine really stands out. The menu comprises much of Indian cuisine, from the southern specialties of *idli* and *dosa* to the northern naans and tandooris. While these options are all very good, the *parathas* (fried whole-wheat bread) and the vegetarian options are truly impressive.

Other Location

895 Willow Street, San Jose (South Bay); (408) 993-8730

ITALIAN

A16
Marina
2355 Chestnut Street
(415) 771-2216
$$

Ever since it opened, there has been bumper-to-bumper traffic at A16. Named for the highway that connects Naples to Bari, A16 specializes in the cooking of Campania. So of course there is pizza cooked in the wood-fired oven, and co-owner Christophe Hille is even recognized by the Naples-based AVPN (Associazione Vera Pizza Napoletana.) As with any certified Neapolitan pizza, when the pie is pulled from one of the two wood-burning ovens that flank the open kitchen, it is still malleable enough to be folded in four without breaking. Mozzarella and tomato comingle on top, forming pools of sauce. In a word it is *delicioso!*

In addition to its fidelity to the cooking of a single region of Italy, A16 also seeks out the best ingredients, like produce from Mariquita Farms near Santa Cruz, rare breed meats from Heritage Foods USA, and *burratta* flown in from Gioia Caseificio in Los Angeles. Recommended appetizers include tuna preserve and red peppers with a drop of red wine vinegar, and the ricotta and chard involtini with olive oil and radish salad. Or choose the excellent tripe prepared Neapolitan style with tomatoes, onions, and white wine. And don't miss the house-cured salumi. Among the special pasta dishes are *maccheronara*, a type of homemade *strozzapreti* with a tomato ragù and ricotta salata. And for a main course, the top sirloin roast with rosemary, green peppercorns, and *mosto* is delicious; so are the braised pork breast and the house-made fennel sausages served with grilled bread. But try anything that sounds appealing—this is a menu to mine.

Co-owner Shelley Lindgren, former sommelier at Fleur de Lys, has constructed a nationally acclaimed wine list that focuses almost solely on the lesser-known Southern and Central Italian wines, from Umbria southward. Always gracious, Lindgren will enthusiastically match the wines to your meal, if you like.

As noted travel writer Norman Lewis wrote in 1944, "Food, for the Neapolitans, comes even before love, and its pursuit is equally insatiable and ingenious." Come and experience the love at A16, but be sure to make a reservation first.

Acquerello
Russian Hill
1722 Sacramento Street, between Polk Street and Van Ness Avenue
(415) 567-5432
$$$$

The interior of Acquerello reminds one of an old church and beautifully sets the stage for food that is both formal and uplifiting. Chef Suzette Gresham and front-of-the-house impresario Giancarlo Paterlini have been serving the faithful since 1990.

Gresham's dishes range from regional Italian to more elaborate and modern interpretations of traditional recipes. The appetizer of dill and fennel-crusted loin of seared tuna topped with tonnato sauce is excellent. One of most interesting pastas is small macaroni with foie gras scented with black truffles. Fabulous *spaghetti alla chitarra* appears on the menu every now and then as well.

Meat and fish courses include a branzino served over artichokes, olives, arugula, and potatoes, all dressed with a red wine–pancetta vinaigrette; and wrapped timpano of braised lamb shank in a red wine reduction.

Paterlini has put together a fine wine list with bottles from some Italian greats like Angelo Gaia, and he and his staff have the magic touch of knowing when to be there for guests and when to leave them alone, an art that comes from years of experience.

Da Flora
North Beach
701 Columbus Avenue, at Filbert Street
(415) 981-4664
Dinner Tuesday to Saturday; closed Sunday and Monday
Cash preferred; no cell phones
$$

This Venetian-inspired, highly personal *osteria* is on the northern out-skirts of the labyrinth of cafés in North Beach. Devoted locals consider this a culinary sanctuary. The Murano glass chandelier, dimmed to a seductive golden hue, Fortuny lamps, crimson red walls, flickering can-dles, and a nibble of focaccia and a sip of amarone induce a near-religious epiphany for many.

The menu changes weekly and lists dishes inspired by owner Flora Gaspar's upbringing in Venice. Chef Jen McMahon has traveled exten-sively through the Veneto and even Budapest to perfect such luminous dishes as house-made sweet potato gnocchi in a sherry cream sauce with bits of pancetta; squid ink risotto; pan-seared double-cut pork chops with roasted peaches and cipollini onions; and chicken *paprikás* over home-made tagliatelle. Truly superb are co-owner Mary Beth Marks's house-made focaccia drizzled with olive oil and sprinkled with sea salt, and her desserts, including mascarpone and white chocolate cheesecake and tan-gerine granita dotted with pomegranate seeds.

Gaspar, well-versed in the regional and historical influences of Italy's nearly eight hundred grape varietals, navigates us mere mortals through a selection of more than a hundred Italian wines. Da Flora's seductive atmosphere and remarkable food and wine make for a delightful and savory evening.

Delfina
Mission

3621 18th Street, between Dolores and Guerrero Streets
(415) 552-4055
Open nightly; at peak times, reserve well in advance.
$$

Craig Stoll and Anne Spencer's Delfina, in the Mission district, is a roaringly popular neighborhood restaurant that has fans across not only San Francisco but the country as well. The name of the restaurant was borrowed from Da Delfina, an exceptional Tuscan restaurant in the picturesque hillside town of Artimino, where Stoll trained. He learned his lessons well and recreates authentic Tuscan cuisine here at home. Like Da Delfina's ribolitta, Stoll's version of this bread-thickened minestrone is classically Tuscan. And like the best restaurants in Italy, ingredients get the respect they deserve here at Delfina. Stoll buys many products from small local producers with whom he has developed strong relationships.

A few menu items have become classics and are almost always available, like the grilled squid with white beans, the tripe Florentine style, and the roasted Fulton Valley chicken. But many selections change with the seasons, so the chilled sweet pea soup with mascarpone might be around for only a few weeks in spring; the fresh favas, a few months. Typical pastas include a spinach *fazzoletti* (handkerchief-cut pasta) with a ragù that is both clean and savory, or a tagliatelle with pesto and summer squash. For dessert enjoy a glass of vin santo with a slice of rhubarb *crostata*, or the wildly popular buttermilk *panna cotta*.

The wine list, expertly crafted to complement the menu, offers a dozen by-the-glass and many more interesting and reasonably priced bottles. Spencer runs the front of the house with a kind of warm, efficient generosity that filters through the staff, but be aware that the restaurant is a bit crowded and noisy.

Dopo
4293 Piedmont Avenue

Oakland   *EAST BAY*

(510) 652-3676

$$

If pressed most young chefs will tell you they secretly dream of opening a small restaurant with a dining room that feels like home. The owners of Dopo, graduates of the renowned Oliveto, have succeeded in doing just that. The place is tiny and casual, with eight small tables and a hardwood counter that looks into an open kitchen. Reservations aren't taken, so groups linger outside the door, waiting for a space to sit, inadvertently livening up this part of Oakland's typically sleepy Piedmont district.

Dopo's Jon Smulewitz understands how to cook with local, organic ingredients. He expertly rolls his own pastas and grinds and stuffs his own sausages. The menu is short, with a list of antipasti (like Spicy Pork Sausage with Escarole) that changes daily, pasta (like Tortelloni with Oysters and Chervil), and, of course, the pizzas for which they have become famous. The wine list is equally brief, containing only a dozen tasty and inexpensive Italian reds and whites, all of which are available by the glass.

The counter is a wonderful place to sit with a glass of wine, watching the cooks transform a lump of dough and pile of wild chanterelles into a bubbly, thin-crust pizza. At Dopo you could have a meal that any Piedmontese—both the Italian or Oakland version—would be proud to serve at home.

Eccolo
1820 Fourth Street

Berkeley   *EAST BAY*

(510) 644-0444

$$-$$$

After nearly a decade of yearly trips to Northern and Central Italy, Chef Christopher Lee has opened Eccolo, where he takes the same perfect ingredients he used downstairs at Chez Panisse for sixteen years and puts his own spin on the most special dishes he's encountered throughout his travels.

First courses on the seasonal menu might include *panzanella*—the Tuscan tomato-and-bread salad with cucumber, spring onion, and celery—

or the ever-changing *fritto misto*, sometimes with pigeon livers, chicken thighs, spring onion, and lemon. Almost every day there is a handmade pasta: nettle tagliatelle with spinach and sweetbread-and-borage ravioli are typical examples. *Bollito misto*, a traditional mixed boil of brisket, beef tongue, and chicken, is served regularly on Sunday nights with bright salsa verde and a piquant tomato-caper sauce.

Perhaps Eccolo's signature, though, is the house-made charcuterie. After many years of practice with Tuscany's lauded butcher, Dario Cecchini, Lee expertly cures hams from Oregon's Laughing Stock Farm with Sicilian sea salt, aging them for sixteen months to make rosy prosciutto. He's now experimenting with an array of heritage breed pork varieties like the Red Wattle, the rarest breed in the United States.

Sweets at Eccolo are equally simple and true to *la cucina italiana*. Superb *gelati* and *sorbetti* are on the menu daily in sometimes surprising combinations. The concise wine list is well chosen and affordable, consisting of two dozen or so regularly changing wines from all over Italy, with a strong focus on Piedmont, the Veneto, and Tuscany.

Incanto
Noe Valley
1550 Church Street, near Duncan Street
(415) 641-4500
Closed Tuesday
$$$

Proprietor Mark Pastore, Chef Chris Cosentino, and Sommelier Claudio Vallani have teamed up to produce what is surely one of San Francisco's Slowest restaurants. With great passion, the chef makes several kinds of bread daily. But perhaps most unusual is Cosentino's use of the cuts of meat that most other chefs ignore: everything from the pig's tail and ear to beef liver and heart.

Incanto also makes exceptional mortadella, *salame al lardo*, country pâté, and other *salumi*. The pasta changes often, as does much of the menu. The *fazzoletti* (handkerchief-cut pasta) with pork ragù and the *agnolotti* with squab and chicken livers with morels and balsamic vinegar are superior dishes. Much of the antipasti and pasta benefit from herbs and vegetables that are grown on the roof of the restaurant. For the main courses, a smart diner will ask the waiter what unusual dishes Cosentino has cooked up from what he's found at the market that day.

Vallani has put together a great wine list, including several dozen wines by the glass. The list is an excellent representation of every part of the Italian peninsula, with some Italian enological gems.

Oliveto
5655 College Avenue, at Shafter Street

Oakland   *EAST BAY*

(510) 547-5356

$$$

Sometime around the rainy, midwinter days of late February or early March, people who appreciate the hog from snout to tail make their way up the stairs to the sophisticated but relaxed dining room at Oliveto. There during Oliveto's whole-hog dinners, they'll meander through a menu featuring salametto, soppressata, and other salumi cured in-house. The menu might offer a terrine of pickled pork ears and a mixed fry of pork trotters, brains, artichokes, and spring garlic enlivened with Meyer lemon. And, of course, there is a host of dishes made from the more accessible parts— fresh-roasted ham, pork scaloppine with wild mushrooms, and, for around $30, a groaning chaoucroute garni for two.

Founding chef Paul Bertolli, who was influenced by a celebrated stint at Chez Panisse and regular trips to Italy, made Oliveto famous by making nearly everything served at the restaurant—from the pasta to the balsamic vinegar—by hand. Bertolli recently left Oliveto to open his own salumeria, but his simple, soulful approach continues under Paul Canales, who has formally been named chef after running the kitchen for several years.

The café downstairs is the perfect spot for an impeccable sandwich of fennel salami with mustard, or a cup of coffee with the regulars from the Rockridge neighborhood. And if you don't make it to Oliveto for one of their special whole-hog dinners, don't worry. Oliveto gets a 250-pound Iowa-grown hog every week or so, and they use almost every bit. It's the only way, they say, to justify killing such a beautiful beast.

For more information about the Whole Hog and other special dinners, visit www.oliveto.com.

Poggio
777 Bridgeway

Sausalito   *MARIN*

415-332-7771

$$–$$$

Larry Mindel's Poggio in Sausalito is a welcome respite of grace in a town clogged with kitsch, tourists, and subpar eateries destined for ruin. In the Bay Area, complimentary valet parking provided by charming valets is unexpected and portends future delights inside. Sip an icy martini in an inviting chocolate-hued booth and take in the decor: rich, dark wood paneling and curved, creamy-white vaulted ceilings suggest nautical influences and add coziness to an otherwise gargantuan space.

Chef Chris Fernandez's simple and rustic food might arrive a little late to your table, but you'll forget entirely with a bite of the dishes that issue from Poggio's wood-fired rotisserie, grill, and mammoth roasting oven. Savory *Ceppo all'Amatriciana* defies the carb-conscious; blistered pizzas reflect a familiar "less-is-more" technique; and delicate petrale sole is simple but spectacular served with buttered spinach and potatoes. Coax someone in your party to order the wood-roasted whole fish: the tableside presentation is a testament to both finesse and speed. And pay close attention to the salads and vegetables. Most are organically grown on the owner's property in Sausalito and include an array of greens grown from seeds imported from Italy.

Poggio is meant to be a Sausalito hang-out and is open for a self-service breakfast beginning at 6:30 A.M. Lunch follows from 11:30 to 5:30—a most unusual offering for a restaurant of this caliber.

Quince
Japantown

1701 Octavia Street, at Bush Street
(415) 775-8500
Closed Monday
$$$

Michael and Lindsay Tusk are a stylish thirty-something couple with top-drawer connections in the Bay Area restaurant world. When they opened Quince in late 2003, familiar faces from Chez Panisse and Oliveto could be found at the stoves and in the dining room (both as servers and diners). Michael cooked at both restaurants under Paul Bertolli, and his ethereal pasta dishes show lessons well learned. Ravioli Filled with Beet Greens rivaled the delicate perfection of a Tuscan grandmother's. Pappardelle with Duck was toothsome and perfectly sauced.

But don't stop at pasta. The antipasti are beautiful, seasonal, and composed with a fine hand. A fish and shellfish antipasti plate included anchovy, sierra mackerel, white shrimp, and razor clam, each presented in a manner befitting their special characteristics, while artichokes *alla romana* were perfectly cooked and herbed. Main courses range from top sirloin roast with two varieties of cornmeal-crusted fried squash to a delicate steamed northern halibut to locally raised heritage breeds of poultry.

While the food is serious, in the best sense, it is never pretentious, and the same can be said for the entire operation. Lindsay manages the dining room while Michael runs the kitchen, and it is one of the most pleasant and adult dining rooms in San Francisco. Situated in an old apothecary in a residential neighborhood, Quince is light, airy, and comfortable, with just enough decorative touches, including white Venetian glass chandeliers and generous flower displays. Service is professional and hospitable without being overly chummy. Quince is one of San Francisco's best.

Rose's Café
Pacific Heights
2298 Union Street, at Steiner Street
(415) 775-2200
$$–$$$

Rose's is full of light at almost all hours of the day. In the late afternoon it turns from sunny café into a gracious bistro by merely laying white tablecloths and small votive candles on each of the twenty-plus tables.

Freshly baked pastries and focaccia accompany breakfasts of homemade granola or oatmeal, spinach scrambled eggs, or thin-crust breakfast pizza with prosciutto and fried egg. Lunch means abundant salads, more thin-crust pizzas, and sandwiches. A favorite when in season is steamed fresh local wild salmon stuffed into homemade pita, oozing with aioli and assorted organic greens.

At dinner young couples head to the tiny bar to taste wine, and then move on to the antipasti like Bruschetta with Gorgonzola, Radicchio, and Honey, or one of the many fresh pastas. The Chopped Salad with Gorgonzola Vinaigrette followed by Herb-Roasted Chicken on an enormous mound of crunchy fresh arugula makes for a satisfying meal out. There is rarely room for dessert; just enough for bites of their thin but rich chocolate cake, soaking in a pool of crème anglaise.

Rose's is a place where you can return week after week without ever tiring of its food. The host and waitstaff will begin to recognize you and always seem genuinely happy to have you back.

NOTABLE

Albona
North Beach
545 Francisco Street, at Mason Street
(415) 441-1040
Closed Sunday and Monday
Complimentary valet parking
$$

When homesick or in need of some mothering, head for Bruno Viscovi's Albona, the cozy Istrian restaurant on the northern edge of North Beach. The first sup of the thick, aromatic minestrone soup affirms that all can be right in the world. Follow it with *crafi Albonesi*, plump ravioli filled with cheeses, pine nuts, raisins, and nutmeg, served with a cumin-infused sirloin tips sauce, a combination that reveals the Istrian peninsula's Orient Express connections.

Angelino's Restaurant
621 Bridgeway, at Princess Street
Sausalito   *MARIN*
(415) 331-5225
$$

Located in Sausalito with a view of the bay (if you are lucky enough to get a window seat), Angelino's is the creation of Pasquale Alfonso and his son Alfredo. While the produce is not organic, the fish is always fresh. Fish appetizers from squid *fritto misto* to the seafood salad to the catch of the day are reminiscent of those you might find at an *osteria* on the Amalfi Coast. Angelino's is packed with old-timers for Friday lunch, but you might also spot Carlos Santana, whose studios are just down the hill.

Antica Trattoria
Russian Hill
2400 Polk Street, at Union Street
(415) 928-5797
$$$$

Ruggero Gadaldi, chef-owner of Antica Trattoria, comes to Polk Street via Bergamo in Northern Italy. The atmosphere of his trattoria is warm and friendly—if a bit loud when it's full—and simply made dishes like the Fennel, Blood Orange, and Red Onion Salad and the Black Pepper Pappardelle with Wild Boar Ragout have drawn a devoted clientele.

Brindisi
Union Square
485 Pine Street, at Kearny Street
(415) 593-8000
$$

Brindisi boasts lovely murals depicting various maritime scenes. Proprietor Antonio Spinoso runs Brindisi with Puglian Chef Fabrizio Protopapa, who prepares exceptional fresh fish dishes, such as Grilled Sliced Octopus or Octopus Carpaccio with Grilled Lettuce and Black Olives. He also makes by hand exquisite pastas, including a special orecchiette to which he adds broccoli rabe and bread crumbs.

Frantoio Ristorante
152 Shoreline Highway
Mill Valley   *MARIN*
(415) 289-5777
$$-$$$

Visit Frantoio in the fall to watch the annual olive crush from the comfort of the dining room. Frantoio is the only restaurant in the state with an in-house olive oil production facility, and the enormous granite press imported from Italy steals the show. Owner Roberto Zecca grows his own olives near Sacramento and sells his oil in the restaurant.

Ideale
North Beach
1309 Grant Avenue
(415) 391-4129
$$-$$$

A resident of San Francisco for nearly twenty years, Maurizio Bruschi is originally from Rome, where his grandmother had a trattoria (Da Nonna Serafina) and where he began cooking. The menu has an assortment of appetizers and typical Roman pizzas. *Penne all'amatriciana* with pig cheeks and the lasagna with meat sauce are good choices for *primi*. For a second course, try the milk-fed piglet or the Roman-style lamb.

L'Osteria del Forno
North Beach
519 Columbus Avenue
(415) 982-1124
Closed Tuesday
Cash only
$$

Susanna Borgatti and Vally Teltamanti have created a homey little space that serves wonderful food. Start with antipasti like the *insalata rustica* with tuna, white beans, and celery, or a baked pasta, one of several focaccia sandwiches, or a thin-crust pizza. The pork braised in milk is a house specialty. If you go, bring your patience, as you will likely have to stand in line in front of the restaurant, waiting for a table.

Prima Ristorante
1522 North Main Street
Walnut Creek   *EAST BAY*
(925) 935-7780
$$$

What started as a wine-and-cheese shop in 1977 has grown into a full-fledged dining establishment, and arguably one of the finest in Contra Costa County. What sets Prima apart, in addition to its competent and professional staff in both the bar and the dining room, is its great wine list. Heavy on Italian vintages but not lacking in any area, eating at Prima can feel like eating in a wine library. The staff loves to talk wine; they are knowledgeable and enthusiastic, eager to share their knowledge, but not pushy. And Chef Peter Chastain, who with his wine director recently purchased Prima from the original owners, has made fresh ingredients the focus of the menu. He makes his own noodles, and the optimal dining experience at Prima is best obtained by asking for the chef's menu.

Ristorante Marcello
Outer Sunset
2100 Taraval Street, at 31st Avenue
(415) 665-1430
Closed Monday
$$$

Don't expect cutting-edge Italian cuisine at Ristorante Marcello. This place defines the old school Italian-American restaurant. The standards are all there: veal piccata, veal Marsala, veal scallopini, all the veals, in fact—no surprises there. What makes Marcello's special is Marcello himself, the congenial, Lucchesi owner and proprietor.

Go on a Friday or Saturday night, with a reservation, when the place is hopping with long-time, older, mostly Italian patrons. Go in time to enjoy a drink at the grotto bar. And go during mushroom season when Marcello, a forager of the first order, will have brought back loads of porcini from his secret spots. They can be found in the excellent fried porcini appetizer, adorned with salt and a light squeeze of lemon, and in a ragu served over noodles. You will end up ordering more than one of each. Begin your meal with Marcello's own minestrone, and have the Frank's salad, shrimp and avocado with house dressing, named for a waiter who has since passed away. The wine list has been hand-picked by Marcello and includes some unusual finds at unusually reasonable prices. Everything is brought to you by tuxedoed waiters, many who could be stand-ins straight from central casting.

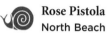

Rose Pistola
North Beach
532 Columbus Avenue
(415) 399-0499
$$-$$$

While North Beach, San Francisco's Little Italy, is dominated by Italian restaurants of every stripe, Rose Pistola may be closest to the original spirit of the place. Ingredients are fresh and local, and the dishes are based on the cuisine of the area's Ligurian immigrants. No Italian-American food here. Specialties include *farinata,* a chickpea pancake from the wood-burning oven, and the delicious *cioppino,* a seafood stew originated by North Beach fishermen. Whole fish are cooked in a variety of ways, with a choice of accompaniments, and sparkling hot and cold appetizers offer something for everyone. The place is also stylish, with an open kitchen, a bar, and sidewalk seating.

Vivande Porta Via
Japantown
2125 Fillmore Street, at California Street
(415) 346-4430
$$-$$$

Carlo Middiones's homage to his Sicilian culinary heritage is a bustling café brightly decorated with ceramics and filled with Italian foodstuffs. Like an authentic *salumeria,* you'll find real mortadellas, salamis, and hams; dozens of prepared food items; and a breadth of international cheeses. The sit-down menu features fresh house-made pastas and hearty regional meat dishes, but don't expect cutting-edge cuisine here; tradition rules. Do be prepared for the prices, though, which for dinner range from $14 to $24 for entrées, perhaps just a little too steep for a casual café.

JAPANESE

Delica rf1
Embarcadero
Ferry Building Marketplace
One Ferry Building, Shop 45
Embarcadero, at Market Street
(415) 834-0344
Takeout only
$$

Delica rf1 is an American outpost of a well-known Japanese chain that combines the European delicatessen concept with the tradition of *Sozai:* meals made up of many small dishes, reflecting a way of eating that is balanced and healthy. While most recipes are not strictly traditional, they are based on old methods of Japanese cooking.

Located in the Ferry Building, Delica rf1 offers a variety of beautifully prepared meals to take away. They have a daily selection of salads—some vegetarian, some not. *Hijiki*, black seaweed salad with *edamame*, is my favorite, and it's loaded with iron. Other offerings include curry rice (a Japanese interpretation of the Southeast Asian dish), *onigiri*, rice balls with seasonings, and salmon spring rolls. The croquettes are fried to perfection using fresh panko made from Acme Bakery's organic *pain de mie* (which makes a world of difference) and filled with potatoes, scallops, or shrimp.

The space is minimal and sleek with warm wooden touches. The bento box is a great deal, and I suggest buying two or three small containers of different salads, a fried item, and a rice ball for a perfect meal. Be certain to try one of the Ito-En chilled teas: this is one of the few places in America that carries them.

Ino Sushi
Japantown
22 Peace Plaza, Suite 510
(415) 922-3121
$$$$

From the first step into the formal entry you know Ino Sushi is different. The mud-plaster walls, the traditional white cedar post-and-beam construction, and the half-curtains that open into a small, lively dining room all make this restaurant feel closer to Japan than almost any other in San Francisco.

And then there is Chef-Owner Ino-san. In constant banter with his wife, who serves the four tables, he makes his way to and fro behind the bar, chatting with customers and deftly assembling sushi for the entire restaurant. Settle in at the bar, wipe your hands and face with the hot

towel, decide how much you want to spend, and order *omakase* (chef's choice).

Ino-san might start you with a fragrant bowl of clam miso soup and then proceed to sushi. Mild white fish will come first: perhaps one each of *tai* (sea bream), *hirame* (flounder), and *suzuki* (sea bass). The fish is pristine, and like the place itself, the sushi is small and precisely constructed. He reaches over and sets the sushi in front of you, directly onto the wooden ledge offset from the cedar bar. The flavors strengthen as the meal progresses. Next might come *hamachi* or *maguro*, and then mackerel two ways: one slightly cured in vinegar and wrapped with a paper-thin sweet white seaweed (just flown in from Kyoto) and the other sliced to show off the silver skin, with a dot of ginger, a few rounds of scallion, and a squeeze of lemon. There is a foil-lined electric grill off to the side that Ino-san uses to quickly toast nori seaweed as he needs it. It's a wonderful detail, and the crisp, barely warm nori elevates the jewel-like *ikura* (salmon roe) and pungent *uni* (sea urchin) roll. If it's available, try his signature roll with whole grilled *shisamo* (small smelt with roe) and *shiso* leaf—a warm and hearty finale. Wash down the meal with beer or any of a dozen sakes. House-made adzuki bean and agar *yokkan* and a cup of hot tea send you on your way.

Kappa
Japantown
1700 Post Street, Suite K
(415) 673-6004
Dinner only; closed Sunday
$$$$

Don't be dismayed by the difficulty of finding this very special restaurant. Located above Denny's in Japantown, you enter this tiny place through a door in the hallway of the Club Nikko. With only ten counter seats and one private room, Kappa offers some of the finest Japanese food in town. The owner, Mr. Kimura, works behind the counter, and his kimono-clad wife meets you with unrivaled Japanese hospitality.

No sushi is served here; instead the restaurant practices the *koryori* style of eating. The menu is made up of many small dishes that are eaten side by side. You either order from an à la carte menu or from the prix fixe menu for $75. There are no wasted motions here: Every part of each dish is integral to the taste and look, and many ingredients, like the *shiro kombu*, are flown in from Japan. Our last visit here was in midsummer, and the menu reflected the season and weather. We began with a cold eggplant dish with incredible hand-shaved bonito flakes, which imparted a delicate smoky flavor. The highlight of the meal was the grilled *shisamo*, a member of the smelt family that is filled with roe and eaten whole. We closed our meal with a steaming bowl of *ochazuke* (a bowl of rice with savory seasonings and hot tea poured over it) and delicate pickles. Finish with the *wagashi* (Japanese sweet *mochi*) and a perfectly brewed cup of green tea.

A well-edited sake selection is served in fine crystal cups. The service is attentive without being intrusive, and the serving dishes are unique. Take note of the hand-carved ice in the water glasses. Be sure to ask for counter seating—the small private room doesn't do justice to the wonderful food being served. Reservations are strongly suggested.

Kiss Seafood Japanese Restaurant
Pacific Heights
1700 Laguna Street, at Sutter Street
(415) 474-2866
Closed Monday
$$$–$$$$

Hidden on the ground floor of a condominium complex on the outskirts of Japantown, Kiss is a tiny enclave for Japanese businessmen and enthusiasts of *nihon ryori*. There are only twelve seats, and Naka-san prepares everything, from the pristine sushi to the grilled *hamachi kama*. The six-course tasting menu includes jewel-like sashimi, *chawa mushi* (a steamed savory custard), and any number of other traditional preparations.

Maki
Japantown
Kinokuniya Building of the Japan Center
1825 Post Street, between Webster and Laguna Streets
(415) 921-5215
Closed Monday
$$$

Though located on the second floor of the Japan Center Mall across from Kinokuniya Books, this tiny gem of a restaurant is hardly pedestrian. The restaurant specializes in *wappa meshi,* a bed of rice topped with delicately seasoned vegetables, fish, or meat and cooked in a bamboo steamer. My favorite is the salmon *oyako wappa,* which highlights salmon, salmon roe (*oyako* means "parent and child"), and herbs. The *wappa* comes with several side dishes that change seasonally. The night I went, my side dishes included a perfectly cooked *chawan mushi* (savory custard with shrimp, *mitsuba,* and a ginkgo nut), miso soup, and lightly flavored pickles. The daily specials can be a revelation: a bite-size piece of white fish, wrapped with nori, delicately fried, and served with *dashi* and grated daikon.

The menu also offers sushi, sashimi, elaborate bento boxes, and other cooked delicacies. My companion had the steak teriyaki, and it came with the same side dishes as the salmon *wappa*. It was a generous portion of chewy, well-flavored (not overflavored as most teriyakis are) meat and rice.

The sake selection is top-notch, and I highly recommend the Otokoyama served chilled in a beautiful decanter in which the ice is kept separate from the sake so as to not dilute it. *Shochu*, distilled grain alcohol served with lemon or plum, is hard to find in this country, but here it is served hot or cold. With just twenty-one seats, I prefer to sit inside rather than outside (in the mall); if you feel the same way, be certain to make reservations in advance and request your preference at that time.

O'Chame
1830 Fourth Street
Berkeley   *EAST BAY*
(510) 841-8783
Closed Sunday
$$

Located on bustling Fourth Street in Berkeley, this popular spot offers fantastic noodles and other Japanese dishes in a beautiful, serene main room and on a great outdoor patio. The menu here is limited but well articulated, with owners David and Hiromi Vardy offering dishes that are inspired by Japan but that draw on the bounty of the Bay Area.

Begin your meal with fresh organic greens and pristine tuna sashimi with rice vinegar dressing. The soba (buckwheat) or udon (thicker flour) noodles come in an aromatic bonito-based broth and with a choice of pork loin, trout, shrimp, or fried tofu *(aburage)*. Don't forget to sprinkle on the five-spice mixture from Kyoto found on your table in the bowl with the tiny spoon. Main dishes are less traditional but still delicious, such as Grilled Flatiron Steak with Collard Greens and Edamame, served with a bowl of rice.

Japanese teas are expertly brewed in iron pots and served in beautiful bowls that fit perfectly in your hand. A very good selection of wine, sake, and beer is available. Bento boxes are a delicious bargain and available for takeout during lunch, but quantities are limited, so arrive early.

Tanto
1063 El Camino Real
Santa Clara   *SOUTH BAY*
(408) 244-7311
Closed Monday; lunch only on Saturday and Sunday
$$$

When the Japanese want to go out for some good drinks and some tasty nibbles to accompany them, they head to an *izakaya*. And when Santa Clara Valley residents want an authentic Japanese experience, they can do no better than head to Tanto, the best *izakaya* this side of Tokyo. An *izakaya* is a lot like a Japanese tapas bar. The plates are small, they are shared between diners, and they are always accompanied by drinks.

In a land where California rolls and Philadelphia rolls have become standard fare in Japanese restaurants, Tanto provides the real experience. Although sushi does not make an appearance on the menu, it is not missed. Categories include sashimi, braised dishes, seared dishes, deep-fried dishes, soups, and much more. Recent highlights were braised black pork belly (a heritage breed of pork, imported from Japan, that's incredibly rich and flavorful); a seared duck breast with a spicy mustard sauce; and a silken glazed omelet of crab and shiitake mushrooms.

The best way to order here is to give the chef a price limit and let him call the shots. You might not know what is coming, but it is guaranteed to be good.

Other Location
1306 Saratoga Avenue, San Jose (South Bay); (408) 249-6020

Uzen

5415 College Avenue
Oakland   *EAST BAY*
(510) 654-7753
$-$$

Select sushi first from the hand-written specials menu that features the best of what Chef-Owner Kazuo Han has found that morning at the fish market in San Mateo. It might be rare tuna, young yellowtail, trout, butterfish, Spanish mackerel, or sockeye salmon. Or look for these exceptional items: fresh sweet shrimp, presented with caviar and a *shiso* leaf, or a spicy scallop roll. Or ask Chefs Han and Toshi for *omakase,* or chef's choice—an option not listed on the menu, but frequently requested by Uzen's many Japanese patrons.

Sushi is Uzen's specialty, but the restaurant has also perfected many cooked dishes. In addition to prawn and vegetable tempura, try the soft-shell crab or shiitake versions. Buckwheat soba noodles come either hot or cold and arrive with a carved bamboo shaker of Japanese hot pepper. Look to the specials sheet, too, for dishes like sea bass baked in miso sauce.

Uzen's "special meal" would not be complete without chilled sake served in hand-blown glasses—no two are the same—that Chef Kazuo imports directly from Japan. At the end of the meal, you will be presented with a slice of fruit or sweet *mochi* that is shipped from Hawaii and offered in several flavors: honeydew, mango, or white chocolate.

Yum Yum Fish

Outer Sunset
2181 Irving Street, at 23rd Avenue
(415) 566-6433
Closed Monday
$-$$

Thankfully, the fog that is whipped up by Ocean Beach, wrapping the Outer Sunset like a thick sweater, also obscures this culinary destination; otherwise it would be impossible to get a seat at Yum Yum. Built on sand dunes once filmed for desert scenes in 1930s Hollywood films, this neighborhood is thriving—one of the few middle-class, multiethnic enclaves left. The main drag is Irving Street, and the area around Yum Yum is the happening hub. Walk alongside Asian schoolgirls gabbing into mobile phones, and Russian seniors happily ignoring traffic laws. Go past dim sum storefronts, Vietnamese *pho* restaurants, a Middle Eastern green grocer who sells four kinds of feta, a real Irish bar, and into one inconspicuous shop that really is yummy.

While most sushi restaurants buy cuts of fish to save money, Yum Yum is actually a fish shop. So sushi, sold on the side, is fresh as can be and dirt cheap, the result of a restaurant buying the whole fish. Dining at one of the three on-site tables, you will be rewarded with a pot of toasted rice tea. Enjoy earthy miso soup and simple rolls. The hot, crunchy shrimp tempura roll is always a reliable choice, and the spicy tuna roll manages to butter and heat up the tongue at once. Warm barbequed eel is plummy, *hamachi maki* deserves two yums-up, and the salmon belly is house smoked. An anomalous Provençal fish stew owes its provenance to all the scraps left over at day's end, and to the fact that the retail fish manager is an enterprising Frenchman. Catch-of-the-day specials are truly that.

If eating next to a cold case of recently deceased fish leaves you unsettled, consider doing takeout. Golden Gate Park is only two blocks away, and Ocean Beach a short bike ride.

NOTABLE

Hama-Ko
Cole Valley
108B Carl Street, near Cole Street
(415) 753-6808
Closed Monday
$$

With no sign out front, plain white paper window shades, and a discreet door, Hama-Ko has been serving excellent sushi for more than twenty years. The sushi chef, Mr. Kashiyama, and his wife, in her starched, crisp pinafore apron, oversee the seven tables and four-seat sushi bar like it is a part of their home. And it is just the two of them, so during peak hours patience and understanding can be a necessity; but what you get in return is well worth it. Fish is purchased from the wholesaler every morning, so the menu is merely a guideline to what might be available on any given day.

Sushi Gourmet
215 Strawberry Village Shopping Center
Mill Valley   *MARIN*
(415) 381-8521
Closed Sunday
$$

Located in Strawberry Village, the low-slung terra-cotta-roofed shopping center parallel to Highway 101 in Mill Valley, Sushi Gourmet is well worth getting off the highway for. The small space, just five tables and a handful of seats at the sushi bar, is spotlessly clean and inviting. In addition to excellent sushi there are plates of cooked food like grilled calamari or eel served over rice and steamed black mussels steeped in sake. The *an kimo* (steamed monkfish liver) pâté is excellent, and make sure to check the board for other specials, as well as details on their interesting sake selections. For those who might shy away from a place proclaiming itself as "gourmet," please note that the name of the restaurant is a play on the owner's name, Go, combined with *mi,* meaning "flavor" in Japanese.

KOREAN

Brother's Korean
Richmond
4128 Geary Boulevard
(415) 387-7991
$-$$

While Brother's is one of a number of Korean barbecue restaurants along Geary Boulevard in Richmond, it is set apart by its enormous popularity and welcoming staff. On a weekend night, the dining room is reliably packed, despite the bad lighting and underwhelming decor (think Formica tables and cafeteria chairs). This is a good place to bring a large group. Everyone gathers around a central superhot charcoal brazier—masterfully set into a recess in the table by the unflappable fire bearer—and takes turns grilling sliced and marinated beef or pork. This is primal around-the-campfire conviviality. The meats are preceded by a delicious tofu soup and accompanied by more than a dozen *pan chan,* or side dishes. These include the requisite kimchee, pickled cucumbers, and sesame oil–infused dried seaweed, all of which are best eaten with steamed rice. With a big bottle of Hite, a crisp Korean lager, nothing could be better.

Although the meat is the main attraction, don't miss the *bi bim bop,* or "special rice in stone pot." The seafood selection is particularly good: rice cooked in a large stone bowl and topped with squid, scallops, shrimp, and a whole egg. The bowl arrives at the table blistering hot, and once the egg is cooked, you mix its contents together with sweet red chile paste. For variety, you might also try the cold buckwheat noodles in a beef broth or any of a handful of other traditional Korean dishes. Roasted barley tea is served to everyone, and the meal ends with a custard-sized bowl of *shik gae,* a sweet, glutinous rice drink. You may not want to wear your favorite sweater here—you'll carry the smoky atmosphere with you out the door.

New Korea House
Japantown
1620 Post Street, at Laguna Street
(415) 931-7834
$$

When you approach 1620 Post Street you will notice that there are two restaurants next to one another, both called Korea House. To make matters more confusing, both are owned by the same family and have similar menus. However, New Korea House is the more energetic and convivial of the two; and if, like me, you gauge a Korean restaurant by the *pan chan* (side dishes), then New Korea House is right up there with the best. You would be hard-pressed to find more plentiful and delicious offerings anywhere. Included are delicious kimchee, the refreshingly funky fermented cabbage, bean sprouts, tofu, fish cakes, and pickled cucumbers.

Meats are the specialty of the house, which you grill yourself on the tabletop brazier. New Korea House offers variations on the hot rice bowl dish *dol sot bi bim bap* and noodle dishes like *jap chae;* there's something for everyone, from tofu-eating vegetarians to hearty meat eaters. My favorite is *pa jun,* a crispy scallion pancake, which is listed without explanation or description on the menu. Servers here are helpful for those who've never experienced Korean food before.

Pyung Chang Tofu House
4701 Telegraph Avenue, at 47th Street
Oakland   *EAST BAY*
(510) 658-9040
$$

Pyung Chang has established itself as an underground favorite in the East Bay. While one can order Korean standbys like *bulgogi,* Pyong Chang Tofu House, true to its name, specializes in *soon doo boo,* or hearty tofu soups. Thick with vegetables, silky tofu, and a red, chile-infused broth, the soup arrives at a vigorous boil in stone bowls. A dozen varieties are available—some with pork, kimchee, beef, or squid. They are accompanied by steamed rice, which also comes in very hot stone bowls. For those who have grown up in Korean households, Pyong Chang is one of the only restaurants in the Bay Area to offer comfort food in the form of *biji,* a stew made from ground soybeans, kimchee, and pork.

The dining room is utilitarian, with high ceilings, empty walls, and rough-hewn tables—charred at the end by the scalding dishes. Chef and owner Jasmine Shin changes the *pan chan* (side dishes) frequently, and once you've ordered, the young, efficient, and perpetually bored-looking servers bring a half dozen earthenware dishes to the table. There is always kimchee, in its familiar napa cabbage form and in a crunchy version made with rounds of daikon. The small chilled dishes of potato braised with sweet rice wine and soy sauce, or bean sprouts dressed lightly with sesame oil exemplify the home-cooked flavors of the restaurant.

When the meals come to an end, the servers pour hot roasted barley tea into the rice bowls of their Korean customers to create a kind of after-dinner digestive drink. Non-Koreans are more often encouraged to pry the crispy rice crust from the inner surface of the still-hot stone bowls. While these browned crisps are just the thing to soak up the last savory spoonfuls of broth, don't hesitate to do as the Koreans do and wash the rice down with some hot roasted barley tea.

Sahn Maru

4315 Telegraph Avenue, at 43rd Street
Oakland   *EAST BAY*
(510) 653-3366
$$

As a college student of chemistry, the chef-owner, Hyung Ryul Yoo, and his buddies began cooking for each other in Korea, but eventually everyone recognized Yoo's cooking skills and let him do the honors. He later attended culinary school and opened a restaurant in Seoul that he ran for eighteen years in the trendy neighborhood of Gang Nam. There he specialized in a preparation of duck and goat stew. Eventually he brought these specialties to the States, first with a restaurant in San Francisco, and now with Sahn Maru.

For those who are used to the ubiquitous Korean barbecue, Sahn Maru comes as a welcome change of pace. The popular stew features "black" goat (black is a color that denotes health in Korean cuisine) and arrives at your table either as a single portion in a bubbling hot pot or in a larger casserole dish set atop a gas burner if you are seated with a group. The color of the stew, as the name suggests, is dark; the pieces of goat are tender and gamy and are meant to be dipped in a sauce of sesame oil, mustard, and chile paste. Sesame leaves help flavor the dish, but Yoo is evasive about how exactly he seasons the dish. The stew is so delicious it's no wonder he protects his spicy secrets.

Not only does Sahn Maru offer goat and duck specialties, but there are other stone-pot dishes and a great seafood pancake appetizer perfect for sharing with a group. The *pan chan* are delicious: spicy and salty in all the right ways, so as not to overpower the taste of the vegetables. You might ask for the traditional mook—a jelly made from ground acorn and seasoned with soy sauce, sesame oil, scallions, and sesame seeds. While every dish might not be as adventurous, Yoo devotes great care and attention to everything that arrives at your table, from the house-made kimchee to the locally produced tofu in the *soon doo boo*.

NOTABLE

Choi's Restaurant

930 El Camino Real
Santa Clara   *SOUTH BAY*
(408) 260-0303
$$

You could easily make a meal of the *pan chan* at Choi's. Of course you will find the kimchee bean sprouts, *jap chae,* (sweet potato noodles mixed with vegetables and beef), spinach, potatoes, and some items that change weekly. Each is made fresh and tastes out of this world. When you're finished with one, don't be shy about asking for more of what you like. Try the *bulgogi* (grilled beef), or *kimchee jigae* (spicy tofu soup), which provide clients with yet another opportunity to make use of the *pan chan.* A large menu includes many of my childhood favorites. They also serve great, boozy *soju.*

Korean Palace
2297 Stevens Creek Boulevard
San Jose   **SOUTH BAY**
(408) 947-8600, (408) 279-9686
$$

While you can find *naeng chae* (jellyfish salad), small intestine and *gob chang jungol* (vegetable casserole), and *bosam* (steamed pork wrapped in cabbage leaves) at different restaurants in the Bay Area, it's unusual to find them as you do at Korean Palace, all served under one roof. But not to worry; they serve other dishes too, including the more common *dol sot bi bim bap* (rice, beef, and vegetables mixed together in a stone pot with chile paste), *bulgogi* (thinly sliced barbecued beef), and various stews like *kimchee jigae* and *soon doo boo jigae* (spicy tofu stew), which make nightly appearances. Like the menu, the seating and facilities are extensive, accommodating up to 150 people in the separate banquet hall.

Koryo Wooden Charcoal BBQ
4390 Telegraph Avenue
Oakland   **EAST BAY**
(510) 652-6007
$$$

Koryo Wooden Charcoal BBQ offers standards in Korean barbecue fare from short ribs *(kalbi)* to thinly sliced beef *(bulgogi)*. You will often find their tables packed with older Korean men huddled around sizzling beef, a good sign for a Korean restaurant. Customers rarely wait long for their food at Koryo, and in the world of Korean cuisine that is the best indicator of good service. The fast service is also an added bonus of eating at Koryo for lunch during the work week. They have reasonable lunch specials starting around $6. This is a bargain, considering that you get several dishes of *pan chan* in addition to your actual meal. For those looking for a whole night of entertainment, there is a karaoke place next door, as well as a café where you can surf the Internet or sit on plush sofas with your friends and make plans for your next visit.

Seoul Gomtang

3801 Telegraph Avenue
Oakland   *EAST BAY*
(510) 597-9989
$$

Every New Year's Day, I looked forward to my grandmother's *mandoo* (handmade dumplings), prepared in the Kaesung royal banquet style. As is traditional for the first meal of the New Year, the dumplings are placed in a simple broth with *dduk* (sticky rice cakes), toasted sesame seeds, and thinly sliced scallions. This year I found myself, upon a friend's recommendation, at Seoul Gomtang for dumpling soup. While my grandmother's *dduk mandoo guk* will remain sacred in my memory, Seoul Gomtang served up a satisfying alternative. Their menu also offers some specialty items like *gom tang* ("bear soup"), which is actually made with beef or oxtail in the case of *koree gom tang*. For those who don't read Korean, it's the only Korean restaurant on the corner of MacArthur and Telegraph in Oakland, not to be confused with the chain burger joint across the street.

Destino   *(Peruvian)*
Hayes Valley
1815 Market Street
(415) 552-4451
$$

On a less touristy part of Market Street, just before the Castro, lies one of San Francisco's South American jewels. The warm and intimate room, with its stucco walls and close quarters, makes you feel as if you are in a small restaurant in Peru. And so do the tasty pisco sours, the country's national drink, and the boozy *caipirinhas* made with cachaça cane rum and lime.

The menu features mostly *platos pequeños,* or tapas-sized selections. My friend, who is from Miraflores (a residential section of Lima, Peru), helped me select the most traditional dishes. These included *conchitas a la Parmesana,* broiled day-boat scallops with garlic butter, Parmesan cheese, and lemon sauce; the tuna ceviche, served in a martini glass; and *antichuchos de corazon,* marinated skewers of beef heart in a tangy *ají panca* sauce. For an entrée try the *lomo saltado,* stir-fried lamb sautéed with Roma tomatoes, red onions, and topped with French fries, all on a bed of rice. To finish, you can't go wrong with the *tres leches de fresas,* citrus sponge cake soaked in three types of milk.

 ## Limón   *(Peruvian)*
Mission
524 Valencia Street
(415) 252-0918
$$

This is one of the Peruvian restaurants now open in the city, thanks to the culinary skills of the Castillio family. Most of the menu selections are inspired by Mother Castillio's family recipe collection and given a slight fusion touch by her son, whose cooking has been recognized by the James Beard Foundation.

The signature dish, *ceviche limón,* is a generous sampling of raw fish marinated in lime juice, served with yams and Peruvian corn. Peru is home to more than three thousand varieties of potatoes, and this ingredient shines in another appetizer, the *papa a la Huancaina:* potatoes served on a bed of lettuce with an *ají amarillo* cheese sauce and olives. Special main dishes include the *tartara de atun:* perfect bite-sized sushi-grade ahi tuna with diced pears, roasted bell peppers, and pine nuts, and given an Asian flare with a sesame oil and *ají amarillo* vinaigrette.

As with any great restaurant, especially in San Francisco, good raw ingredients are responsible for a good dish, and Limón is a perfect example of this principle. They even have a Niman Ranch pork chop on the menu. Anchored in the traditions of conviviality and authentic food, Limón should surely be a destination on any San Francisco culinary tour.

Mochica   *(Peruvian)*
SOMA
937 Harrison Street
(415) 278-0480
Closed Tuesday
$$

Mochica takes its name from a pre-Incan Peruvian Indian tribe, whose males honed their culinary skills to impress their women (something I've always tried to explain to my son). The recently opened restaurant has an elegant feel, with a high ceiling and walls adorned with Picasso-like paintings. They also have an excellent selection of Californian, Portuguese, and South American wines. Or you may want to try the traditional pisco sour.

Chef-Owner Carlos Altamirano uses his French culinary skills to add a bit of fusion to his Peruvian dishes. My friend, a Peruvian architect, helped me navigate the menu, and we started with the *pulpo a la oliva* (braised octopus in white wine and fish broth, tossed with olives and a *salsa criolla*) and the *choros a la chalaca* (New Zealand green mussels topped with tomatoes, onions, and Peruvian corn, and marinated in lime juice).

The Peruvian staff is helpful and recommended an entrée of *parihuela* (Peruvian seafood bouillabaisse with garlic, tomatoes, red onion, *ají limo, ají panca,* brandy, and shrimp), served family style with a generous sampling of fish and shellfish, and the *ají de gallina* (shredded chicken cooked in a creamy *ají amarillo* sauce with hard-boiled egg and toasted nuts), a traditional dish of Peru.

Platanos   *(Pan-Latin)*
Mission
598 Guerrero Street, at 18th Street
(415) 252-9281
Closed Tuesday
$$

Plantains are a staple ingredient in Latin American cuisine and can be found fried as a chip, mashed as a side dish, or sweetened for dessert. Owner Lisa Lazarus opened her restaurant in November 2002, naming it after this versatile fruit. The dining room is lined on two sides by floor-to-ceiling windows, which provide a very inviting, open-air feeling. And the ornate palm ceiling fans rotate slowly overhead, giving the dining room a tropical feel.

Starters like *tostones con dos salsas* (green plantains, twice-fried and smashed into flat rounds) are served with two dipping sauces: a garlic-cilantro sauce and a spicy Mayan pumpkin seed sauce. Another starter, *empanadas de carne* (turnovers made with corn *masa* and stuffed with sirloin, chicken, capers, olives, potatoes, and anchovies), is made for sharing. The generous portion size allows these tapas to become the meal, with enough for everyone to get a taste. Entrées include *pollo en mole poblano* (chicken simmered in dark chocolate mole sauce and sautéed Blue Lake beans) and *cochinita pibil* (pork chunks braised with orange juice, tomatoes, and achiote). This is served with stewed black beans, rice, and guacamole.

Platanos has an excellent beer selection, including Ximou, a Brazilian black beer. The wine list features plenty of Spanish and Argentine selections. The fruity sangria, served in a large carafe, is always a good choice. For dessert, try the *Azteca* (dark chocolate cake spread with cayenne, coffee, and cinnamon), served with an espresso custard sauce and whipped cream.

NOTABLE

Balompie *(Salvadoran)*
Mission
3349 18th Street, at Capp Street
(415) 648-9199
$

At Balompie, the onomatopoeic word for *soccer* in Spanish, soccer flags of local and international clubs and vintage photos of famous matches line the walls. Two television sets show game replays, and during important matches fans crowd in to watch. It is not quite as full but still bustling during mealtimes, when the chefs serve delicious Salvadoran specialties. You can hear your *pupusas* being patted to order, and they are filled with meat, cheese, or with the less familiar *loroco* (the bud of a Salvadoran flower) and served with an herby cabbage slaw and salsa. You might also want to try the *enchiladas de pollo* and *bistec Salvadoreno*. Balompie is small (there are only twelve tables) and sweet, with friendly service.

El Perol *(Peruvian)*
Mission
2590 Mission Street, at 22nd Street
(415) 550-8582
Lunch only
$

Owned by Augusto and Nancy Molero, this Peruvian family restaurant serves lunch in the Mission with family-style seating under tables with umbrellas. Signature dishes include *ceviche mixto* (marinated fish in lime juice, cilantro, onions, and garlic) and *papa a la huancania* (medallions of potato with feta and ricotta cheese sauce). Served with the meal is a special Peruvian drink, *chica morada,* which is made from dried purple corn boiled with allspice, cinnamon, clove, and dried fruit. Augusto says it takes four hours to prepare this complex drink, so savor it slowly.

Fina Estampa *(Peruvian)*
Mission
2374 Mission Street, between 19th and 20th Streets
(415) 824-4437
$$

Fina Estampa is a Peruvian restaurant that has been a mainstay in the Mission district for more than fifteen years. You can judge a Latin American restaurant by their chips and salsa, and at Fina they are superb. The weathered black awning that greets you and the decaying interior have seen many busy days, and locals still pour in for delicious *camarones al ajo* (sautéed prawns in white wine and garlic sauce) and *arroz con pollo* (chicken with cilantro sauce mixed with rice). They also have a nice selection of beers.

Fonda *(Pan-Latin)*
1501 Solano Avenue, at Curtis Street
Albany **EAST BAY**
(510) 559-9006
$$$

This buzzing, upscale pan-Latin restaurant on Solano Avenue specializes in *antojitos,* the South American equivalent of tapas. Don't miss the Jicama and Cucumber in Lime and Cayenne, a great way to start your meal. The *tostaditas* of Niman Ranch pork, the selection of ceviches, and the *vuelve a la vida* (Veracruz-style seafood cocktail) are all delicious. The bar mixes a mean mojito, though you might be tempted by the extensive list of rum- or tequila-based cocktails. The front opens up to the street in nice weather, while the upstairs features a more loungelike setting. All told, Fonda makes for a festive night out.

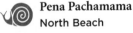 Pena Pachamama *(Bolivian)*
North Beach
1630 Powell Street
(415) 646-0018
Closed Monday and Tuesday
$$$

A friend in her late eighties coyly recounted a World War II dinner at Amelio's—then one of the finest restaurants in San Francisco, noted for its excellent food and, not least, its private rooms upstairs. Her companion was about to ship out. She was in love. . . . If these walls could speak!

Today, the two-story building in North Beach still swings, but now it's to the beat of world music, and the fare has shifted from French-Italian to the mountains of Bolivia. Run by Eddy and Quentin Navia (Quentin is the founder of the famous Andean ensemble Sukay), Pena Pachamama serves tasty dishes based mainly on chicken, potatoes, and beef, with Andean spices, reasonably priced wines, beer, and sangria. Surprisingly, the ingredients are mostly organic, including produce and Oregon Country naturally raised beef. A three-course dinner for $29.95 includes a musical performance. The Craftsman-style rooms upstairs are still there, charmingly furnished for lounging as well as dining, and available for spill-over crowds or private parties.

Radio Habana Social Club *(Cuban)*
Mission
1109 Valencia Street
(415) 824-7659
$

Cuban owner Victor Navarrete and his partner Leila Mansur opened the Radio Habana Social Club in 1999. The atmosphere is in keeping with lively Valencia Street, with hundreds of objects of art hung on the wall: everything from Desi and Lucy photos to Salvador Dalí prints. Over the years customers have been placing postcards and business cards in the wallpaper, making this social club a fun place to soak up the history of its clients. The *chile lindo empanada,* Cubano sandwich, and grilled meats are all worth trying. There are only five tables at this cozy venue, with a long bar that serves great drinks.

San Miguel *(Guatemalan)*
Mission
3263 Mission Street
(415) 641-5866
$-$$

Typical handcrafted straw baskets, straw hats, and slingshots from Guatemala hang from the ceiling and give San Miguel a homey feeling. Dishes not to miss are *pepian* (chicken with a roasted pumpkin seed sauce and cilantro) and *camarones al mojo de ajo* (prawns in a butter and garlic sauce). The rice and beans are excellent too.

Taqueria La Bamba   *(Salvadoran)*
2058 Old Middlefield Way
Mountain View   **SOUTH BAY**
(650) 965-2755
Cash only
$

Don't expect a white tablecloth at La Bamba. You'll be lucky if you can even sit down. Most people get food to go. The food is lighter and fresher than you'll find at most Latin restaurants. We tend to order the regular burrito with black beans and extra salsa. Our friends swear by the *carne asada* (seasoned beef) filling, but we tend toward the grilled chicken. The result is a perfectly packed and balanced construction, with a fluffy texture and fresh, savory lightness—absolutely addictive. The owners are from El Salvador, and they make excellent *pupusas* from sweet masa, pork, and cheese. A few of these delicacies make a meal. Prices are cheap, and the food is unforgettable.

MEXICAN

Don Pico's Original Mexican Bistro
461 El Camino Real

San Bruno   *SOUTH BAY*

(650) 589-1163

$$

The deliciously spicy aroma that assaults your senses when you enter Don Pico's Original Mexican Bistro is enough to make you forget the miserable traffic on El Camino Real. What began twenty-nine years ago has come of age under the influence of Chef-Owner Isaac Mejia, the son of the founder. He incorporates flavors and techniques from his travels and has fully embraced fresh, local ingredients. He makes everything from scratch, from the stocks that form the basis of the sauces to the guacamole he makes twice daily. Chicken is gently cooked and hand-pulled. Refried beans are made with three types of beans instead of just the standard pintos. The veteran kitchen staff at Don Pico's, many of whom have been there for more than two decades, aren't daunted by this labor-intensive style of cooking and wouldn't have it any other way. "It's a labor of love," says Isaac.

And love is what you will feel when you take your first bite of *enchiladas rancheras* or a rare sirloin steak with fried potatoes, beans, and *pico de gallo*. You might also choose one of the five or six fresh seafood dishes offered daily. It is the attention to detail in all aspects of food preparation that makes the dining experience at Don Pico's unique, satisfying, and memorable.

El Balazito
Bernal Heights
2560 Marin Street, at Bayshore Boulevard
(415) 824-6684
Closed Sunday
Cash only
$

There may not be a better fish taco, and certainly no better place to eat a fish taco than at El Balazito, a tiny taqueria hidden behind the do-it-yourself car wash just off Bayshore next to the 101 freeway on-ramp. The weather here is some of the best in the city, and while you eat you get to watch gearheads lovingly bathe their custom rides to soothing jazz piped in from an office located over one of the car wash bays. It's a perfect place to reacquaint yourself with the muscle cars of the Nixon era. Beronio Lumber is just across the way, so lots of construction workers drop by. Good sightseeing all around.

Now, about the tacos. Chunks of fish served on a soft, warm corn tortilla, sprinkled with perfectly chopped onions, cilantro, and a healthy hit

of *pico de gallo*. A taco and a drink can be had for less than $5 (sadly, there is no beer), and thin, crispy tortilla chips are included. You can help yourself to limitless amounts of *pico de gallo* and what everyone simply calls jalapeño, a fiery hot, pickled carrot, onion, and jalapeño relish. Fillings for the rest of the tacos and burritos are ordinary.

You can sit outside at the counter or eat inside a renovated car wash portal. I found out at a recent visit that the owner of the car wash is responsible for cranking out the jazz. "You know why I do it?" he asks. "Because everyone loves it. People tell me all the time they love to come here, relax, eat something, and listen to the music." The festivities end at 5:00 P.M. daily.

Estrellita Restaurant

971 North San Antonio Road
Los Altos   *SOUTH BAY*
(650) 948-9865
Closed Sunday
$

The restaurant was founded in 1958 by Maria Bustamante and family when Bustamante began serving burritos in the living room of her rented Victorian home. As her popularity grew, she moved her restaurant into a shop next door, where it still stands. Two decades later, Nancy Corlay, a native of Chiapas, purchased Estrellita and has integrated recipes from her home state into the menu. Goat and rich, sinister moles make their way onto the rotating menu.

Try the *sopes* (five tiny homemade corn masa patties, topped with beans, *salsa fresca*, tomatillos, and cheese) or one of the more unique and popular entrées like the Chicken Oaxaca (boneless chicken marinated for three days in a blend of orange juice, chiles, and achiote, a tangy paste made with annatto seeds and other Yucatecan spices).

Estrellita has a full bar, a scant wine list, and a choice of a few Mexican beers. The house-made sangria is fruity and delicious. One of the more interesting beverage choices is called *Michelada*—Modelo Especial beer on ice with fresh lime juice, salt, pepper, and a dash of Tabasco, with an optional splash of House Silver Tequila.

The dining room is warm, casual, and comfortable, with glass-top tables covering Mexican blanket tablecloths. Service is efficient and friendly, attracting dedicated customers.

La Palma Mexicatessen

See Ethnic & Specialty Markets, page 248.

La Taqueria
Mission
2889 Mission Street
(415) 285-7117
$

Most people in San Francisco are passionate (and some fanatical) about their favorite taqueria. It should come as no surprise that this one tops many lists. It's a no-frills kind of place, with large wooden, bench-style tables at which you grab a seat after ordering at the counter and wait for your number to be called.

La Taqueria has been dishing out delicious tacos since 1974, and the formula still works today. Fresh corn tortillas are griddled lightly and then loaded with juicy, well-seasoned meat. Depending on which taqueria fanatics you ask, you'll hear that La Taqueria has the best *carnitas* (pork), *carne asada* (beef), or chicken tacos around. One produce-obsessed friend of mine loves La Taqueria simply because of their avocados.

Another beloved item at La Taqueria is the *agua fresca.* Their version is perfectly sweetened, and each glass includes bits of fresh fruit. Depending on the season, you'll find mango, watermelon, strawberry, or other fresh fruits. Other beverage options are *horchata,* a rice-cinnamon drink, or *tamarindo,* a tamarind fruit drink.

Maya
SOMA
303 Second Street
(415) 543-2928
$$$–$$$$

Chef Richard Sandoval started cooking in his parents' restaurants as a teenager in his native Acapulco. With encouragement from his grandmother, he headed north and trained at the Culinary Institute of America. Now proprietor of six restaurants nationwide, Sandoval's cooking, which he calls "modern Mexican," stays true to the fresh, local ingredients of his childhood. The chicken at Maya is free-range, the salmon is wild, and the vegetables are locally sourced.

The atmosphere at Maya is upscale, with a large bar that serves a half-dozen variations on the margarita. You might start with the *callos de hacha* (seared diver scallops) or a bowl of roasted corn soup with dumplings of *huitlacoche* (corn smut). For a main course the *huarache de huachinango,* with two handmade corn tortillas stuffed with large chunks of red snapper and oyster mushrooms, is delicious. The local emphasis also extends to the ample wine list, which is heavy on Californian wines.

Mi Lindo Yucatan
Mission
401 Valencia Street, at 15th Street
(415) 861-4935
Cash only
$

At about the time the drug-riddled Valencia Street housing projects came down, Mi Lindo Yucatan opened its doors across the street—both very fortunate occurrences. Mi Lindo Yucatan offers a glimpse into the fertile Yucatecan kitchen. Crispy chips and two salsas (one fiery hot, habanero-infused; the other smoky and mild) arrive at your table before you've even had a moment to settle in. Do try to resist them, as you want to save room for what is to come.

You will want to order the *tostadas de ceviche* (crispy tortillas topped with shrimp marinated in coconut milk, citrus, and cilantro). It's sublime. Order the *cochinita pibil,* a gorgeous bowl of slow-cooked pork with achiote peppers and served on a banana leaf. *Pibil* is destined to become a part of everyone's culinary vernacular. Yucatecans eat a lot of turkey, and you would be wise to order the *relleno negro de pavo* (turkey stewed in black mole). Though it looks one-dimensional and slightly drab, it's not. And the pickled red onions, a common garnish at Mi Lindo Yucatan, will add any needed flair. A basket of warm, pillowy, handmade tortillas accompanies the meal.

Other Location
4042 24th Street, near Castro Street, San Francisco (Castro);
    (415) 826-3942

 ## Mijita
Embarcadero
Ferry Building Marketplace
One Ferry Building, Shop 44
Embarcadero, at Market Street
(415) 399-0814
$

Celebrated Chef Traci Des Jardins of Jardinière has returned to her Mexican roots with this taqueria in the San Francisco Ferry Building. Borrowing from the nickname her Mexican grandmother gave her as a child, Des Jardins has taken her culinary skills and devotion to sustainability with her to Mijita. As with many taquerias in San Francisco, you stand in line to place your order at the counter, but you won't find overstuffed rice-and-bean burritos here.

Mijita serves delicious tacos and quesadillas made with tortillas of organic masa, which are patted and cooked on the spot. Fillings include local fish, Niman Ranch meats, and traditional Mexican cheeses. The sauces and salsas are complex and balanced, and the Guacamole Salad and Jicama Salad are pristine. Attention to detail and tradition extends to the pink pinto beans, a locally grown heirloom variety from Oaxaca. While the tortillas are delicious, for me the greatest treat is the *sopa albondigas,* a tomato-based broth with vegetables and beef and pork meatballs. On a foggy San Francisco day, I can think of no better lunch than a bowl of this soup and Mijita's spectacular view of San Francisco Bay.

Mijita's commitment to sustainability extends beyond ingredients, and the chef pays her workers well. Given that this restaurant is healthy for diners, workers, and the environment, the prices, while a little steeper than most casual Mexican restaurants, are almost miraculously low.

Nick's Crispy Tacos
Russian Hill
1500 Broadway, at Polk Street
(415) 409-TACO, (415) 409-8226
Cash only
$

A few piñatas and some tropical-themed oilcloths transform this place every day from a swanky, chandelier-dripping club by night into a burrito

bordello by day. Order any of the tacos "Nick's way"—a soft taco surrounds a crispy taco, inside of which is melted Monterey jack cheese, fresh pinto beans, and choice of filling. (The pork and beef come from Niman Ranch.) Everything's topped with a heavy dollop of guacamole. The fish taco, served Baja style—delicately fried and served on a bed of shredded cabbage mixed with a creamy lime mayonnaise—is a must, and it should be eaten on the spot. There is always a trio of *aguas frescas,* plus a house-made *horchata* that's sheer sugary perfection. Better yet, order a margarita made from top-shelf tequila and freshly squeezed lime juice. Take your order outside or make yourself at home in one of the sought-after plush booths and watch the gym wear–clad Polk Street crowd scarf up Mexican favorites.

Picante
1328 Sixth Street, at Gilman Street
Berkeley   *EAST BAY*
(510) 525-3121
$

Picante is not your usual Mexican restaurant. It's owned by a *gringo,* Jim Maser, who happens to be Alice Waters's brother-in-law and whose deep understanding of the cuisines of Mexico comes from frequent trips to the country and occasional classes with Diana Kennedy.

With booths and tables and an outside patio, the place is family-friendly and is busy right up until its 10:00 P.M. closing time. The tortillas are made from organic masa and come hot off the *comal,* the tamales are soft and delicious, and the house-made chips are excellent—especially when scooping up guacamole. One of our favorite dishes is the *sopa Azteca,* a deep, rich chicken soup with tortilla strips, avocado, and chicken, which is served with chopped raw onion, Mexican oregano, and lime. It's a meal in itself. The *rajas* tacos with strips of roasted poblano chiles, sautéed onions, and *queso fresco,* and the *manchamantele* tacos with chicken in red mole are also delicious. On weekends come for the *huevos rancheros.*

You can enjoy beer on tap, an excellent margarita, or the milk-and-almond *horchata.* The Mexican chocolate angel food cake is divine.

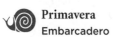

Primavera
Embarcadero
Ferry Plaza Farmers Market, rear plaza
Ferry Building
Embarcadero, at Market Street
Saturday 8:00 A.M. to 2:00 P.M.
$

For what may be the best Mexican food in the Bay Area, head to the back plaza of the Ferry Building during the Saturday morning farmers' market. Primavera's owner Karen Taylor has studied with Diana Kennedy, and her cooks turn out unsurpassed regional dishes right on the spot in their tiny outdoor kitchen.

There are only about six choices on the menu, but they are all fabulous. My personal favorite is the fish taco. While the tortillas themselves are so good they could make a meal on their own (Taylor grinds organic corn and makes her own masa with a minimum of lime), these tacos are heavenly, piled high with lightly breaded fried fish, guacamole, fresh cabbage, a few radishes, and fabulous salsa. The menu items change with the seasons, and other options include *huevos rancheros* with pumpkin seed salsa, or *chilaquiles* (eggs scrambled with tortillas). The seafood ceviche tostadas are fresh and spicy, and the *carnitas* tacos are made with Niman Ranch pork. Their famous tamales are always a good choice, especially accompanied by the *pepita* (green pumpkin seed salsa).

Once you receive your order, take your plate and head for a seat along the water. On a sunny Saturday morning, it just doesn't get much better than this. The only drawback to this restaurant on the bay is that it exists only on Saturdays from 8:00 A.M. to 2:00 P.M. You can take Primavera home, though. They sell packaged stone-ground organic corn tortillas and tamales to go.

Tacubaya
1788 Fourth Street, at Virginia Street
Berkeley   *EAST BAY*
(510) 525-5160
$

Tucked away on Berkeley's upscale Fourth Street, Tacubaya is a sophisticated take on the taqueria by Dona Savitsky and Tom Moniz, who own Doña Tomas in Oakland.

Mexico City street snacks are prepared with organic, carefully sourced, and deftly combined ingredients. The chalkboard menu lists tacos, tortas, beans, and rice—much the same fare as many a local taqueria, but the approach is decidedly different. The *al pastor* is marinated pork cooked on a vertical spit or *trompa* (more commonly seen grilling lamb for *shawarma*) and sliced off at the edges, which helps it develop a toothsome caramelized crunch. Ordered as a soft taco, the Niman Ranch pork is tender and slightly charred, redolent of chile, spice, and vinegar. A squeeze of lime sets off the richness of the pork, and it's topped with avocado salsa. Other tacos feature beef tongue with tomatillo salsa, and crisp fried organic chicken with cheese and cucumber salsa. The shredded pork *tamal* is paired with a thin, delicately fruity *mole rojo,* but it's the *tamal vegetariano* that is a revelation, even for a dedicated carnivore. Zucchini and corn mingle in moist, light masa under a blanket of *queso fresco,* arbol chile salsa, and warm *crema.*

Stop in before noon on weekdays or 4:00 P.M. on the weekends to enjoy classic Mexican breakfast dishes, or swing by anytime and sample the phenomenal *churros.* Crispy on the outside, soufflé-light and creamy on the inside, dusted with sugar and cinnamon, these slender batons are served three to an order. Tacubaya is rarely empty until later in the afternoon, and the lunch rush can slow the counter line to a crawl.

NOTABLE

Cactus Taqueria
5642 College Avenue, at Ocean View Drive
Oakland   *EAST BAY*
(510) 658-6180
$

Catering to the stroller-and-sweater set in Oakland's affluent Rockridge neighborhood, Cactus offers the usual tacos and burritos but with an emphasis on good ingredients. The chicken is from Fulton Valley Farm in Petaluma, and the beef and pork from Niman Ranch. The tacos are satisfying in their many incarnations of fish, chicken, or meat. Eat the piping hot *quesadilla suiza* or their cheesy, crisp-fried taco on the spot. They don't travel, and it'll give you a chance to check out the latest in baby fashions.

Casa Sanchez
Mission
2778 24th Street, at York Street
(415) 282-2400
$

While you can buy Casa Sanchez's chips and salsa in many groceries and corner stores around the city, they are best enjoyed fresh from the fryer while you sit on the sunny back patio of their 24th Street restaurant. And if you get a tattoo of their logo (a little man riding on an ear of corn), you can enjoy free food for life!

El Huarache Azteca
3842 International Boulevard, at 39th Avenue
Oakland   *EAST BAY*
(510) 533-2395
$

Flouting the conventional wisdom that the best taquerias are the grottiest, El Huarache Azteca is possibly the cleanest, most beautifully decorated taqueria in the Fruitvale area, yet one of the best. The restaurant is decorated with long wood picnic tables and sepia-toned murals of Aztec warriors. Their specialty is Mexico City–style *antojitos,* the small masa-based snacks that Americans think make up the entire canon of Mexican cuisine (well, that and melted cheese). But aside from the chips on the table, the owners make few concessions to American expectations. Try the restaurant's namesake, the *huarache,* a sandal-shaped "pizza" with a thin slick of refried beans and finely crumbled *queso fresco.* Or the *gorditas,* thick tortillas filled with braised *chicharrón,* cheese, and shredded lettuce. Or a quesadilla—this one a fresh corn tortilla pinched at the edges and griddled until crisp, stuffed with corn and fresh *huitlacoche* (corn fungus). Weekends are for lamb *barbacoa,* slow-roasted in maguey leaves, a delicate *consomme de barbacoa* to go with it, and chile-red *posole.*

El Toro Taqueria
Mission
598 Valencia Street, at 17th Street
(415) 431-3351
$-$$

There's a lot of noise (ceaseless meat cleavers on the chopping block), and not much English is spoken here. The hallmark of commitment in the restaurant world is an on-premises proprietor, and El Toro has an exemplary one, sporting a wonderful ill-fitting toupée. The burritos are too big and beany, but the tacos are simplicity perfected. Some of the many possible ingredients include rich, juicy tongue, beef with *nopales* (cactus leaves), and crisp roast pork.

El Chachanilla
Mission
2948 21st Street
(415) 550-9410
$

Out of a tiny, almost Prohibition-style sliding glass window on 21st Street emerge some of the tastiest tacos in the Mission. A large, arched awning shades the window, and its underside also serves as the menu board. Offerings range from the usual *carnitas* to tongue, intestines, and eyes. Yes, eyes. You can try almost any body part here. Load up your tacos with any of the six salsas that line the counter under the window and sit in the sun at one of the two ramshackle tables on the sidewalk to enjoy them.

Pancho Villa Taqueria
Mission
3071 16th Street, at Valencia Street
(415) 864-8840
$-$$

Although it feels a bit like a cafeteria, there is always fresh, good food and a seat to be had at this cavernous taqueria near many of the Mission's most popular bars. The menu offers all the traditional fare and a wide selection of house-made salsas. The place provides a perfect quick fix when you are in the neighborhood, and it's open until midnight.

A WALKING TOUR
OF THE MISSION

Toward 16th and Mission Streets is where you'll find many of the bars and restaurants where San Francisco's young hipsters hang out. But for food lovers on a quest for Mexican cuisine, 24th Street is the place to start. Step off the BART train at 24th and Mission Streets in the middle of the day, and you're immediately assaulted by the sights, sounds, and smells of the center of San Francisco's Latino neighborhood. Within a few blocks of here, you will find many of the best taquerias in the city, as well as the best Mexican food shops and bakeries and, in case you're in a festive mood, piñatas.

Within a block on Mission Street, you'll find La Taqueria, La Corneta, and El Farolito, if you need a couple of tacos or a burrito to fortify you for the short tour. Then walk down 24th Street and take in the hustle-bustle of the produce stores, butchers, and small groceries. Take time to enjoy the murals that adorn almost every wall along the way. Head to La Victoria Bakery (24th, at Alabama Street) for a *pan dulce* to satisfy your sweet tooth. Or if it's a warm day, stop the ice cream man pushing his cart and enjoy a fruity Mexican popsicle (mango is my favorite) as you stroll. A must-see is La Palma Mexicatessen (see page 248). Stop by Galeria de la Raza (24th, at Bryant Street) to see their current exhibition of Chicano/Latino art, and be sure to check out their gift shop for all manner of arts and crafts, especially Day of the Dead merchandise. Pick up a *Milagros* or have one of the ladies light a candle for you at the Candle Light Shop (24th, at Mission).

As you head back up 24th Street, pop into Precita Eyes Mural Arts and Visitors Center (at Harrison Street) to find out more about the murals and the history of the Mission, or call ahead to find out about guided tours ([415] 285-2287).

If you happen to be in San Francisco in late May, don't miss Carnaval. The parade winds up 24th Street, down Mission Street, and ends with a block party on Harrison Street. The festivities encompass all the cultures of the Americas, including everything from Mayan dancers with tall feathered headdresses to a parade of low-riders showing off their hydraulic lifts. Any time of year, however, the Mission is nothing if not colorful.

—*Tatiana Graff*

EAST OAKLAND'S
TACO TRUCKS

Oakland's Fruitvale district boasts the highest percentage of Latinos in the East Bay, and local residents like Emilia Otero have worked hard to protect and promote the rich cultural expression of the neighborhood. Recently the Oakland City Council passed ordinances to regulate and legitimize this motley crew of entrepreneurs, primarily comprised of immigrants, for their own livelihood and safety and for everyone's enjoyment.

Frequented by those who are in the know, the taco truck scene in this East Oakland enclave has all the elements of an authentic culinary adventure, one that is reminiscent of a stroll through the streets of Mexico City. The army of trucks, carts, and wagons—emblazoned with mystical tropical waterfalls, hand-painted shrimp, slick airbrushed renditions of giant overstuffed *tortas,* and colorful signs offering the day's specials—disappears each evening, only to reappear the next morning. Other trucks appear around dusk and linger on the streets well into the night. On corners, in alleys, and in parking lots, this legion of mobile eateries, ranging in appearance from charming dilapidation to grand embellishment, invites you to stop and investigate what each vendor has to offer. From the stout, frowning ladies on cell phones selling hot corn on the cob and tamales out of plastic coolers, to the proud, mustachioed proprietor of a taco window extolling his handmade pickled cow's feet, the personalities abound as you walk down International Boulevard in search of fresh, cheap, handmade food.

After, before, or during a taco excursion on International Boulevard, be sure to treat yourself to a sample from one of the roving fresh fruit pushcarts. Vendors offer such delicacies as *elotes* (hot corn on the cob, slathered with mayonnaise, chile powder, and cheese), plastic bags full of tropical fruit doused with lime and chile to your taste, and *atoles* (masa-thickened and brown sugar–sweetened hot beverages). To soothe your chile-scorched mouth, buy a fresh fruit ice from a truck or seek out the refreshing *raspado* at the ice cream counter at Four Star Pizzeria. This icy relief made with condensed milk and nuts or fruit will have you coming back to try every different flavor.

El Ojo de Agua
Fruitvale and East 12th Streets
Oakland
The best taco trucks graduate into real restaurants. El Ojo de Agua is halfway there. The small truck used to station itself in a parking lot on International Boulevard and 38th Avenue, but did well enough to move to

the busier corner of 12th Street and Fruitvale Street, where it now has picnic tables and parking spaces for visitors. Going upscale hasn't spoiled the quality of El Ojo de Agua's tacos, though. Doubled-up tortillas the size of sand dollars are covered in a couple of tablespoons of meat, a thin layer of *salsa verde*, and a sprinkling of chopped onions and cilantro. El Ojo de Agua is well known for its pork *al pastor* (marinated and slow-roasted), chorizo, and velvety braised tongue, but the shredded chicken and crispy roasted tripe are equally good. Half the appeal is the strength of the truck's salsa, as tart as it is piquant.

And when it gets hot out, your day is not complete without a *liquado de papaya*. A Mexican favorite, a *liquado* is a cross between a smoothie and a milk shake. Papaya is by far the best, but they also come in walnut, strawberry, and coconut. With easy access from the freeway, plan to stop by on your way back from picking up a friend at the Oakland International Airport and welcome them to the Bay Area with a *torta* or taco and a delicious *liquado*.

La Fortuna
San Pablo Dam Road
San Pablo
Take comfort and shelter at this taco truck down the street from Windy Gates mobile home park. Located in the lot of a gas station, La Fortuna shares her good luck in the form of tasty *tortas* on just-right soft buns, and some of the best spicy pickled carrots you will eat out of a little tinfoil package.

La Torta Loca
36th Street and International Boulevard
Oakland
Open Tuesday to Sunday 9:30 A.M. to 8:00 P.M.
Even though it isn't on wheels, I knew I had to eat at this storefront window so I could embellish my stories with the phrase, "So, I was at the Crazy Sandwich . . ." Thankfully this ten-year-old establishment, specializing in *antojitos* and *tortas,* is, to borrow from urban slang, "crazy good." With quesadillas, flautas, *huaraches,* tostadas, and tortas, all made in a sandwich press, the large selection of handmade snacks and larger selection of fillings and toppings overwhelm you with possibilities. One afternoon I simply eavesdropped on my neighbors and copied their order: a *huarache al pastor* with *nopales.* This combination was nowhere on the menu, but I was delighted how the tangy cactus cooled the bite of the spicy pork and tempered the richness of the fried masa. Let this venture teach you to try things you might not see, and to listen to the locals.

Los Michoacán

33rd Street and International Boulevard
Oakland
Open every day 8:00 A.M. to 8:00 P.M.

At first glance, the faded signage and glossy flyers in the window make Los Michoacán look more like a weathered tour bus than an old taco truck serving exceptional braised meats prepared by the careful hands of Flaviano Sorriano. Saturday and Sunday bring large, comforting bowls of braised goat in piquant broth and heaps of tripe in the *menudo*, served with chopped onions, dried oregano, and plenty of lime. After watching the lady in the back of the truck making thick tortillas on the weekends, it's obvious why the plastic-covered tables in the lot are filled elbow to elbow and the *menudo* runs out by noon. Jesus, Flaviano's son, takes the orders on weekends, polices the parking lot, and is, of course, learning to cook food in the *estilo casero*, or homemade style, that his father learned from his family in Apatzingan, Michoacán.

Mi Grullenese

30th Street and International Boulevard, in the Goodwill
parking lot
Oakland
Open every day 9:00 A.M. to 12:00 A.M.

The sight of two taco trucks parked within twenty feet of one another is perplexing, yet the proximity and the long lines in front of each truck only attest to the popularity of the duo with the same name and same menu. Mi Grullenese has bargain prices, and the six choices of meat come two ways on griddled corn tortillas or on a toasted Mexican sandwich roll with lettuce, tomato, onions, and mayo.

Tacos El Gordo

High Street and International Boulevard
Oakland

Easily spotted toward the east end of International Boulevard by its bold neon sign, Tacos El Gordo is not to be missed. Always busy, especially late at night, El Gordo boasts a fully visible kitchen inside the small truck it inhabits. Place your order at the left-hand window and watch the three cooks prepare it while you wait to pick it up on the right.

On a recent visit, the truck was staffed by three women who were a force to be reckoned with. One was busy peeling tomatillos for the tangy salsa, and another one gently coaxed *saudero* (roasted beef) around the *comal* (the large round skillet used for cooking just about everything). The third, a woman seriously confident with her knife skills, tirelessly diced the meat with a cleaver on a board that has been well worn by the blade. Our tacos came out piping hot and sprinkled with very fresh chopped cilantro and diced onions. If you are a vegetarian, ask for a quesadilla and you won't be disappointed.

Tacos Los Primos
South 23rd Street
Richmond
Open every day 9:00 A.M. to 8:00 P.M.

If you never go to Richmond for anything else, go there for Tacos Los Primos. Pull into the parking lot where the truck is positioned in front of a supercool rainbow mural, place your order at the window, get your goods, and take them back to your car for a feast. This represents the new generation of drive-ins, and you will most likely be parked near some cute young lovers, loving the food. You get the sense that you've stumbled onto something secret and special, and when they call your number you know why. The plates are generous but not overly stuffed with meat or weighed down with grease. The cilantro and radishes are fresh, the meat well seasoned, the mini-tortillas thrown onto the grill (my favorite touch), and the spring onions grilled to perfection. Tacos like these will disappear in minutes, though the smell in your car may last until the next day.

—Michelle Fuerst and Clair Ptak

MIDDLE EASTERN

Medjool
Mission
2522 Mission Street, at 21st Street
(415) 550-9055
$-$$

Medjool is the grand centerpiece of a newly opened hotel and hostel in the Mission. Magnificently carved dark wooden doors separate the all-day café from the spacious restaurant, lounge, and mezzanine areas. The menu of small plates transports you to the Southern Mediterranean, highlighting the flavors of the region: fried sumac-dusted squid; mussels in *chermoula* sauce; and the harissa-crusted hanger steak.

One gets the impression that the heart and soul of Medjool's menu is inspired by the gentle touch of generations worth of family meals. The Medjool sampler is a great way to start with delectable versions of the trinity of Middle Eastern starters—hummus, baba ghanoush, and tabbouleh served with house-made pita. The light smokiness of the baba ghanoush is particularly memorable and comes from just the right amount of charring on the skin of the eggplant. Tender lamb *kefta* is aromatic and accented perfectly with an irresistible pine-nut-and-tahini sauce.

The one-page wine list offers some very reasonably priced selections that match the food well. There is some outdoor seating on the sidewalk, as well as a balcony upstairs, and the owners plan to add a rooftop deck in the future.

Yaya
Russian Hill
2424 Van Ness Avenue
(415) 440-0455
Closed Monday
$$

Yahya Salih, a native of Iraq, has been cooking in the Bay Area since the late 1980s, including a stint with Jeremiah Tower at Balboa Café. This explains why his "Mesopotamian" cooking, while honoring the centuries-old traditions of the great civilizations of the Middle East, also has a Californian influence in the form of an abundance of fresh vegetables and a lightening of certain dishes. His Middle Eastern salad of mixed greens and feta with sumac and rosewater vinaigrette is beautifully balanced, refreshing, and thoroughly satisfying. Ravioli stuffed with dates, cardamom, and cinnamon, served with yogurt and walnut sauce, are a sensual combination of textures and contrasting flavors. A favorite is the dolma plate, which features an array of vegetables stuffed with diced lamb, rice, tomato, parsley, allspice, and ginger. There are also wonderful, piquant preparations of meat, fish, and chicken and delicious desserts like baklava with *mouhalabia* (a custard) and *kanafa*, a rosewater-scented shredded phyllo pastry stuffed with Arabian cheese.

The restaurant's interior sports murals of different Mesopotamian landmarks and a color palette of amber, green, and blue. Lapis blue glass and brass lamps light the room, and the overall effect is warm and relaxing.

Yahya is also a very well liked and soulful person. Given our involvement in his homeland, he desires to tell us about his culture through his food. After you've enjoyed his heartfelt offerings, if it's a slow night and he's in the dining room, he might even read your coffee grounds and tell you a little about yourself as well.

Zand's

1401 Solano Avenue, at Carmel Avenue
Albany   *EAST BAY*
(510) 528-8600
$

"Persian food is a slow, slow food," says Monier Attar, the owner of Zand's Middle Eastern deli and market. Unlike most deli-and-market combinations, Zand's is a comfortable place to sit down with friends over a falafel sandwich or a platter of *olivieh,* a delicious Persian chicken-and-potato salad, or *kookoo sabzi,* a vegetable soufflé. After spending time at one of the

simple tables, it would be difficult to leave without a cup or two of Attar's secret tea blend, inherited from her father, and one of her excellent éclairs. Surveying the full shelves, Attar admits that "everything has a fan, but the napoleons and cream puffs have their own customers."

Her emphasis on pastries is not surprising, since it's where she got her start in Iran in the 1970s. When her bakery was closed by the government as a penalty for her refusing the veil, she set out for America with her two young children.

In the market you will find not one, but three brands of pomegranate syrup, as well as feta from Bulgaria, Greece, and France. There are cookies of all kinds, dried roses, matzoh, menorah candles, an entire rack of Persian music CDs, and the pickled lemons that Attar was finally able to import after seventeen years.

Zatar
1981 Shattuck Avenue
Berkeley   **EAST BAY**
(510) 841-1981
Closed Sunday
Cash only
$$

Zatar is the product of the passion and hard work of its owners, Iraqi-born Waiel Majíd and his wife, Kelly. The interior is narrow with high ceilings and mural-painted walls and is adorned with ceramics from the owners' many travels.

Happily, much of what they serve in this comfortable room is harvested from their home fruit and vegetable garden. Accordingly, the menu is Mediterranean in inspiration and dictated by the season. Meals begin with a basket of warm, fresh flat bread served with olive oil and *za'atar,* a Middle Eastern spice mixture of sumac, thyme, sesame, and sea salt. Classic dishes, such as falafel with hummus and *dolmades,* are anything but commonplace. The falafel, made with fresh chickpeas, is lightly fried, and perfectly crusted with crushed coriander seeds. The *dolmades,* both vegetarian and lamb, are stuffed with aromatic rice and toasted pine nuts and simmered in tamarind and lemon.

For the main course the chicken *kuzi* is a good choice for a foggy Berkeley night—the phyllo pastry is filled with chicken, basmati rice, plump dried apricots, caramelized shallots, and crunchy roasted almonds. It arrives warm and sweet, a beautiful little package accompanied by a few colorful roasted vegetables.

The wine list is decent and reasonably priced, but perhaps the more adventurous choices are the many nonalcoholic drinks, such as tamarind with rose water and lemon. The creamy rice pudding with orange water, topped with toasted almonds, and the baklava are perfect endings for this Mediterranean feast.

NOTABLE

A La Turka
Tenderloin
869 Geary Boulevard, at Larkin Street
(415) 345-1011
$-$$

A La Turka is the proverbial hole-in-the-wall eatery. Despite the restaurant's modest ambience and marginal neighborhood, Turkish-born Naim Sit cooks fresh home-style food with a light hand. He makes his own flat bread, and the *dolmades* are among the best we've had. The Black Sea pies, which are similar to calzones, are stuffed with spinach, feta cheese, ground beef, or chicken and are made to order. Or try their *manti,* homemade ground-beef ravioli with yogurt and tomato sauce. Some other traditional dishes include kebabs, lentil soup, and baba ghanoush. Turkish beer and wine are available, and the restaurant is open late.

Mediterranean Wraps
425 California Avenue, at Mimosa Lane
Palo Alto   *SOUTH BAY*
(650) 321-8189
$

Healthy, delicious, inexpensive, quick food—these are not words often heard together when describing a restaurant, but they perfectly portray Mediterranean Wraps. A tiny space with a few small tables, it boasts a mixture of Jordanian, Lebanese, and Greek fare with recipes that are derived from the owners' own home cooking. Specials change from day to day depending on the whim of the cook. Don't miss the traditional falafels, *dolmades,* and tabbouleh, and the very special *kafta kebab,* a mixture of fresh ground beef and lamb with diced onions, parsley, and Middle Eastern spices.

New Kapadokia Restaurant
2399 Broadway, at Winslow Street
Redwood City   *SOUTH BAY*
(650) 368-5500
$$

Turkish hospitality is legendary, and it is mandatory that any stranger be welcomed into a home, even if that person happens to be your enemy! Your meal begins with a tray of appetizers brought to your table, and servers give a careful explanation of each one. All the dishes, from the homemade baklava to the bread, stay true to Turkish recipes. Entrées include stuffed vegetables, grilled kebabs, and stewed meats, as well as other classic Turkish dishes. Even the wines, beers, and sodas are Turkish, a good sign when you are looking for an authentic experience.

Paul K
Civic Center
199 Gough Street, at Oak Street
(415) 552-7132
Dinner only; closed Monday
$$

Paul K offers inspired Armenian-influenced Mediterranean food in an intimate candlelit space that seems far away from the crush of people outside in the theater district. Warm home-baked pita and hummus arrive promptly at each table. Highlights include a *meze* taste platter with a delicately flavored combination of lamb riblets; smoky roasted baba ghanoush and pomegranate dips; and feta, olives, and artichokes. Main courses include rib-eye steak rubbed with chile *harissa*, and pan-roasted bluenose bass in a tomato-cumin sauce.

Yumma's Mediterranean Restaurant
Inner Sunset
721 Irving Street, at Eighth Avenue
(415) 682-0762
$

On this busy stretch of Irving Street, within walking distance of the UCSF Medical School campus, dozens of eateries compete for the student dining dollar. Yumma's is a top contender. This tiny grill serves Middle Eastern street-food standbys—*shawarma*, kebabs, and *kefta*—made with quality ingredients. The lamb and beef are from Niman Ranch, and the chicken comes from Rocky Range. Accessorize your selection with sumac-dusted onions and hummus, crunchy pickles, cucumber and tomato salad, and fiery hot sauce. Eat in Yumma's pleasant backyard patio, weather (that is, fog) permitting, or, better yet, get it to go and picnic in the Golden Gate Park Arboretum just a couple blocks away.

OTHER EUROPEAN

Bocadillos *(Spanish)*
Financial District
710 Montgomery Street
(415) 982-2622
Closed Sunday
$$$

It only takes a single trip to Bocadillos to understand why the Spanish have created a culture around the tapas bar. It's a place to meet friends for a quick bite or to while away the evening. It's not unlike the British pub, though the food is much better. And Basque-born Gerald Hirigoyen has been able to successfully transport this special feeling to Bocadillos. There are a lot of tapas bars around, and none have been able to capture that elusive spirit—until now. On one of those rare hot evenings, if you find yourself at Bocadillos, you'd swear you had landed on the Iberian Peninsula.

Stop in for a glass of Albarino and a nibble of cured *salumi* or serrano ham before dashing off to dinner elsewhere. Or you can simply relax and settle in for the night. Get the *pimientos de pardon* (small, flavorful green peppers) given a quick sauté, and a plate of the *patatas brava* to liberally dip in the accompanying *romesco* sauce. The luscious flatiron steak with the tangy *chimichurri* sauce will please everyone, and despite any protestations, yours or otherwise, order the pig trotters. You will not regret it.

The welcoming staff is eager to help you with wine pairings. Bocadillos is a great place to acquaint yourself with the delights of the Spanish bodega and the Spanish character.

Kokkari Estiatorio *(Greek)*
Jackson Square
200 Jackson Street, at Front Street
(415) 981-0983
Closed Sunday
$$$

Kokkari, named after a small fishing village on the island of Samos, serves honest Greek food in a rustic if somewhat theatrical setting. The large main dining room is furnished with handsome overstuffed chairs, solid wooden tables, a large fireplace, and a long, packed bar.

The Greek spreads, always tasty, are nearly upstaged by the lightly grilled house-made pita. The watermelon salad is a lovely starter on a warm day, its juiciness tempered by spicy arugula and briny feta. Or you may also want to try the grilled octopus salad with frisée. For main courses, the *moussaka* is one of the best I've tasted in the States—the tangy yogurt béchamel beautifully melds together the lamb, eggplant, and potatoes.

The wine list is enormous, sorted as New World and Old World. It includes many Greek varieties, and the bartenders are glad to pour tastes: the Santorini Sigalas is spritzy and lots of fun. Or you may want to stop in just for an ouzo—the selection is truly impressive, and the bartenders are happy to explain the differences.

Pipérade   *(Basque)*
Embarcadero
1015 Battery Street, at Green Street
(415) 391-2555
Closed Sunday; lunch served Monday–Friday only
$$

Gerald Hirigoyen and his wife, Cameron, run one of the best little bistros in San Francisco. Named for a traditional Basque dish, Pipérade is warm, stylish, and embodies the bonhomie of its owners, who are almost always on the premises.

Hirigoyen first came to the attention of San Francisco diners when he opened Fringale in 1991. The unpretentious atmosphere and honest Basque-inspired food transported diners to their favorite European bistros and brought Hirigoyen local and national fame. In 2002 Hirigoyen sold his share in Fringale and opened Pipérade—a restaurant that feels

entirely his in every way. While Hirigoyen's cooking is influenced by California tastes and ingredients, a true Basque spirit remains, and his dishes are not to be found anywhere else in the city, with the exception of Bocadillos, his new tapas bar.

Small plates alone can make a satisfying meal: Warm Piquillo Peppers with Goat Cheese, Raisins, and Moscatel Vinaigrette; Braised Oxtail with Cornichons, Chopped Egg, and Fresh Herbs; *bacalao* (salt cod) fritters with aioli; and Dungeness crab salad *txangurro*, with apple, curry, and *piment d'Esplette* are all winners.

Big plates are equally adventurous and satisfying and include *pipérade* (a stew of peppers, tomatoes, onion, and garlic served with serrano ham and poached egg) and Atlantic cod with potatoes, *riojanas*, chorizo, thyme, and onion. Hirigoyen trained as a pastry chef, and his cakes and tarts are lovely, but my personal favorite is a walnut and sheep's milk cheese gratin: sweet yet nourishing, simple yet supremely satisfying.

Speisekammer *(German)*

2424 Lincoln Avenue, at Park Street
Alameda **EAST BAY**
(510) 522-1300
Closed Monday
$$

The word *speisekammer* means "pantry" in German, and owners Peter and Cindy Kahl have created an atmosphere of enjoyment, or *gemutlichkeit,* a word that has no equivalent in English but connotes all around well-being and conviviality. The staff is friendly, and the customers are clearly at ease as they sip superior-quality German and Belgian beers and munch on dense, organic German rye bread called *schrotbrot.*

Tangy side salads of carrot, beet, and cucumber and plates of smoked, air-dried ham served with cornichons give a taste of Germany. The pickled herring is a standout among the appetizers. The highly flavored food is best matched with German wines, including a good selection of Rieslings or one of the many beers. Speisekammer keeps eleven on tap and seven varieties in bottles. All are German or Belgian and are served at the correct temperature in the correct glasses.

Sauerbraten (long-marinated, slow-roasted tri-tip beef), Wiener schnitzel (thin-pounded pork or veal that's breaded and fried), and cabbage stuffed with ground pork are all delicious. Many of the entrées come with golden fried potatoes or *spaetzle* (little dumplings). Or try the crispy potato pancakes served with a smooth cinnamon-apple compote. Don't skip the sauerkraut, which is tender and bursting with cumin seeds.

Suppenküche   *(German)*

Hayes Valley
601 Hayes Street, at Laguna Street
(415) 252-9289
$$

With bare plank tables and generous swaths of candlelight that practically require you to gather around with friends for a communal meal, Suppenküche unites the hopping Hayes Valley with toothsome Teutonic food in a congenial setting. It's the perfect antidote to the cold Pacific wind outside.

The menu is palpably meaty yet fresh, and the portions are huge and can be shared among light eaters. Fresh pea soup, when offered, is tasty and seasoned with white pepper. The half chicken, roasted to order and served hot with red wine sauce and potato pancakes, is irresistible. Cheese *spaetzle,* salty and rich, is a must. Sit in the candlelit recess around the freestanding bar, if you're in the mood for just a drink. The broad beer list includes all the usual staples, as well as Belgian, Czech, and German brews.

Those with murky pasts as dark microbrew–swilling fratboys, take note: German men actually drink light beers, while the darks, which are sweet, are generally the province of the women.

NOTABLE

B44   *(Spanish/Catalan)*

Financial District
44 Belden Place, between Bush and Pine Streets
(415) 986-6287
$$$$

Tucked into the Financial District on an alley between Bush and Pine, Belden Place is a little piece of Europe in downtown San Francisco. Café lights serve as a canopy over the street, and heat lamps make outdoor dining a year-round possibility at the European-inspired restaurants that dot the block.

From the minute the waiter puts down bread and a dipping sauce of chopped olives in olive oil, you know that chef Daniel Olivella will give you a real taste of Catalonia. The paella (there are nine variations available) are authentic and delicious, as is the roasted rabbit *ala Catalana,* but we think the appetizers are the main reasons to come. Try the piquillo peppers stuffed with crab meat, salt cod fritters, fresh fried anchovies with Meyer lemon aioli, sautéed Atlantic cod cheeks, and a salad of romaine hearts with *romesco* dressing. A great selection of Spanish wines pairs perfectly with the hearty food.

The Basque Cultural Center *(Basque)*
599 Railroad Avenue
South San Francisco SOUTH BAY
(650) 583-8091
Closed Monday
$$

As the establishment's name suggests, the Basque Cultural Center is part of a banquet facility and community center, meaning there's plenty of parking, a casual setting, and lots of fluorescent lighting. Originating in the Pyrenees region of France and Spain, Basque shepherds made their way to the American West in the early twentieth century. Although few shepherds remain, and the Basque hotels in San Francisco have closed, the Basque Cultural Center carries on the tradition of the bachelor eating club.

Taking the best of hunter's-style French and Spanish flavors with a solemn nod to pastoral roots, dishes like duck confit and rack of lamb are offered with green salad, potato-leek soup, and sides of cheesy potatoes and ratatouille, all for less than $20. The restaurant also offers a family-style dinner with two entrées, soup, salad, and dessert for a fixed price. Each Thursday they serve veal cheeks and *poulet cordon bleu*—a full meal for two. The wine-by-the-glass selection is a little thin, but when you can have a Rioja Gran Riserva for $38, go for the whole bottle!

Evvia Estiatorio *(Greek)*
420 Emerson Street
Palo Alto SOUTH BAY
(650) 326-0983
$$$

Greek tradition reigns here, and the menu changes seasonally. Standout appetizers, known as *mezes,* include the Grilled Octopus, Spanakopita, and the unusual and delicious Yogurt Dumplings with Pork Belly. *Moussaka,* of course, leads the entrée choices. *Kokinisto me manestra* (an aromatic braised lamb shank over orzo, served with Myzithra cheese) is fall-off-the-bone tender and juicy. A Greek version of ravioli is outstanding, as is the feta mint pasta stuffed with yellow wax beans, fava beans, and Kalamata olives and served in a leek-lemon broth. Evvia is popular and busy, so reservations are strongly advised.

Katia's Russian Tea Room   *(Russian)*
Richmond
600 5th Avenue, at Balboa Street
(415) 668-9292
Closed Monday and Tuesday
$$

Chef-Owner Katia Troosh's warm presence is part of the magic at this wonderful Russian restaurant. Katia and her daughters, although efficient hosts, take the time to linger in the dining room, chatting with guests. And several nights a week the crisp, feminine ambience is enlivened with the sounds of a live guitar and accordion.

Begin with the borscht, then move on to the fragrant, lovingly made blinis with smoked salmon, caviar, and sour cream. Katia's is a favorite with local Russians, who come for the *pelmeni* (meat dumpling), *piroshki* (meat turnovers), stuffed cabbage, and beef Stroganoff. When you are sipping tea from the elegant tea service, nibbling on your napoleon, and savoring your berry pudding, you'll feel as though you've been on a short vacation and will not want to say *dasvidania*.

Walzwerk   *(German)*
Mission
381 South Van Ness Avenue, at 14th Street
(415) 551-7181
Closed Sunday and Monday
$$

Located across from a car dealership and garage, and flanked by rather nondescript row houses, the surrounding environs of 381 South Van Ness Avenue are hardly the San Francisco one sees on postcards. But if you're in the mood for delicious, hearty East German fare, you've come to the right place.

Walzwerk oozes proletarian charm with a very hip edge. Stepping through the door is like going back in time, with Soviet-era East German memorabilia adorning every nook and cranny and mismatched tables and chairs, plates, silverware, and glasses. The menu showcases German classics like red beet soup, grilled bratwurst with sauerkraut, and a trio of salads—red cabbage, green cabbage, and carrot slaw. Naturally, there are mashed potatoes. Also look for a revolutionary vegetarian schnitzel and a vegetarian cabbage roulade.

The beverage list includes all three of the former East German beers available in the United States.

THAI

Suriya Thai Restaurant
Mission
1432 Valencia Street, between 25th and 26th Streets
(415) 824-6655
Dinner only; closed Monday
Cash only
$$

At the far southern end of the Valencia Corridor, Suriya Thai Restaurant feels like it is much farther away, transporting you to a quiet corner of Bangkok or Chiang Mai. Wooden animal carvings, antique furniture, and tropical plants fill the dusty pink room. The menu is not typical; it's the carefully crafted and innovative cuisine of Chef-Owner Suriya Srithong. He grew up in the northern Thai city of Chiang Mai, and his two main influences were the delicious home cooking and street food of his childhood and the eighteen years he spent sailing around Southeast Asia in the Thai Navy. His menu is a combination of Thai classics like *pad thai, tom yum koong* (hot and spicy shrimp soup), and green papaya salad; street food from his childhood like *roti martabark* (a sweet stuffed crepe); traditional regional dishes rarely found in restaurants in the United States like *khao soi*, a special noodle dish from Chiang Mai; and innovative dishes that Chef Srithong has created himself, like Pacific Rim Ginger Sea Bass or Suriya Emerald Noodles (homemade noodles with chicken and peanuts). Influences from his travels can be seen in such dishes as Thai *samosas* or the popular Money Bags appetizer—prawns and chicken bundled in crispy rice wrappers and tied with green onion strings.

Thai House Express
Tenderloin
901 Larkin Street, at Geary Street
(415) 441-2248
Open till 2:00 A.M.
$

Thai House Express is a regular hangout for local chefs and line cooks. They come in for two reasons: They serve less common but perfectly executed Thai dishes, and they're open until 2:00 A.M. The interior of this Tenderloin restaurant is trendier than one would imagine given its location. The space is airy, with high ceilings and modern abstract art, and the servers are sassy and efficient.

Among the uncommon dishes, there's the braised pork leg with mustard greens, a meltingly tender slow-cooked pork shank infused with aromatic spices such as galangal and star anise. It is one of the few mild dishes here, and a comforting respite from the rest of the very spicy food.

Other dishes include *kanom gen num ya,* which is a red curry base made with lots of loose crab meat and fish that has the texture of a *bourride;* it comes with fish balls and is served with rice noodles, bean sprouts, and basil. The fried rice with fermented pork sausage or dry fermented fish is also excellent. Other good choices are the yellow curry with chicken and potato (a milder curry that allows the flavors of ginger and lemongrass to shine through) and the green papaya salad with dry salted crabs (although the crabs can be an acquired taste). Noodle dishes are another strong point.

Beer and wine are served, but because of the heat of the food, ordering a Thai iced tea is the way to go.

NOTABLE

Krung Thai

580 North Winchester Boulevard, near Forrest Avenue
San Jose   *SOUTH BAY*
(408) 248-3435
642 South Winchester Boulevard, near Moorpark Avenue
San Jose   *SOUTH BAY*
(408) 260-8224
$-$$

Krung Thai is so good that it draws a bustling crowd every day in two locations just three blocks apart. The lovely dining room and inspired food, like Pork-Stuffed Squid with Striped Eggplant in a rich green basil curry, have kept regulars coming back since 1988. The pure, authentic flavors are spicy, but a friendly staff keeps water glasses full. Skip the pedestrian wine list and try a Thai beer or classic iced tea.

Osha Thai Noodle Cafe
Tenderloin/Lower Nob Hill
696 Geary Street, at Leavenworth Street
(415) 673-2368
Open Sunday through Thursday till 1:00 A.M.; Friday and Saturday
till 3:00 A.M.
$$

I have been eating the *larb gai* (spicy chicken salad), Green Papaya Salad, and Green Curry Fried Rice at Osha's original location in the "Tender-Nob" for more than five years now and have never been disappointed. The food is fresh, delicious, and as spicy as you could possibly dare to have it. The young, cell-phone slinging crowd stays late: Osha serves until 3:00 A.M. on the weekends, and until 1:00 A.M. during the week. Osha's stylish new sibling on Valencia Street looks like it could double as a nightclub and has some of the same classics, but also some nouveau Thai creations and a beer and wine license. The Valencia Street Osha is open until midnight.

Other Location
819 Valencia Street, San Francisco (Mission);
(415) 826-7738

Sai Jai Thai
Tenderloin
771 O'Farrell Street, between Larkin and Hyde Streets
(415) 673-5774
BYOB
$

Sai Jai started out as a hole-in-the-wall restaurant that had a reputation for serving some of the most delicious, pristine Thai curries and noodles around. A couple of years ago it had a very stylish makeover, but the food (especially when the mother of the family is cooking) is still some of the best in San Francisco. Thanks to a semi-open kitchen, it is easy to see why: all the freshly cut ingredients, curry pastes, and spices are laid out by the stove, and everything is cooked to order. The Roasted Duck in Red Curry with lime leaf, basil, and coconut milk is absolute perfection, and in complete harmony alongside fresh bamboo-shoot slivers and bell pepper. The *pad thai* isn't too sweet, the noodles are cooked just right, and the flavors are fresh and bright. The *larbs* are top-notch, though be careful: In true Thai tradition "medium spicy" is definitely not mild! Sai Jai Thai has no beer and wine license at this time.

THAI TEMPLE

Every Sunday morning the Thai Wat Mongkolratanaram Buddhist Temple in Berkeley is transformed into an outdoor market with long family-style seating under a tent and vendors lined up under a semipermanent structure. Sales from the market help support the temple, much of the food is donated, and all the labor is volunteer.

The format is simple: Change your money into tokens and peruse the line of vendors selling their wares. The vendors officially open at 9:00 A.M., though it is prudent to get there early, as long lines usually form by 11:00 A.M. In the first stall to the right of the money exchange sit ladies chatting away at various griddles, frying up flat taro-coconut fritters and little half-spheres of coconut-chive custards. Both are good and can be bought separately or in a combination dish for three tokens.

Farther to the right is the boat-noodle stand. Here you have a choice of medium or wide vermicelli noodles. Once you get your steaming bowl of noodle soup, visit the table full of condiments. The Thai people I've had noodles with generally start by pouring in a healthy amount of sugar. Then follows the chile powder, vinegar with jalapeños, and finally fish sauce with the very spicy little Thai chiles.

At the next stand, where there is usually a long line, you'll find vegetable and meat curries like stir-fried pumpkin, green curry chicken, and beef *panang*. The pork *kapow* is an outstanding mix of spicy ground pork and vegetables, flavored with basil.

Packaged Thai sweets and freshly cut mangos are in the next stall. Among the many sweets are egg yolks cooked with sugar and shaped into flowers. Many people come only for the mango and sticky rice. In winter, when mangos are not in season, a coconut-egg custard tops the rice. The custard is eggy, and like many Southeast Asian desserts, sweet and slightly salty.

Now for my favorite, and the real reason for getting up to eat Thai food in the morning: papaya salad. It can be made vegetarian, but for me, what's the point if it doesn't have the pungency of fish sauce and dried shrimp?

The last stall is a favorite of lovers of fried chicken and sticky rice. You get a mound of sticky rice and a chicken leg, accompanied by a small cup of sweet-sour sauce with chopped peanuts. For a few tokens extra, you can get sweet potato, taro, and banana fritters on the side.

It's not fancy, it's not expensive—but a trip to the Temple can be a religious experience.

—*Emily Su*

Thai Temple
1911 Russell Street
Berkeley   *EAST BAY*
(510) 849-3419

VIETNAMESE

Ana Mandara

Fisherman's Wharf

891 Beach Street, at Polk Street

(415) 771-6800

$$$

Most San Franciscans are used to mining the Tenderloin (part of which was recently rechristened Little Saigon) for some of the best Vietnamese food in the city. Ana Mandara is the exception: This swank restaurant is located in touristy Ghiradelli Square and owned by no less than Don Johnson, of *Miami Vice* fame. And although Executive Chef Khai Duong honed his skills at Le Cordon Bleu in Paris and Le Bernardin in New York, don't worry: The food here is not only delicious, but also traditional. Standout starters include the Grilled Five-Spice-Scented Baby Spare Ribs; the Banana Blossom Salad ("You have to buy the right banana blossom," says Duong), tossed with shredded chicken and slices of grapefruit; and the Ceviche of Striped Bass, served with crispy shallots and crunchy cucumber. For the main course, the clay pot of *Mekong basa* (Vietnamese catfish), gorgeously presented on spiraled layers of lightly blanched snow peas, is mandatory. "It is a very traditional Vietnamese dish," says Duong. "It is what many Vietnamese people eat every day." Now you can too.

Bodega Bistro

Tenderloin

607 Larkin Street, at Eddy Street

(415) 921-1218

BYOB

$$

Bodega Bistro opened not a moment too soon, what with lines stretching around the block at the Slanted Door and with the unfortunate closing of Pacific Restaurant No. 2. Bodega Bistro is Chef-Owner Jimmie Kwok's first restaurant, though you would never know it. Kwok is from Hanoi, and his loyalty is firmly planted in the cuisine of North Vietnam, which he claims is "lighter and more delicate" than that of the South.

Start with his green papaya salad, a mound of julienned papaya tossed with toasted peanut shards and red chile, and the secret ingredient—tiny squares of dry-cured beef. Follow with the crab spring rolls fried crisp and accompanied with a generous plate of fresh lettuce, mint, perilla, and other assorted herbs. Wrap a roll in a lettuce leaf with some herbs and dip the whole packet in Tuong Ot Toi chile garlic sauce—a revelatory juxtaposition of hot and cold, oily and fresh. The pork "bun" is also excellent and consists of a bowl of charbroiled pork and pork meatballs in a flavorful sauce served with rice noodles. Squab under Kwok's command is not

unlike Peking duck and is also eaten wrapped with lettuce and herbs. Give Kwok a day's notice if you want a whole crab or lobster, and he will serve them with the most fabulous garlicky noodles.

Bodega Bistro has a limited selection of wines, but you are welcome to bring your own. Prosecco works especially well with the starters, but Kwok will set the pace with whatever you've brought along. His aim is to make you feel at home. One evening a friend's husband arrived very late, well after the kitchen had closed, due to flight delay. "You want some *pho*?" Kwok asked, "I always have *pho*. I think you need some *pho*." I think we all need Kwok.

Cam Huong
725 International Boulevard
Oakland   *EAST BAY*
(510) 444-8800
$–$$

You could come to Cam Huong only for their *bahn mi* (Vietnamese sand-wiches) and leave happy. Their version is excellent: a crisp French roll stuffed with barbecued pork, roasted chicken, or pâté, marinated carrots and daikon, cucumber batons, and fresh cilantro, plus mayonnaise and a drizzle of soy and fish sauce. This is a fusion food born out of France's century-long occupation of Indochina, and at Cam Huong there are more than a dozen varieties. The bread is baked up the street at a sister bakery and arrives fresh several times a day. The pâté and head cheese in the pork combination sandwich are house-made, and the ham is cured in the back. They are only $2 apiece, and a sandwich and a cup of sweet, milky Vietnamese iced coffee makes a fine lunch. Most customers take their orders to go.

But the *bahn mi* is only part of the story here. Owner Huong Luu has made the most of a small space, and few people work as hard. First thing in the morning she ensures the deli cases are filled to capacity with Styrofoam takeout dishes of *bun nem nuong* (house-made Vietnamese sausage over vermicelli); *com tam thit nuong cha* (steamed cakes of ground pork, egg, and mushrooms over broken rice); *bahn cu cai* (shrimp, pork, and daikon dumplings stuffed in tender, steamed rice-flour wrappers); and salad rolls stuffed with shrimp, mint, and basil.

In the drink cooler at the back of the shop, behind several Formica tables, you'll find fresh soymilk, pressed on-site daily, and a handful of Southeast Asian sodas. But it's the homemade *che*, or desserts, that will catch your eye. These confections are probably unlike anything else you've eaten, each a little abstract expressionist masterpiece.

Other Location
920 Webster, Oakland (East Bay); (510) 444-8800

Slanted Door
Embarcadero
Ferry Building Marketplace
One Ferry Building, Shop 5
Embarcadero, at Market Street
(415) 861-8032
$$–$$$

In April 2004 Charles Phan's Slanted Door settled in the newly remodeled Ferry Building, the restaurant's third location in less than ten years. The restaurant seats 150 people in the dining room and 20 at the bar, and there is a 34-seat cocktail lounge facing the bar. Slanted Door is always packed, and even if it were twice the size, it would still book weeks in advance.

Phan has become a sort of San Francisco legend, a household name to just about everyone in the Northern California food scene. Born in Da Lat, Vietnam, in 1962, Charles Phan and his family left in 1975 and relocated to Guam. It was from Guam that the Phans moved to San Francisco in 1977, an event of historic significance for Northern California food lovers.

Phan's restaurant is one of the few Asian restaurants in the country that is committed both to age-old traditional cooking technique and pristine,

locally sourced organic ingredients. Much of his produce comes from the farmers' market on the plaza, and the ingredients sparkle, especially in classic items such as the Salad Rolls, the Shaking Beef, and the Caramelized Shrimp—all of which have remained on the menu for years. Or you may want to try his chicken clay pot, with chiles and fresh ginger and chicken from Hoffman Farms in Petaluma.

The restaurant's Olle Lundberg–designed space is modern and comfortable, and it affords spectacular bay views. Despite the restaurant's expanded size, booking far ahead is essential—though you can order the full menu in the lounge. Service is knowledgeable and attentive, but it can be strained at the restaurant's busiest times. Go with a group of friends; most people eat family style, which enables everyone to taste a wide variety of dishes.

The restaurant also recently opened a to-go counter called Out the Door at the back of their space, featuring items such as Vietnamese sandwiches and soups.

NOTABLE

Irving Café and Deli
Inner Sunset
2146 Irving Street, between 22nd and 23rd Avenues
(415) 681-2326
$

Irving Café and Deli is about as basic as dining gets in San Francisco. One small room serves as both dining room and kitchen. The Vietnamese barbecue pork sandwiches are sublime—for me, the best in the city. A glass-fronted refrigerator offers unique canned drinks (such as grass jelly) and desserts in an array of colors unknown to nature. There are three folding chairs and a couple of stools at a counter across the window, through which you can watch the passersby on Irving Street.

Lotus Garden
Mission
3452 Mission Street, at 30th Street
(415) 642-1987
$$

This hole-in-the-wall Mission restaurant might not attract great crowds, but it is worth a visit just for the Raw Beef Salad—a dish that should be put in the Valhalla of San Francisco dishes. Resembling a mint-and-basil-topped carpaccio, this plate defines the word *awesome.* Classics like the spring rolls, live crab in tamarind sauce or roasted with garlic, beef *luk luk,* eggplant with curry, and pork chop are excellent.

Saigon Sandwiches
Tenderloin
560 Larkin Street, at Eddy Street
(415) 474-5698
Takeout only; cash only
$

Bahn mi (Vietnamese sandwiches) might be one of the world's most perfect creations. The *bahn mi* at Saigon Sandwiches are made with freshly baked and reheated baguettes, choice of chicken, barbecued pork, or pâté, plus cilantro and perfectly seasoned pickled carrots. In the *bahn mi* wars, it has risen to favored status, and for $2, I challenge anyone to find a better value anywhere. This establishment is the poster child for the term "hole in the wall," so you might not want to go here for a big birthday party.

Tu Lan
SOMA
8 Sixth Street, at Market Street
(415) 626-0927
Closed Sunday
$

Don't let the grimy exterior of Tu Lan or the general unseemliness of the neighborhood surroundings put you off. Make your way past the colorful parade of street life and take a seat at the counter. That way you'll be where the real action is: in front of the blackened workhorse stove, with all burners firing. Business is brisk; orders are fired, seasoned, tossed, and plated or packed to go in what seems a matter of seconds. The Vietnamese shrimp or beef salad is a perennial favorite, as is the shrimp fried rice. Portions are huge, and luckily, beer is available.

Vung Tau II
1750 North Milpitas Boulevard
Milpitas   *SOUTH BAY*
(408) 934-9327
$$

Named after a resort island just off the coast from Ho Chi Min City, Vung Tau II offers one of the broadest Vietnamese menus around. So it's no surprise that in this Silicon Valley town, with the Bay Area's densest concentration of Vietnamese expatriates, lunchtime finds the restaurant crowded with more people waiting at the door.

If possible, forgo the standard fresh spring rolls and go for the more unusual options, including the Shrimp Cakes with Fish Sauce. Crisp on the outside and tender inside, the coconut-batter cakes are wrapped with aromatic herbs and dipped in a sweet vinegar sauce. Or try the crunchy Green Papaya Salad with Sweet Dried Beef. Both the steamed vermicelli and the flat-sheet noodle with grilled prawns are fantastic.

Beverages are typical of what you might find in Vietnam. Try a fruit shake to get an idea of the popular Vietnamese smoothie, and finish with a fruit, bean, and jelly dessert.

Yummy Yummy
Inner Sunset
1015 Irving Street, between 11th and 12th Avenues
(415) 566-4722
Closed Tuesday
$

Yummy Yummy is a small, unremarkable-looking restaurant on a quiet section of Irving Street. It has a devoted if not fanatical following, not only because the place is so aptly named, but also because unlike so many other similar joints—where getting your food involves flagging down waiters, who most of the time will not acknowledge your needs, much less your empty water glasses—the servers at Yummy Yummy are friendly and attentive. They'll take the time to steer you toward something you've never tried before like *goi bo* (raw beef and herb salad) or *bahn khot* (pan-fried rice cakes with shrimp, coconut, and fish sauce) that you wrap with herbs in lettuce. And of course, there are the dozen varieties of *pho*, beef noodle soup that comes piping hot with or without rare steak, well-done beef flank, tendon, or beef balls. It's some of the best around, almost a miracle considering the rudimentary kitchen. And if you need an extra bowl to share the soup, it'll arrive right away, with a smile.

PART TWO

SPECIAL FOODS
&
NIGHTLIFE

BARBECUE

Bo's Barbecue

3422 Mount Diablo Boulevard

Lafayette   *EAST BAY*

(925) 283-7133

Open till 9:00 P.M.; closed Sunday

$$

A barbecue joint doesn't quite seem to fit in the staid suburban hamlet of Lafayette, but Bo's is well worth the trip across the bridge and through the tunnel. It's exceptional, in part because owner Bo McSwine (really, that's his name), an ex-hippie Berkeley radical, makes his barbecue from only the finest, most sustainable ingredients. Most locals order to go, but if you choose to sit, you can eat inside or out and enjoy a great selection of imported beers and unusual California wines.

The brisket is amazingly tasty, and the ribs and chicken are good too. If you like to gnaw on bones, the beef back bones are the way to go. The house sauce, available in medium and hot versions, is so good you'll want to devour it with a spoon, or slather it on the pork ribs and sausage links. Fresh sides include potato salad, corn, and French bread, and for dessert, sweet potato pie. But we recommend filling up on the meat. It's what Bo McSwine does best, and he learned the art of cooking it from his grandmother in Mississippi.

Brother-In-Laws Barbeque

Western Addition

705 Divisadero Street, at Grove Street

(415) 931-7427

Closed Monday

$

Most days Divisadero Street, from about Fell Street to Golden Gate Avenue, is brought to you in full Odorama. Barbeque Odorama, that is, courtesy of Brother-In-Laws, the venerable Western Addition institution that has been putting out fine barbeque for about the last twenty years. The oak wood smoke billows out the chimney and drifts over the neighborhood, riling up appetites all along the way. Though they have a worn-out sign in front, it is unnecessary; this smoke plume is really their calling card. The place itself is a bit ramshackle, which adds several notches of authenticity. Pork are the ribs of choice here, and you order by the slab: full or half. We like to slather a half-hot, half-sweet combination of their BBQ sauces onto our ribs. The sides are somewhat unremarkable, and there is not much room to eat in, so if you can resist breaking into your takeaway bag, the food is best enjoyed at home in a stain-forgiving environment.

Chef Edward's
1998 San Pablo Avenue, at 20th Street
Oakland   *EAST BAY*
(510) 834-9516
$

The first thing most people mention when asked about Chef Edward's is
Chef Edward himself—a charming man with a commanding presence.
The second thing they will mention is the beef brisket. It is so tender you
can leave your knife on the napkin: The meat falls off the bone of its own
accord. Edward's is a no-frills restaurant with a long counter, framed accolades along the walls, and a massive cleaver with which Chef Edward deftly
chops those meaty ribs and shoulders. You have a choice of delicious sides:
traditional accompaniments like black-eyed peas, potato salad, greens,
and Mama's special pickled coleslaw. You can eat at the restaurant, but
most people do takeout or have the food delivered for special parties,
church and charity events. Chef Edward's is an East Bay establishment
with reliably great barbecue and exceptionally gracious service.

Doug's BBQ
3600 San Pablo Avenue
Emeryville   *EAST BAY*
(510) 655-9048
Takeout only
$$

Doug's BBQ has become an Oakland mainstay, with its exquisitely slow-
cooked pork and beef ribs, house-made link sausage, and juicy deep-fried
turkeys. And the 25¢ slices of sweet potato pie are reason enough to go.
The sides, which include a tangy potato salad and cabbage slaw, are fine,
but the pork ribs, especially when they're coated with Doug's well-honed
special sauce (available in hot or mild), are something to write home

about. Sparse in the extreme, there's nothing frivolous about this place. It's all about the sweet and delicious slabs of ribs cooking in the kitchen's enormous smoker.

Everett and Jones
126 Broadway, at 2nd Street
Oakland *EAST BAY*
(510) 601-9377
$$

The smoky aroma creeping down Broadway like a sweet Southern drawl is enough to cause many vegetarians to consider coming back to the other side. Oak burns in the "Super Q" smoker out back, behind Everett and Jones's stark storefront, calling out to passersby day after day: Come and get it! The menu, equally austere, is simple to navigate. Unless you haven't eaten for days, order an unassembled sandwich, which is more or less a smaller version of the plates/platters. Choose between chicken, beef, link sausage, or the signature falling-off-the-bone ribs. All are served in a pool of barbecue sauce, hot, medium, or mild, which is made every few days in small batches by Mary Everett, the daughter of founder Dorothy Everett. Both sandwiches and plates come with a generous mound of creamy potato salad, sweet with pickles and onions.

Memphis Minnie's BBQ
Lower Haight
576 Haight Street, at Fillmore Street
(415) 864-7675
www.memphisminnies.com
Closed Monday
$-$$

Bob Cantor came to barbecue serendipitously. In his native Brooklyn he was originally hired to rework a menu at a local restaurant, and in the course of his research he fell in love with this truly American cuisine. Few foods in American cuisine are as regionally diverse as barbecue, with numerous styles to be found throughout the country.

Cantor set out to educate himself about barbecue and spent more than three years traveling to all the barbecue hot spots around the United States: Texas, Kansas City, and, of course, Memphis. Along the way he spent hours in kitchens working under the watchful eyes of the old masters. The result of this odyssey is Memphis Minnie's, which serves an assortment of the diverse styles of Southern barbecue. It is considered by barbecue expert Lolis Eric Elie, of the *New Orleans Times Picayune,* to be "the finest barbecue restaurant in the state."

The meats at Memphis Minnie's are slow-cooked, meaning the time ranges from four to eighteen hours over white oak logs at 185 to 250 degrees Fahrenheit. The menu offers no surprises, but what is served meets the standards of the most discerning barbecue aficionados. Some favorites include the Texas Beef Brisket, Pit-Smoked Beans, and the Memphis Sweet Smoked Pork Sandwiches. You can also order meats by the pound.

Cantor's continuing education program consists of annual treks to the Southern Foodways Alliance Symposium (more information can be found at www.southernfoodways.com) and regular trips to Texas.

Perry's Food for the Soul
185 Pelton Center Way
San Leandro   **EAST BAY**
(510) 614-5576
Closed Monday
$-$$

San Leandro, a leafy suburb of Oakland, has the feeling of bucolic small-town America. Luckily, it's much more diverse than most small towns and offers the visitor some soulful soul food, including Stephanie Perry's storefront in the Pelton Center strip mall.

In an enormous stainless steel smoker imported from Kansas City, Perry keeps a fire of apple wood stoked. The ribs, chicken, beef links, and tri-tip that she slowly barbecues come out gently smoked and incredibly tender. The dry rub and the barbecue sauce (mild or spicy) create a pleasant resonance in your mouth, yet don't overpower the meat.

Today Perry's repertoire includes fried catfish, scrumptious candied yams, baked beans, and a potato salad full of crunchy celery and egg, all of which she learned from her father. She also makes succotash, crispy fried okra, and a popular jambalaya on weekends. Her individual sweet potato pies are famous, and her pecan pie is irresistible.

Perry's is the sort of place where the menu varies from day to day, and popular foods, such as the corn bread, often sell out within an hour of opening. Go to Perry's with an open mind; whatever they have on hand is likely to be delicious. Takeout is usually the way to go except on Sunday, when churchgoers crowd the place dressed in their Sunday best.

Perry's father died a few years ago, and the dessert menu now features Daddy Perry's Peach Cobbler. His daughter ponders what new recipes she'll be making in the coming months. She's been experimenting with smoking whole turkeys. She's planning her next marketing trip to Jack London Square in Oakland, where she buys ingredients such as collard greens. She says she also dreams of opening a place in Berkeley. But on one point, she's firm: "This is what I'm going to do for the rest of my life."

BARS, PUBS & TAVERNS

A Coté
5478 College Avenue, at Taft Avenue
Oakland   *EAST BAY*
(510) 655-6469

Though it has only been around for a few years, A Coté feels like a long-time fixture in the neighborhood, with its unassuming facade and a comfortably dark interior dominated by a sweeping bar. Despite a respectable offering of small plates like *pommes frites* and mussels, A Coté is really all about the drinks. This is immediately clear when you receive the menu, three-quarters of which is devoted to wine, beer, and spirits. You'll hear no complaints, though, as it's a truly impressive list.

On a recent trip we ordered the Figuon cocktail (a fig-infused French aperitif with vodka and lemon juice), which is just as fun to drink as you might imagine. In fact, many of their specialty cocktails are created with unusual aperitifs and liqueurs.

The wine list is refreshing for its representation of wines from small producers. The story is much the same for beer, and there are dozens of Belgian ales available, with no fewer than five brewed by real Belgian monks (not merely contract-brewed for the monastery).The bartenders are both knowledgeable and congenial and are usually happy to pour several samples to help ease you through your ordering indecision.

Albatross Pub
1822 San Pablo Avenue, between Delaware Street and Hearst
   Avenue
Berkeley   *EAST BAY*
(510) 843-2473
Cash only

A large stone fireplace casts an amber light on the wood-paneled interior of the Albatross, creating a cozy atmosphere not unlike the inside of a full pint glass. It's easy to see why Berkeley's oldest pub still pulls in crowds of all ages and from all corners of the East Bay. With fourteen draft and fifty bottled beers to choose from, it's like being at home, only with more beer (although there are no well drinks and no blenders, they do have a limited number of select liquors for those who prefer a more potent swill). The patrons are friendly, fun, and extremely casual—if not a bit competitive. An assortment of board games for all skill levels, from chess to Connect Four, can be checked out from behind the bar. Sunday's Trivia Night always packs the house, but local grad students make winning tougher than you'd expect. For those with more brawn than brain, there's a darts tourney every Tuesday across six well-kept dart lanes. Large, round oak tables make this the perfect place for a big group of friends; the smaller booths, however, when paired with, say, Chutes and Ladders, are a great way to warm up a nervous first date.

Bacar
SOMA
448 Brannan Street, between Third and Fourth Streets
(415) 904-4100

Legendary for its wine program created by Co-Owner Debbie Zachareas, Bacar came on the South of Market scene at the end of the dot-com bubble, and unlike the bubble, it survived. With its tri-level seating, brick-and-mortar walls, steel beams, and floor-to-ceiling glass wine storage system, Bacar is hip and urbane. Live jazz starts nightly at 9:00 P.M. in the bar, and Chef-Owner Arnold Wong, of EOS fame, oversees an Asian-accented Mediterranean menu. With a list of 1,400 wines—85 offered by the glass—you'll need a glass of wine just to figure out which wine to drink.

Bix
Financial District
56 Gold Street, at Montgomery Street (alleyway between Pacific
    and Jackson Streets)
(415) 433-6300

From its clandestine entrance off an alley in historic Jackson Square to its art deco interior and perfect martinis, Bix is one of the sexiest spots in San Francisco. If you're alone, the crush at the bar might be the best spot; if not, try for a table on the balcony. There's live jazz nightly and a menu of updated American classics from noted chef Bruce Hill. It's an ideal stop for a flirtatious bite early or late.

Beach Chalet Brewery
Outer Richmond
1000 Great Highway, between Fulton Street and Lincoln Way
(415) 386-8439

The bar at Beach Chalet is as far west as you can go in the Lower 48 without dropping into the Pacific Ocean. This historic building, designed by Willis Polk, originally opened in 1925 as a changing room for Pacific swimmers. It recently received a much-needed makeover, including restoration of the fabulous WPA murals by Lucien Labaudt. The highlight of the Beach Chalet is the beer, which is brewed on-site. There are a half a dozen styles to choose from, and for a small deposit, you can take home a half-gallon growler jug of your favorite brew, perfect for serving during a Giants or 'Niners game.

Black Horse London Pub
Cow Hollow
1514 Union Street, between Franklin Street and Van Ness Avenue
(415) 928-2414
Cash only

It was two years before my friend Bill received his time card, and still it was not without controversy. Another patron who had been attending the Black Horse London Pub with the same degree of regularity as Bill did not receive one. You see, not everyone gets a time card.

If deemed worthy, regulars are given a time card. They punch in when they arrive and punch out when they leave. After five hundred hours on the clock, you receive a free beer. After a thousand hours, your time card is retired.

BHLP is about the size of a postage stamp and was the conception of beer enthusiast Joe Gilmartin. In 1996 Gilmartin overcame Union Street zoning restrictions and obtained a "beer only" liquor license by converting this one-time deli into a deli and, oddly, Irish cultural center. According to the city, the BHLP is a deli that serves beer; but to us it's a community center, and for the lucky few, something akin to a job rewarding you with free beers.

Buena Vista Café
North Beach
2765 Hyde Street, at Beach Street
(415) 474-5044

Opened in 1889, the café sits on an ideal corner of Hyde Street, where the cable car turns and the bay views are spectacular. It is a lively café, crowded with both tourists and locals, and is credited as the birthplace of Irish coffee in the United States. As the story goes, fifty years ago the then-owner of the café set out to recreate the much revered Irish coffee served at Shannon Airport in Ireland. After experimenting with various Irish whiskeys and the consistency of the cream, he arrived at the recipe we go back to the Buena Vista to enjoy today.

C. Bobby's Owl Tree
Union Square/Theater District
601 Post Street, at Taylor Street
(415) 776-9344
Closed Sunday through Tuesday
Cash only

The Owl Tree, perched on the corner of Post and Taylor, is just the place to relax after running around the city or to grab a drink before heading to one of the Indian restaurants down the street. True to its name, owls take center stage at this comfortable, oddball place, from the shape of the menus to the bric-a-brac that lines the walls. The no-nonsense owner-bartender keeps his bar extraordinarily clean and the occasional unruly patron in line. I come for the ice-cold Bitburger, but he also makes fine cocktails and is generous with the baskets of Chex snacks and Wet Naps.

Café Rouge
See California, page 23.

César
1515 Shattuck Avenue, between Cedar and Vine Streets
Berkeley   EAST BAY
(510) 883-0222

A space that might otherwise be cold with its poured concrete floors and cool blue tiles, once it begins to fill with people (as it reliably does) César quickly warms up. In fact, the noise can often reach deafening levels as the night wears on. A further peril is the often longish wait if you don't arrive early. However, it's clear why César draws such a crowd. Not only is it a boisterous outpost in the often staid and residential North Berkeley neighborhood, but its cocktails are some of the best in the East Bay. César offers a full range of standards such as cosmopolitans, martinis, mojitos, and margaritas, and all are consistently excellent. There is also an extensive wine list that includes favorites from the local importer Kermit Lynch, as well as a fine selection of beers.

César offers a tapas menu, including *jamon serrano,* grilled spring onions with *romesco,* and salt cod and potato *cazuela.* Perhaps the most popular dish, though, is the one piled high with splinter-thin fried potatoes with herbs and sea salt and served with garlicky *aioli.*

Doña Tomas

5004 Telegraph Avenue

Oakland   *EAST BAY*

(510) 450-0522

Closed Sunday and Monday

I often admit to a certain finickiness when choosing bars in the East Bay. In fact, a night out can often resemble a sort of Goldilocks experience: this one's too noisy, that one's too precious, and that one reeks of disinfectant and bad beer. It was a happy occasion, then, to find this bustling, richly hued bar adjacent to the equally bustling restaurant of the same name in Oakland's Temescal neighborhood.

Seated at the bar alternately admiring the vibrant iconography of saints decorating the walls and the bartender's tattooed arms, you'll find a wide variety of tequilas plus an impressive selection of potent mezcal. Cocktails include the Doña Colada or the El Low Rider (indistinguishable from a Sidecar, but all the more appealing for its name). There are a respectable number of wines by the glass and Mexican beers, as well an exciting array of nonalcoholic drinks like guava juice and tamarind *agua fresca.*

Just as the tequila is going to your head, you can order small plates of *costillas de res* (beef short ribs with mole sauce) or *sopes* with chanterelles. Other standards include a generous serving of guacamole in a rough stone mortar, ceviche made with ahi tuna, and quesadillas with *queso Oaxaca,* avocado, and *epazote.* There are plenty of appetizers to share if you really are there mostly to drink; however, you can also choose from full plates like *pescados con tomate y Serrano crema* (sautéed cod cheeks) or *carne asada con chimichurri.* The service is patient and skilled, and Doña Tomas uses local, organic meats, poultry, and vegetables. What more could a fussy patron ask for?

Eagle Tavern
SOMA
398 Twelfth Street, at Harrison Street
(415) 626-0880
Cash only (ATM available)

With an interior that is best described as "vintage biker club," a tattooed, unruly crowd that veers from leather to urban-hipster lesbian, and laconic, laid-back service make the Eagle Tavern one of San Francisco's most enduring and eccentric gay bars. Part of its success is the building itself, a collection of sheds with outdoor spaces on different levels, much of which is covered with sculpture, posters, and urban artifacts. The drinks are nothing out of the ordinary but inexpensive; the bartenders are of the musician-philosopher persuasion and make everyone feel welcome.

Music is one of the big draws. Under the direction of Doug Hilsinger, the "Thursday Night Live" series at the Eagle has turned into one of San Francisco's most popular music venues. On other nights the DJs, especially Andy Castle, play intelligent and well-researched mixes of rock, punk, old-time country, and soul (no disco).

EOS Restaurant and Wine Bar
Lower Haight
901 Cole Street, at Carl Street
(415) 566-3063
$$

EOS offers forty wines by the glass, predominantly from California and France. The entire wine list, consisting of some four hundred wines, is excellent, with wines carefully selected from high-quality and unusual estates.

The menu is small but good. Try oysters on the half-shell served with mignonette sauce and horseradish *concasse,* the Thai Spiced Sweet White Corn Succotash and Fresh Water Prawns, and the homemade Red Curried Duck and Pork Sausage. The waitstaff can seem a bit brusque but are nonetheless quite knowledgeable and prepared to talk about wine.

Ferry Plaza Wine Merchant
See Wine Retailers, page 294.

1550 Hyde Wine Bar & Café
See California, page 26.

Incanto
Noe Valley
1550 Church Street, near Duncan Street
(415) 641-4500
Closed Tuesday

If you're looking to have an Italian wine experience, you should spend an evening drinking the first-rate wines at Incanto. Claudio Villani, one of the most innovative sommeliers in the city, was the first to place an identification coaster under each wine goblet with the name and origin of the wine. Villani is extremely helpful with his clientele, discussing wine and explaining the history of each estate. Incanto has a list of thirty to forty Italian wines by the glass and around three hundred wines on its entire list—certainly one of the best in the city. You'll enjoy an enchanting, that is, an *incantevole* evening, dining on appetizers prepared by the tireless Chris Cosentino, and chatting with Claudio Villani. For more about Incanto, see Italian, page 93.

Li Po
Chinatown
916 Grant Avenue, at Washington Street
(415) 982-0072
Cash only

The first time I visited Li Po, a heavily eyelined, mid-to-very-late-middle-aged Asian woman who took prolonged drags off of a thin, brown cigarette, was tending bar. There was a gigantic gilded Buddha in the corner. The room was dark. Shadowy. And very smoky. When I couldn't decide what I wanted to drink, she gruffly recommended some kind of homemade plum wine that she had behind the counter. "Be careful! It's very strong!" warned a seasoned patron, who was hunched over his drink. I was twenty-three. I had just arrived from Peoria. I had never been anywhere more exotic than Li Po.

Recently we had predinner cocktails at Li Po to celebrate my forty-third birthday. The Buddha was still there, but not nearly as big as I remembered. The bartender was nondescript, and smoking is no longer permitted. A video poker machine had been installed. Worse yet, three fraternity guys held sway at the far end of the bar. Nonetheless, Li Po still retains its charm. Once an opium den, always an opium den, after all.

Nectar Wine Lounge
Marina
3330 Steiner Street, at Chestnut Street
(415) 345-1377

Nectar has a broad wine list of nearly eight hundred wines drawn from all regions of the globe. Located in the affluent Marina District, Nectar is small (with seating capacity of forty-five) and welcoming, though at times cramped. Its by-the-glass service is superb, with approximately three dozen choices, primarily French, Californian, Australian, and Spanish. The food menu is small and international but is interesting and well done, marrying well with the wines.

The Pied Piper Bar
Financial District
In the Palace Hotel
2 New Montgomery Street, at Market Street
(415) 512-1111

When you have a hankering for something old school, be it dark wood, cocktails, or great art, make a beeline for The Pied Piper Bar inside the Palace Hotel. Maxfield Parrish painted the mural-sized rendition of the bar's namesake, The Pied Piper, for the grand reopening in 1909, after the earthquake and fire of 1906. The vivid $20,000 commission, now valued at around $2.5 million, was based on the fairy tale and includes the faces of Parrish's children as well as his mistress. Don't miss this San Francisco landmark (rated as one of the world's seven best bars by *Esquire* magazine), where the cocktails are all $10 and you can get tasty snacks, a sirloin burger, or an order of sweet corn crab cakes for a reasonable price. The bar also serves a variety of wines by the glass.

Pier 23 Café
Embarcadero
Pier 23, Embarcadero, at Battery Street
(415) 362-5125

When the sun is out and you have a free afternoon, head over to Pier 23. Located along the Embarcadero, Pier 23's best feature is its back patio, which juts out over the Bay propped up by stilts . It's worn and likely suffering from dry rot, but it's a prime spot to take in some rays and some booze. Pier 23's got a full bar, choice brews on tap, excellent margaritas, ESPN, and live music six nights a week. Jimmy Buffett would like it here.

You can get a competent bite to eat at Pier 23 too. The cracked crab or steamed clams go well with the atmosphere. And remarkably, if you sit in the front room, you will be treated to sit-down, white-tablecloth service.

Ruby Room
132 14th Street, between Madison and Oak Streets
Oakland   *EAST BAY*
(510) 444-7224

Across from the public library, two red floodlights mark an otherwise nondescript facade. Inside the Ruby Room, however, much more effort is made in the name of ambience. Red candles, red light bulbs, and plenty of smoke make for a lighting that is both flattering and good for developing photos. Red pleather banquettes line faux-rock walls, and a pool table nestled in the back presents a perfect opportunity for strutting around in front of the seated crowds. A predominately younger set, cool and arty, flocks to the Ruby Room for two reasons: first, for the drinks, which are cheap, big, stiff, and generally served by an attractive bartender; second, for the music. DJs, many from local indie radio station KALX, spin a different genre almost every night of the week. DJ Kitty's classic soul on Wednesday nights is likely most popular, but honky-tonk, punk, funk, and '80s nights are equally danceable. That's right, I said dance: it's too dark for anyone to actually see you dance, and too loud for you to hear them make fun of you. So brush up your robot moves and hit the floor.

Specs Twelve Adler Museum Café
North Beach
12 William Saroyan Place, off Columbus Avenue, close to
    Broadway
(415) 421-4112
Cash only

Specs Twelve Adler Museum Café is the bar's formal name, but most people simply call it Specs. Opened in 1968, it is one of the few remaining locales from North Beach's Bohemian past. It is a dark and gritty, though well-preserved bar. And it's virtually impossible to not get lost pondering the eclectic decor. Every inch of the place is covered: flags billow from the ceiling and pictures and knick-knacks cover the walls. Signs, such as the one that reads REALITY IS A TEMPORARY ILLUSION BROUGHT ON BY THE ABSENCE OF ALCOHOL, reflect the flavor of this North Beach favorite.

Tommy's Mexican Restaurant
Richmond
5929 Geary Boulevard, at 23rd Avenue
(415) 387-4747

While the food is OK, Tommy's is worth a trip just for the margaritas. Sit at the bar and order chorizo and eggs to absorb one of their delicious margaritas or any one of about a zillion tequilas. You can even join their tequila tasting club. The place is crowded on almost any night of the week, so go in the mood for a party.

Tonga Room
Nob Hill
In the Fairmont Hotel
950 Mason Street, at California Street
(415) 772-5278

Every visitor to San Francisco must make a pilgrimage to the Tonga Room—a tiki-tacky destination bar inside the Fairmont Hotel. Dusty thatched roofs hang over tables, acres of plastic orchids line the walls, and tiki torches light the room. Thrifty devotees come here for the award-winning Pacific Rim Happy Hour—complete with pot stickers, greasy chow mein, and spare ribs—but true Tonga worshippers come for the tropical cocktails and surprise thunder and lightning shower. Hold on to your drinks—you don't want a raindrop to splash into your mai tai.

There's live music after 8:00 P.M. most evenings, with a cover band playing from a stage that floats out into the middle of the lagoon during the sets, then floats back to shore during breaks. Tonga Room is the last of San Francisco's kitschy gems.

Top of the Mark
Nob Hill
In the Mark Hopkins InterContinental Hotel
One Nob Hill, 19th Floor, between California and Mason Streets
(415) 616-6916

The Mark Hopkins was built in 1926, but the penthouse apartment was not converted into a bar until 1939. The story is that soldiers heading out to war in the Pacific would go to the Top of the Mark with their friends for one last toast to the Golden Gate, ensuring them a safe trip home. These days, though you may be grouped in with tourists or socked in by fog, the Top of the Mark is still the best place to take out-of-town guests for an unparalleled 360-degree view. I prefer the relative calm of cocktail hour, but there is live music most nights and a cover charge on Friday and Saturday nights.

Tosca Caffe
North Beach
242 Columbus Avenue, at Broadway
(415) 986-9651
Cash only

Tosca Caffe, one of the most unique bars in San Francisco, is owned and operated by Jeannette Etheredge. Born in China and the daughter of Madame Armen Bali (who owned the famous and sadly departed Russian-Armenian restaurant Bali's), Etheredge spent time in a Japanese prison camp during World War II. Her funny, no-nonsense lines will remind you of Tallulah Bankhead, and she is a genius at working the room and making you feel welcome. She has been a close friend of many of the great ballet dancers, actors, film directors, cops, criminals, and politicians of our time. When they are in town, Mikhail Baryshnikov, Sean Penn, and Sam Shepard can be found hanging out in the private room with its legendary pool table. Her wonderful drinks, like the house cappuccino (hot chocolate and brandy) and the white nun (brandy, Kahlúa, and steamed milk), will warm you up on even the foggiest night.

Vesuvio's
North Beach
255 Columbus Avenue, at Broadway
(415) 362-3370
Cash only

With its entrance of wild murals, paintings, and stained glass, just across the alley from City Light Books, Vesuvio's is a required stop on any beatnik tour of North Beach and ideal for anyone looking for a comforting, dimly lit refuge from the world. Opened in 1949, Vesuvio's was a well-known watering hole for Kerouac, Ginsberg, Cassidy, and other famous literary figures, and their spirit lives on. The wood interior is plastered with memorabilia, there's a colorful group of regulars, and the mezzanine seating and corner looking out over Columbus Avenue is a favorite spot on a quiet afternoon for journal writing or daydreaming.

Zeitgeist
Mission
199 Valencia Street, at Duboce Avenue
(415) 255-7505
Cash only

On the rare sunny afternoon, San Franciscans flock to Zeitgeist's outdoor patio. With its huge backyard lined with long tables and benches, and plenty of space to park your bike, Zeitgeist is the Friday after-work hangout for cyclists of all types. Try one of the huge Bloody Marys; with its forest of pickled vegetables, it is almost as good as a salad. Later on, as the sun goes down and the backyard fills, the grills fire up and there are tasty burgers, sausages, and chicken sandwiches to be had. Zetigeist has many different beers on tap, from local brews to Belgian ales, and pitchers too. As the night wears on, the bikes pour in, so be careful on your way out.

BREAKFAST & BRUNCH

 Boulette's Larder
See Ethnic & Specialty Markets, page 247.

 Café Fanny
1603 San Pablo Avenue, at Cedar Street

Berkeley   *EAST BAY*

(510) 524-5447

$

On a corner of Cedar and San Pablo that's dotted with olive trees stands the worn brick structure that houses Café Fanny. Opened in 1984 by Alice Waters and named for her daughter, it is now run by her brother-in-law, Jim Maser. The café serves an inventive breakfast and lunch. Ingredients are largely organic and originate nearby—as close as next door, from Acme Bread Company to Kermit Lynch Wine. Imagined as an European stand-up café complete with a long zinc counter, Café Fanny also has a few tables outside.

Breakfast is varied and unique: buckwheat crepes, sweet or savory; poached farm eggs with vinegar and oregano or prosciutto; Irish oatmeal; the café's celebrated granola, also named after Fanny; and a slew of house-made pastries. Though the millet muffins have acquired a somewhat cultish following, the fruit crisps and beignets are also a good supplement to the café's staple beverage, a bowl of café au lait.

For lunch, the cooks behind the counter assemble plates of pâté with cornichons, a *croque monsieur* (perfectly crisp), or greens with toasted Sonoma goat cheese. The glass shelves of pastries and cakes, such as the crème frâiche cake or a chocolate *pave,* should not be overlooked. Café Fanny takes the morning and midday meal seriously. Though its dishes are small and simple, they're cooked perfectly with pure ingredients.

 Campton Place
Union Square

340 Stockton Street, at Campton Place

(415) 955-5555

$$-$$$

When tony Campton Place Hotel opened, Chef Bradley Ogden knocked the socks off San Francisco's elite diners with his delicious American breakfast. Several chefs later, the tradition continues, and the corned beef hash with poached eggs is not to be missed. For more about Campton Place, see French, page 63.

Canteen
Union Square
817 Sutter Street
(415) 928-8870
$$

Corned beef hash, steak and eggs, pancakes, bacon, home fries—all the diner breakfast specials can be found at this very special diner. There's also French toast, eggs Benedict, a smoked salmon omelet, and espresso. And it is at the breakfast hour that you can actually walk in unannounced and get to eat. Not to be missed. Breakfast is served Monday through Friday 7 A.M. to 11 A.M.; brunch on Saturday and Sunday from 8 A.M. to 2 P.M. For more about Canteen, see California, page 24.

 ## Desiree
Presidio
Building 39
39 Mesa, Suite 108
Closed Saturday and Sunday
(415) 561-2336
$

It may be a little confusing to find which building Desiree is in, but when you push open the heavy iron door at Building 39 in the Presidio, all you have to do is follow your nose. The pleasant scent of freshly cooked eggs or a grilled Saint George cheese and ham sandwich (and perhaps the squeal from the steamer of the espresso machine) will lead you to your right and down the hall to pocket-sized Desiree. Chef Anne Gingrass traded in all the glitz (she was at the helm at Spago, Postrio and Hawthorne Lane) to keep the many not-for-profiteers at the San Francisco Film Centre, the Thoreau Center for Sustainability and other Presidio denizens well-nourished and centered at breakfast, lunch, and brunch. Poached eggs, house-made granola, morning scones and crumbly coffee cake help many to start the day, while seasonal soups, salads, and sandwiches provide sustenance at the noon hour. Everything is made on-site and in the kitchen downstairs. Ingredients are almost all organic and local: you'll find greens from Maraquita Farms, organic eggs from Petaluma Farms, cheese from Cowgirl Creamery, dairy from Strauss. Gingrass's sourcing is as correct as Chez Panisse, maybe more so. And like many of her Park Partners serving food in the Golden Gate National Recreation Area, such as the Headlands Institute and the Headlands Center for the Arts, the Crissy Center, and the Warming Hut (see page 196), Gingrass celebrates local sustainable food, some of which comes from the Park itself.

To avoid getting lost, log on to the Desiree Web site, www.desireecafe .com, for directions and a detailed map. Beer and wine are available.

Dottie's True Blue Café
Tenderloin
522 Jones Street, between O'Farrell and Geary Streets
(415) 885-2767
$

Dottie's is a bright spot in an otherwise grungy neighborhood. Once inside, you'll find a warm, cozy room with tables filling every nook of this odd-shaped room. You'll be greeted first by a display of the day's house-made scones, muffins, and fruit breads. The simple apricot-and-oat scone is one of my favorites and will certainly satisfy even the pickiest pastry lover. Have a seat and peruse the printed menu of breakfast standards, but be sure not to miss the specials board. It's on the wall near the poster of a topless Josephine Baker.

Dottie's self-described "famous" pancakes are worth any notoriety they receive. These are thick and chewy buttermilk cakes seasoned with just a touch of cinnamon. All egg dishes are served with toasted homemade breads. Buttermilk dill is the house standard, but the whole wheat is equally delicious. In fact, it would be worth a trip to Dottie's just for their bakery items.

Ella's
Pacific Heights
500 Presidio Avenue, at California Street
(415) 441-5669
$

Once you step inside this cute corner restaurant, you'll see the main attraction. There in the glass case before you is an array of house-made baked goods: breads, pastries, and the outrageously tasty sticky buns. They are available to take away, but I prefer to order a sticky bun as an appetizer for two while we wait for more serious breakfast fare. But the all-time favorite for most regulars is the Chicken Hash, a more than generous patty topped with two perfectly cooked eggs. All the breakfast dishes are served with a choice of Ella's house-made breads—white, wheat, rye, or raisin. The two thick-cut slices are perfect for a dollop of jam.

 Ferry Plaza Farmers Market
Embarcadero
One Ferry Building
Embarcadero, at Market Street
(415) 291-3276
Saturday 8:00 A.M. to 2:00 P.M.

If your group can't agree on what to have for breakfast on a Saturday morning, the best answer is to go to the Ferry Plaza Farmers Market. Head straight for the plaza behind the building, as that's where most of the food vendors are found. Those in the mood for pastry can get their fix at Downtown Bakery with a heavenly Donut Muffin. Their fruit tarts are fabulous as well.

Those in need of something more substantial can head back toward the water to find the hot food section. There you'll discover many choices, from *chilaquiles* at Primavera (see Mexican, page 127) to an open-faced Hobb's bacon-and-egg sandwich from Hayes Street Grill (see Seafood, page 217). In season they offer a crab cake that is out of this world. Next door, the Crepe Factory offers lots of sweet and savory buckwheat crepes. A seat outdoors along the pier offers a stunning view of the Bay.

Foreign Cinema
Mission

2534 Mission Street, at 21st Street
(415) 648-7600
$-$$

Foreign Cinema Chefs Gayle Pirie and John Clark make such amazing meals with eggs that they've written a whole cookbook about it. Eggs are the star of the weekend brunch menu, but organic house-made "pop tarts" are also not to be missed. For more on Foreign Cinema see California, page 27.

Garden Court in the Palace Hotel
Financial District

2 New Montgomery Street, at Market Street
(415) 546-5089
$$

The Garden Court in the Palace Hotel might be where Eloise would stop for high tea when visiting San Francisco. You'll feel posh just walking over the threshold, which used to be a carriage entrance when the hotel first opened in 1875. Nearly a century ago the space was transformed into an enormous dining room with a leaded glass dome and Austrian crystal chandeliers. Woodrow Wilson hosted luncheons in this magnificent room before signing the Versailles Treaty, and in 1945 celebrations were held here after the opening session of the United Nations. On Sundays there's an extravagant brunch with live jazz; a perfect opportunity to enjoy the glorious space with friends, or even work out the details for lasting peace of your own.

Just for You Café
Portrero Hill
732 22nd Street, at Third Street
(415) 647-3033
$

In the area formerly known as the Dogpatch, and now called the Third Street Corridor, is a cozy, if a little funky, breakfast spot. This part of the city near Pacific Bell Park has been transformed from an industrial area into an urban office mecca laden with condos. But the food at Just for You has remained consistently good.

Just for You is beloved for its big breakfasts, egg dishes, and fantastic breads. In fact, they make all the baked goods on the premises, including the huge beignets, fried to order and served with a simple dusting of powdered sugar. It's a little taste of New Orleans that's sure to get your morning (or afternoon) started off right. They are especially devoted to their pancakes here, offering buckwheat, oatmeal, cornmeal, and buttermilk.

The portions are generous and the prices good. Some people complain that the service can be surly, but it may just be a rumor started by locals to keep the rest of us away.

Moose's
North Beach
1652 Stockton Street, at Filbert Street
(415) 989-7800
$$

Sunday Brunch at Moose's is lovely, especially if you are seated by the windows looking out onto Washington Square Park. You might even catch a glimpse of the famed wild parrots of Telegraph Hill perched in a tree. For more on Moose's see American, page 18.

Oliveto
5655 College Avenue, at Ocean View Drive
Oakland   *EAST BAY*
(510) 547-5356
$

With clean steel counters and a large wooden table in the center of the café, Oliveto is perfect for breakfast alone with a morning paper, a Mr. Espresso coffee, and the café's exceptionally buttery scones. Or come here with a friend and divvy up the Polenta with Poached Fruit and the café standard of two poached eggs and *prosciutto cotto*. A large group can split the restaurant's unexpected breakfast pizza, to which you must add toppings of pancetta and egg. The outdoor seating facing the BART station is pleasantly scented by flowers from a nearby stand, the restaurant is packed on weekends, and the house-made marmalade is too good to be shared. For more on Oliveto see Italian, page 94.

The Pork Store Café
Lower Haight
1451 Haight Street, between Masonic and Ashbury Streets
(415) 864-6981
$

Pork lovers take note. Here's a breakfast joint where you can enjoy house-made pork sausage patties, high-quality bacon, and, for the hungrier among you, pork chops with eggs and hash browns. While the porcine dishes are the highlight to many of us, The Pork Store offers a wide range of options for all tastes. There are standard egg dishes, pancakes and French toast, and a long list of sides that make it easy to create a breakfast platter exactly to your liking.

My favorite part of the menu is the small box highlighting Southern specialties. You can choose from such classics as biscuits and gravy (vegetarian, if you like) and the "Georgia Ice Cream," two overeasy eggs served over grits with buttery biscuits. Add a side of the outstanding patty sausage for the full Southern experience.

Other Location
3122 16th Street, between Valencia and Guerrero Streets,
   San Francisco (Mission); (415) 626-5523

The Dining Room at the Ritz-Carlton
Nob Hill
In the Ritz-Carlton Hotel
600 Stockton Street, at California Street
(415) 773-6168
$$$$

The Dining Room at the Ritz-Carlton serves a lavish Sunday jazz brunch buffet in a beautiful outdoor garden setting. For more on the Ritz-Carlton see French, page 65.

Rose's Café
Pacific Heights
2298 Union Street, at Steiner Street
(415) 775-2200
$$–$$$
Breakfast at this Italian café includes pizza with an egg, brioche French toast, and polenta. For more on Rose's see Italian, page 96.

Slow Club
Mission/Portrero Hill
2501 Mariposa Street, at Hampshire Street
Brunch 10:00 A.M. to 2:30 P.M. Saturday and Sunday
(415) 241-9390
$

Don't let the out-of-the-way location near the AC Transit bus depot deter you from visiting Slow Club for weekend brunch. From Bourbon French Toast with Blueberries and Walnuts to a frittata with zucchini, tomatoes, and smoked mozzarella, you really can't go wrong. Chef Sante Salvoni always creates menus that highlight local, seasonal ingredients in simple and elegant combinations.

On sunny days, which are frequent in this neighborhood, those with good timing can secure a table on the sidewalk. It's the perfect spot to sip a mimosa made with freshly squeezed orange juice, or the *agua fresca* of the day as you slow down and enjoy a perfectly prepared meal. The menu offers a standard egg-and-meat breakfast for more traditional palates, and several savory options, such as a grilled albacore tuna salad. But by all means, don't miss the home fries, with their lightly crispy exterior and divinely creamy center. And of course, Slow Club's outstanding hamburger is a staple of every meal, including brunch. For more on the Slow Club see California, page 39.

Thai Temple
See Thai, page 152.

Town's End Restaurant and Bakery
SOMA
2 Townsend Street
(415) 512-0749
Closed Monday
$$

Town's End sits in a lovely corner spot overlooking the Embarcadero and the Bay, just a few blocks from the ballpark. While there isn't much of a waterfront view, it's enough to know you're near the water in this sunny part of town. They serve breakfast, lunch, and dinner most weekdays, but the real highlight is the weekend brunch. It can get crowded, so if there's a wait for a table you can grab a pastry from the bakery counter just inside the door and enjoy the sunny lawn out front. But don't fill up, because you're in store for a delicious and hearty breakfast.

Once seated, you'll be greeted by a basket full of miniature scones and muffins baked fresh that morning. Try them with a little house-made apple butter as you wait for your "real" breakfast. You can choose from house-cured gravlax with a bagel, or generous omelets and a side of fantastic local bacon. Wash it all down with some fresh-squeezed juice, and you'll be ready to face the rest of the day.

Zuni Café
Hayes Valley
1658 Market Street, between Franklin and Gough Streets
(415) 552-2522
Closed Monday
$$

Zuni Café is a favorite for Sunday brunch. People-watching, oysters, and fresh-baked scones are among the many highlights. For more on Zuni, see California, page 32.

COFFEE SHOPS & TEAHOUSES

We all know the satisfaction of that morning cup of tea or coffee. But in an era of formula-driven chain outlets on every corner, with baristas slopping overpriced hot beverages into paper cups (horrors), it has become something of a challenge of late to perform our caffeination rituals outside the confines of our own home kitchens. Thankfully one can still find plenty of terrific independently owned cafés in the Bay Area.

The businesses featured in this section have in one way or another stood their ground(s), not only by providing delicious coffee and tea, but also by creating a relaxed and comfortable place in which to enjoy them, whether you are a neighborhood regular or are just visiting San Francisco. Additionally, we've listed a few local retailers who sell a consistently superior quality of coffee or tea for brewing at home.

Atlas Café *(Coffeehouse/Café)*
Mission
3049 20th Street, at Alabama Street
(415) 648-1047

Located in the resurgent, loft-living part of the Mission, Atlas Café is a popular hangout that provides straightforward salads and sandwiches. Their own house coffee blend is organic and fair trade and roasted at Uncommon Grounds in Berkeley. There's an attractive patio setting in back and occasional live music in the evenings.

 ### Blue Bottle Coffee Company *(Coffee kiosks/Retailer/Wholesaler)*
Hayes Valley
315 Linden Street, at Gough Street

Maybe it's the caffeine, but there's something about coffee that inspires zealotry among its fans. Take James Freeman, the bespectacled clarinet player behind Oakland's Blue Bottle Coffee Company. Freeman began · roasting beans at home as a hobby, but unable to keep his fanaticism in check, traded his career as a classical musician to become a full-time roaster. Working out of a tiny space in North Oakland, Freeman roasts just six pounds of beans at a time. All Blue Bottle Coffee not sold within forty-eight hours of roasting is given to charity. Such zeal turns out to be contagious. Witness the line of devotees that stretches from his cart at the Ferry Building Farmers Market on Saturday mornings. Blue Bottle Coffee drinkers sometimes wait as long as twenty minutes for one of Freeman's deeply flavored but never bitter espresso drinks. They are working on a seven-day-a-week kiosk at the Ferry Building, and you can also find them almost daily in Hayes Valley on Linden.

Café Fanny
See Breakfast & Brunch, page 179.

Café lo Cubano   *(Coffeehouse/Café)*
Presidio Heights
3401 California Street
(415) 831-4672

One of the grooviest places to go for coffee is at the unlikely location of the eastern corner of the Laurel Village shopping strip. There you'll find Café lo Cubano, a sort of coffee living room lounge. Relax in the 1950s-style couch or the Eames lounge chair and admire the oil paintings of old Cadillacs or the brown and orange swirls in the shag rug while you sip your expertly made coffee. World beat music is what's playing here, and you can get your Joe in the Cuban vernacular: *cafecito* translates to espresso, *cortadito* is somewhere between a macchiato and a cappucino, and the *café con leche* is akin to a latte. Sugar is added Cubano style, so you may want to stick with the familiar if that is not your thing. And they serve something called a *colada,* which is four shots of *cafecito,* apparently the Cuban version of Red Bull. You'll find the napkins, stirrers, and other accoutrements in old Cuban cigar boxes. The coffee is organic and fair trade. The café is wireless Internet connected.

Caffe Greco   *(Coffeehouse/Café)*
North Beach
423 Columbus Avenue, at Vallejo Street
(415) 397-6261

The baristas are the stars at Caffe Greco. Carlos Chava and Jorge Bivera have been manning the espresso machine for fourteen and thirteen years, respectively. There is a preciseness to their every move, all the way from tamp to steam. They extract a thick head of *crema* every time on the Illy espresso, and they foam the milk perfectly. Of course, they know the regulars' drinks of choice by heart. The best seats in the house are along the windows that look out over the action on Columbus Avenue.

Caffe Puccini
North Beach
411 Columbus Avenue, at Vallejo Street
(415) 989-7033

In addition to hearing the music of Puccini you are likely to hear the music of spoken Italian in this North Beach café. The remaining Italian restaurateurs and shopkeepers of the neighborhood hang out here, along with other old-timers. It is the least legendary or trendy—and perhaps therefore the most authentic—of the area's cafés. They also serve surprisingly good and reasonably priced pasta dishes—far better than some of the tourist-trap restaurants lining Columbus Avenue.

Caffe Roma   *(Coffeehouse/Retailer/Wholesaler)*
North Beach
526 Columbus Avenue, between Union and Stockton Streets
(415) 296-7942

Ambling tourists looking for a coffee spot in North Beach are certainly welcome at *molto Italiano* Caffe Roma, but they might not be able to find an open seat. By 9:00 A.M., scads of locals gather here daily in clustered tables for business discussions, civic meetings, and gossip. Proprietor and chief coffee roaster Tony Azzollini's memory for the names and personal minutiae of more than three hundred regulars defies reason. It might not be the most quickly moving queue in the area, but the warm familiarity of a brief morning chat with Azzollini while you wait for your *crema*-topped espresso is what North Beach is famous for.

Caffe Trieste   *(Coffeehouse)*
North Beach
601 Vallejo Street, at Grant Street
(415) 392-6739

There are few pursuits more enjoyable than sitting with a cup of coffee at a table in front of this café in San Francisco's North Beach neighborhood, surrounded by local poets and watching life on the street. It is a ritual, if not a way of life, for many of the people who make their way to Caffe Trieste every day.

The shop was founded in 1956 by a family of immigrants from the small port city of Trieste. It is lauded as both the first espresso coffeehouse on the West Coast and the place where young Francis Ford Coppola wrote his screenplay for *The Godfather*.

The pictures on the walls memorialize other famous past visitors, like Luciano Pavarotti and Jack Kerouac, as well as many unknown but devoted locals. It is one of the only joints left in North Beach that still maintains an Old World charm, despite being a top tourist hangout. Of course, Caffe Trieste's baristas make excellent espresso, but don't waste your time on the many pastries, bagels, and sandwiches sold here. Food

isn't Caffe Trieste's strong suit, unless you have a taste for some of their creamy, moist tiramisu.

 Cole Coffee *(Coffeehouse/Café/Coffee Retailer)*
6255 College Avenue, at 63rd Street
Oakland *EAST BAY*
(510) 653-5458

Cole Coffee is serious about coffee. So serious that they grind and brew each cup to order. And in case you are not convinced of their devotion to the bean, you need only look up as you grab your lid (and add milk and sugar, if you're a little less serious) and catch a glimpse of the altar above: oversized percolators, ornamented with splashy red caps, worship an even larger grand percolator.

Cole Coffee has something of a cult following, as evidenced by the crowds spilling out onto the sidewalk. They serve fair trade, mostly organic coffee grown from Ethiopia to El Salvador, along with pastries from La Farine and other local bakeries, and poached eggs with toast. The adjacent shop sells coffee and tea by the pound. Some words of caution: This café is not for those with weak stomachs; brews are strong, as can be the attitude of the employees.

Coupa Café *(Coffeehouse/Café)*
538 Ramona Street, between University and Hamilton Avenues
Palo Alto *SOUTH BAY*
(650) 322-6872

For the past fifteen years Arabica Coffee Company of Venezuela has been working to resurrect the traditional methods of growing, harvesting, and roasting coffee beans from the mountainous regions of Venezuela. Only the second shop after the one in Caracas, Arabica opened Coupa Café in Palo Alto to introduce Venezuelan coffee to the United States.

Coupa Café features select Arabica coffees, grown on only eighteen *haciendas* (and bought for a fair price), ranging in flavor from strong and hearty to mild and aromatic. The usual favorites are included in the espresso menu, but all are uniquely Venezuelan. The café mocha has a surprising flavor resulting from the use of spicy Venezuelan chocolate.

Fairfax Coffee Roasters *(Coffeehouse/Wholesaler)*
4 Bolinas Road
Fairfax   *MARIN*
(415) 256-1373

This place can seem "like a coffeehouse flashback, man," but remind yourself that you are in Fairfax, in which case you will realize that this is a compliment. Actually the key owner, Ed Wall, has been absorbed in carefully roasting beans for years, and locals are dedicated to this hangout. He is also involved in a sister roaster, San Anselmo Coffee Roasters, and he and his partner there, Bryan Stubblefield, are much appreciated for their community involvement as well as their coffee prowess. Both locations get aging hippies, laptop users, and power cyclists lining up their bicycles outside to come in and rest or recharge. Welcome to Marin.

Other Location
San Anselmo Coffee Roasters, 546 San Anselmo Avenue, at
   Magnoura Street, San Anselmo (Marin); (415) 258-9549

Farley's *(Coffeehouse/Coffee Retailer)*
Potrero Hill
1315 18th Street, at Texas Street
(415) 648-1545

Farley's is a real, honest-to-goodness coffeehouse on Potrero Hill that has been in business for more than fifteen years. It's just coffee here, plus an assortment of pastries and an extensive magazine stand served up in a general-store atmosphere. What more do you really need? Well, perhaps a bit of art, which adorns the walls in rotating exhibits. And some live music, which happens from time to time, but doesn't overshadow the main attraction—the coffee. The people at Farley's roast their own blends and definitely know what they are doing. All you need to know is what kind of coffee you would like and how much time you have to relax.

Far Leaves Tea *(Teahouse/Retailer/Wholesaler)*
2979 College Avenue, at Ashby Avenue
Berkeley ***EAST BAY***
(510) 665-9409

Located in the Elmwood neighborhood in Berkeley, Far Leaves sells a full range of loose-leaf teas, though it specializes in greener oolongs as well as a healthy selection of canisters, pots, and cups. To avoid sensory overload, defer to proprietor Donna Lo-Christy. Indicate your preferences, and she will prepare several different teas for you to taste. She makes a pot of tea the way any of us would, and it tastes delicious. It's a revelation, though, when she shows you how the same tea can taste when it's made perfectly and the flavors are allowed to bloom in the cup.

Imperial Tea Court *(Teahouse/Tea Retailer)*
Chinatown
1411 Powell Street, at Vallejo Street
(415) 788-6080
Closed Tuesday

On Saturdays the Imperial Tea Court on Powell Street is one of the Slowest scenes around. Men from neighboring Chinatown bring songbirds in bamboo cages, which they hang on hooks from the rafters as they chat and sip tea. A bit intimidating for an outsider, you might ask? Luckily, Roy and Grace Fong's eagerness to show you the best of traditionally made teas from China and Taiwan keeps their teahouses from feeling culturally exclusive. You are welcome to sample individual teas or select from a variety of more in-depth tastings (best to schedule in advance). There are also nuts or cookies available for nibbling, and you can purchase amounts of tea to take home, as well as high-end tea ware.

The new Ferry Building location has a small dim sum menu, which includes a delicate steamed bao with greens. Ferry Plaza Farmers Market regulars congregate on Saturdays in the serene shop, escaping the throngs outside.

Other Locations
Ferry Building Marketplace, One Ferry Building, Shop 27,
   Embarcadero, at Market Street, San Francisco (Embarcadero);
   (415) 544-9830; Tuesday through Friday 10:00 A.M. to 6:00 P.M.;
   Saturday 8:00 A.M. to 6:00 P.M.; Sunday 11:00 A.M. to 5:00 P.M.;
   closed Monday
1500 block of Shattuck Avenue, two doors down from Chez
   Panisse, Berkeley.

Java Beach   *(Coffee and Ale House)*
Outer Sunset
1396 La Playa Street, at Judah Street
(415) 665-5282

The wooden long boards that hang outside this hip venue can mean only one thing: serious surfer hangout. No Gidgets here; instead you'll find actual surfers talking Maverick swells over espresso and coffee, and locally brewed draft beers with a strong neighborhood following.

Lovejoy's   *(Teahouse)*
Noe Valley
1351 Church Street, at Clipper Street
(415) 648-5895
Closed Monday and Tuesday

Many downtown hotels host an afternoon British-style tea service, but if you just want to relax with a nice pot of tea and a decent plate of sandwiches, scones, and Devon cream without having to put your hat and gloves on, this is the place to go. Mismatched teapots and cups from England and Scotland, couches and lace reminiscent of your great-aunt's living room, and a welcoming staff have all helped Lovejoy's maintain a loyal following. While Lovejoy's will sometimes perform miracles to get you seated when they're busy, it is best to call ahead and make a reservation, especially on the weekends.

Momi Toby's Revolution Café   *(Coffeehouse/Café)*
Hayes Valley
528 Laguna Street, between Fell and Hayes Streets
(415) 626-1508

With an old-fashioned screen door and a saloonlike feeling, Momi Toby's has become a Hayes Valley hangout with its special house blend (supplied by Malvina). Rotating artwork by local artists is featured here, as well as live music on the weekend.

Located off the beaten path of this boutique-laden section of Hayes Street, Momi Toby's is the place we keep going back to for their sunny patch of sidewalk seating. It provides a welcome place to relax after you've spent more money than you had planned. If you are over at 22nd and Valencia, check out their outpost in the Mission, with a similarly groovy scene.

Other Location
Papa Toby's Revolution Café, 3248 22nd Street, between Valencia and Mission Streets, San Francisco (Mission); (415) 642-0474

Philz Coffee   *(Coffeehouse)*
Mission
3101 24th Street, at Folsom Street
(415) 282-9155

Philz Coffee has the best drip coffee anywhere. First it is ground and dripped to order. Then there is the added secret ingredient (could it be cardamom?) and the mint leaf. Then there is the location—in a corner grocery store that has all but been cleared out to make way for coffee activities, which includes ample seating for chess. And lastly there is Phil, the fedora-sporting owner. Have him make you his favorite coffee. You will keep coming back.

Reverie Café   *(Coffeehouse/Café)*
Cole Valley
848 Cole Street, at Carl Street
(415) 242-0200

Nestled in Cole Valley, Reverie offers great coffee drinks, tea, and sandwiches. Colorful locals, the Craigslist crew, and a few lucky tourists who meander up from Haight Street can find delicious sustenance here. Order a wine or beer and make your way into the tranquil backyard garden.

Ritual Coffee Roasters   *(Coffeehouse)*
Mission
1026 Valencia Street, between 21st and 22nd Streets
(415) 641-1024

Ritual Coffee Roasters is the place to go to get wired—literally and figuratively. The wi-fi connection keeps a good many patrons engaged with their laptops while the coffee, a tasty, hair-raising blend from Stumptown Coffee Roasters of Portland, sustains the typing at an above-average word-per-minute count. The staff expertly makes all the expected espresso drinks as well as French press coffee by the pot. The café au lait is great, with a perfect milk-to-coffee ratio, and the counter guys are sweet-natured even at 7 a.m. The place is tidy and well-lit, and sports upscale versions of downbeat coffeehouse accoutrements like couches, lounge chairs, and a communal table. And in good coffeehouse form, you can linger all day if you like. You don't have to be digitally obsessed to seek refuge at Ritual Coffee Roasters: we recently noticed a couple in the window with their Joe playing cards.

Samovar Tea Lounge *(Teahouse)*
Castro
498 Sanchez Street, at 18th Street
(415) 626-4700

A recent addition to the tea scene in San Francisco, Samovar Tea Lounge has become a popular alternative to neighboring coffeehouses. The Moroccan-Asian interior is colorful and peaceful. Samovar is distinct in that they offer every tea tradition in the world (except perhaps the one featuring Tibetan yak butter). The tea itself comes from sources that keep a close eye on organic and sustainable growing practices.

Although they have only a tiny reheating-style kitchen, Samovar's food offerings are elegantly presented and every bit as diverse as their list of teas: from samosas with chutney to a bowl of rice and nori with salmon.

Simple Pleasures *(Coffeehouse/Cafe)*
Outer Richmond
3434 Balboa Street, between 35th and 36th Avenues
(415) 387-4022

For those who hanker for the coffeehouses of San Francisco past, Simple Pleasures is just the ticket. I knew I was on to something when I stumbled upon this unpretentious enclave to buy a quick espresso. While there, a neighborhood crony dashed in from outside and exclaimed, "Meter maid!" Counterpersons and patrons alike stood up and fed quarters into *all* the meters outside—just the sort of antiestablishment behavior that fuels us San Franciscans.

The decor is simple: nicked wooden tables, handmade lamps, shelves filled with board games and dog-eared books, a casual smattering of read newspapers, and worn rugs. The coffee is straightforward, not Starbuck-ed. The fare includes light sandwiches, pastries, wine, and beer. Some nights, casual live jazz is performed.

Simple Pleasures is the perfect place to spend a foggy Sunday afternoon before catching a double feature at the nearby Balboa Theatre.

Spike's *(Coffeehouse/Retailer)*
Castro
4117 19th Street, at Castro Street
(415) 626-5573

Spike's is the place to go for coffee in the Castro. The loyal staff at this independently owned cafe are welcoming, even at the opening bell on Sunday morning. They know their espresso machine and you can count on a tip-top, expertly foamed cappuccino or latte to start your day off right. If you have a dog, be sure to bring the pooch along, as Spike's is not just dog-friendly, but positively dog-adoring. And on your way out don't forget to pick up a bag of the Harvey Milk Civil Rights Academy Blend of organic coffee to take home.

Teance/Celadon Fine Teas *(Teahouse/Tea Retailer)*
1111 Solano Avenue, at San Pablo Avenue
Albany **EAST BAY**
(510) 524-1696
Closed Monday

Teance, the retail store, and Celadon, the wholesaler, focus on both traditional varieties and some of the new hybrids that are being developed in China and Taiwan. As a result they have established connections to competition-grade tea sources in Taiwan, which have never before been available in the United States. If you have arrived at this retail store to drink tea, you have a few options: You can either sit at the state-of-the-art tea bar and taste a variety of teas that are available for a small fee (or complimentary, with the purchase of a few ounces afterward) or you can sit at a table and simply relax with a pot, with or without the small sweets that may be available that day. Top-grade porcelain and other tea ware are also available to buy.

The Warming Hut *(Coffeehouse/Café)*
Presidio
West Bluff parking lot, at the end of Mason Street
Building 983, west end of Crissy Field
(415) 561-3042

Reclaimed by the Golden Gate National Recreation Area from the U.S. Army and transformed by the expansive vision and philanthropy of both the citizenry and the Haas Foundation, Crissy Field is now one of the great urban parks in the country. Complete with beach, wetlands, native grassland, a walking/bike path, and head-on views of the Golden Gate Bridge, it's hard to believe this three-mile stretch of real estate right on the San Francisco Bay was once a paved-over, abandoned mess.

Part of this fortuitous peace dividend is The Warming Hut, located about a half mile from Fort Point, the nineteenth-century brick arsenal where Kim Novak was famously rescued by Jimmy Stewart in *Vertigo*. Punctuate a morning jog with a pastry from Noe Valley Bakery and a cappuccino made with organic, fair trade, shade-grown coffee beans. For lunch enjoy a Niman Ranch ham and Straus cheese sandwich, toasted in the panini grill and served with a side of organic mixed greens. Organic sodas and juices are also available. Eat in if the weather is difficult, or outside at one of the many picnic tables with a view.

PRODUCER PROFILES

Mr. Espresso

Frying pans and an electric popcorn popper are good enough for most home coffee roasters, but not for Carlo DiRocco. When the man behind Oakland's Mr. Espresso couldn't find a coffee he liked, he built a full-scale roaster in his backyard and fired it with oak, just as he had learned to do as a seventeen-year-old apprentice roaster in his hometown of Salerno, Italy. These days, DiRocco works out of a West Oakland warehouse, providing beans to many of the region's most exacting restaurateurs and coffee drinkers. While other roasters typically blend their beans before roasting, DiRocco insists on roasting varieties individually to enhance their unique characteristics. It's a process that requires extra time and care, but as DiRocco says, "Preblended coffees have only one flavor. In a good cup of coffee, every bean sings."

—*Jan Newberry*

Graffeo Coffee Company   (*Coffee Wholesaler*)
North Beach
735 Columbus Street, at Filbert Street
(415) 986-2420

If you want locally roasted beans that are very, very fresh, you can walk into this simple retail shop and buy directly from this popular wholesaler.

Silk Road Teas   (*Tea Wholesaler*)

Found in most grocery stores that allow you to buy bulk herbs, the owner of Silk Road Teas is a local who spent years hiking the far reaches of China in search of tea, long before it was easy to get into that country. While you are at the mercy of the storage rules of the individual grocery where it is sold, we find more often than not that Silk Road's offerings are the highest-quality teas in the bulk section.

A HISTORY OF
LATE-TWENTIETH-CENTURY NORTH BEACH
THROUGH ONE OF ITS CAFÉS

When Liliana and Mario Crismani took over the Bohemian Café & Cigar Store in the midseventies—when Carol Doda's silhouette was blinking in her bosomy glory at the intersection of the red-light district and Little Italy, and four bucks bought you a plate of pesto fettuccini—you didn't go to a wine bar in North Beach to swirl Mendocino Syrah in Riedel glasses, nor to blind-taste Medoc premier cru. Wine bars catered mostly to the North Beach-ini, the local patchwork of Piemontese, Genovese, and Lucchesi, dotted with a minority of Triestines and Sicilians. Those customers were perfectly satisfied with the purple juice poured out of half-gallon jugs of California Chianti, Burgundy, or Barbera.

For special occasions and intimate friends, Mario kept a special treat on a back shelf: grappa and brandy disguised in bottles of vermouth. For more typical occasions, like a gathering of fellow *paesani* from east of Trieste, Mario's baritone notes rose over an Italian musical potpourri, and as the night thinned out, one could hear Liliana's crystal voice leading a nostalgic chorus of refugees from Pola, celebrating their homeland. In the afternoon hours, the four tables of the Bohemian were taken by retired immigrants in old sparrow-colored suits, playing *briscola* and sipping tiny glasses of sweet *mandorlato* wine.

Soon, however, a new crowd began gathering on the narrow space between the four stools at the counter, the *calcetto* (table soccer machine), and the pinball machine. It was a mix of young Italian waiters and San Franciscans scouting for ethnic hangouts, local color, and warm atmosphere. Why did so many of them prefer a tiny hole at the corner of Union and Columbus to the fern bars of the era? Because of the foamy cappuccino laced with Vov egg liqueur? Or was it the friendly ironic smile of Mario? The motherly welcome of Liliana? Certainly all that.

The Bohemian's success was also part of a new trend in North Beach. The old locals, fulfilling their American dream, were moving to houses with lawns and barbecues on the Peninsula. Urban hipsters replaced them on the lower slopes of Russian Hill. The old retirees in fedoras abandoned little by little the stools of the Bohemian for the benches in the park. There they sat for hours under the sign LA GLORIA DI COLUI CHE TUTTO MUOVE PER L'UNIVERSO (over the Saints Peter and Paul Cathedral), chatting in murmurs and drawing with the rubber tip of their walking sticks the last chapter of their memories, on the gravel of Washington Square.

Back at the Bohemian the party was in full swing. Italian kids didn't mind coaching Anglo bimbos in the art of *calcetto,* or admitting whiskered WASP executives to their *scopa* games. And for this friendly crowd Liliana came to the Bohemian loaded with *salame cacciatora,* homemade sandwiches, chocolate cakes, crostini. Their kids, Julie and Paolo, were by now helping them serve, feed, and quench the thirst of a happy and increasing crowd. By the end of the seventies, you could see the first Californian cabernets and imported Chianti bottles sitting next to the jugs. With the coming decade, the little cozy hole had acquired a reputation far beyond the boundaries of North Beach and even the city. It was not unusual to hear French spoken at the counter, for the Bohemian was a favorite stopover of foreign students from Berkeley and Stanford. The racks behind the counter were still filled with cigarettes and local brands and vicious Toscani cigars, but the Bohemian Cigar Store had become *Mario's.*

—*Roberto Ballabeni*

Mario's Bohemian Café
North Beach
566 Columbus Avenue, at Union Street
(415) 362-0536

HAMBURGERS, HOT DOGS & SAUSAGES

 Acme Chophouse
See American, page 11.

 Burger Joint
Lower Haight
700 Haight Street
(415) 864-3833
$

Niman Ranch beef is what put Burger Joint on the map. One of the first non-fancy places to use this top-drawer natural beef, the Burger Joint stands were a hit from the beginning. Excellent juicy burgers, best enjoyed with the grilled onions, milk shakes made with local Double Rainbow ice cream, and crispy real French fries make for a perfect meal. The interior sports a vaguely '50s feel and has occasionally changing silhouettes painted by a local artist. The crew is friendly and quick, especially when filling your take-out order. Chicken and veggie burgers are offered, but there is no alcohol. At Burger Joint you can indulge your fast food cravings without compromising your Slow Food meat values.

Other Locations
807 Valencia Street, San Francisco (Mission); (415) 824-3494
International Terminal at San Francisco International Airport,
   San Bruno (South Bay); (650) 583-5863

 Café Rouge
See California, page 23.

Casper's Hot Dogs
5440 Telegraph Avenue
Berkeley   *EAST BAY*
(510) 652-1668
$

Famous for serving extra-long franks in freshly steamed buns, family-owned Casper's has been a staple in the San Francisco Bay Area for more than seventy years. In addition to a fiercely loyal local clientele, fans include ex-mayors, professional athletes, and rock stars like those in the Grateful Dead and Metallica. Built mostly in the 1950s and '60s, Casper's original decor—vinyl-cushioned stools and booths in a distinctive palate of pink, orange, and yellow—is still intact, and photos of the founders hang at each location.

Originally toppings on a Casper Dog were limited to mustard, relish, onions, and tomatoes, but today they include sauerkraut and more unusual choices like mayonnaise or hot sauce. But beneath all those toppings still lies the tastiest hot dog around. One thing that distinguishes Casper's is that the restaurant produces its own dogs, using secret recipes for Polish, spicy Cajun, and even turkey dogs.

There are ten Casper's restaurants located throughout the East Bay, including Oakland, Hayward, Dublin, Walnut Creek, Pleasant Hill, San Pablo, Richmond, and Albany. And if you want to pick up some of Casper's hot dogs for a barbecue at home, you can also find them for sale at some grocery stores.

Joe's Cable Car
Mission
4320 Mission Street, at Silver Avenue
(415) 334-6699
$

You can't miss Joe's. Look for the neon montage of cable car, Golden Gate Bridge, and burger, and the sign that shouts JOE GRINDS HIS OWN CHUCK DAILY. Open since 1965, this is the original burger joint. Burgers are served open-faced, and if you want yours cooked other than medium rare, you need to speak up. Excellent shakes. Excellent outing.

The Original Kasper's Hot Dogs
4521 Telegraph Avenue, at 46th Street and Shattuck Avenue
Oakland   *EAST BAY*
(510) 655-3215
$

There's a magic little triangle of concrete where Telegraph and Shattuck Avenues merge together at 46th Street in Oakland. In the middle of that bit of land there is an even tinier wedge-shaped building—the home of Original Kasper's. Belying its small size, Kasper's has been an anchor in Oakland's Temescal neighborhood since 1929 and has had legions of followers. And many of them, old-timers by now, have been relishing the hot dogs ever since they were kids.

Kasper's offers first-rate hot dogs, including a lemon chicken number that comes with tomatoes, green onions, and Italian parsley. But don't think they have gone all New Age on us. They still have the best old-fashioned, all-beef hot dogs with all the traditional trimmings, including sauerkraut, sliced onions, and pickle relish, and they carry all flavors of Stuart's sodas, including the delicious Key Lime. They also have the requisite chips for crunchy contrast.

After more than seventy years, Kasper's recently closed for renovation. The management promises no messing with the look or taste of the original when they reopen.

Rosamunde Sausage Grill
Lower Haight
545 Haight Street, at Fillmore Street
(415) 437-6851
$

A small place with a few stools and a line out the door because there's no room inside, Rosamunde serves well-crafted sausages from various local makers like Fabrique Delices. Beautifully grilled and served on slightly chewy rolls with a good selection of mustards, their sausages include wild boar and duck with fig, along with *weisswursts* and a very nice beer sausage. Most of the customers take their wursts to the Toronado brew pub located immediately next door. The friendly staff leans style-wise to long hair under baseball caps and vintage Megadeth T-shirts. They also make a good burger here.

Taylor's Automatic Refresher
Embarcadero
Ferry Building Marketplace
One Ferry Building, Shop 6
Embarcadero, at Market Street
(415) 318-3400
$

While the original Taylor's gains a considerable measure of charm from its nostalgic drive-in location in the Napa Valley (open since 1949), the San Francisco address in the landmark Ferry Building tries to recreate the feeling, though the space is much bigger and a tad industrial looking. Never mind the decor, though—the real draw is the drive-in-style food: burgers, fries, and shakes. Taylor's use of premium sustainable ingredients ups the ante, and most of the sandwich menu is a sure bet, including any of the burgers. Steer clear of the tacos and salads, which suffer from a lack of inspiration and execution. The mango shake (if it's available) and the onion rings are delicious. If it's nice out, enjoy your meal picnic style at their large sidewalk dining area that looks out over the Embarcadero.

Other Location
933 Main Street, St. Helena (Napa); (707) 963-3486

World Sausage Grill
Upper Market
2073 Market Street, at 14th Street, across from Safeway
(415) 621-7488
$

If you have been here before you already know the drill and you immediately reach for one of the plastic-coated menu cards and a dry-erase pen to write down your order. There are plenty of choices to be made, with more than twenty locally made sausages, some of them organic, but all of them free of preservatives, nitrates, and artificial flavorings. The sausage runs the gamut from Hawaiian Portuguese to an organic bratwurst to *merguez* (a spicy North African lamb sausage). There are also some chicken options, as well as a seafood sausage—you can even select from among three organic and GMO-free soy versions, all cooked on a dedicated grill that is untouched by the meats.

The long list of possible condiments and sausage dressings varies, from sauerkraut to mango chutney to artichoke mayo or hot chipotle catsup. The French bread buns are made with organic flour and have the perfect chewy quality. Only three house wines are available, but there are a number of beers—six on tap, including the organic Bison Belgium. Organic green salad, *edamame*, two styles of potato salad, mammoth dill pickles, and delicious *cannelè* are other temptations. World Sausage Grill is a bit bigger than your typical hole-in-the-wall place, with seating for fifty.

Zuni Café
See California, page 32.

EAST BAY
WIENER NOSTALGIA

Nothing expresses the East Bay's blue-collar legacy quite like its aging hot dog joints, places resonating with scrappy, rust-belt charm. The formerly lush landscape of wiener stands clustering along Third Street—close to the Oakland docks—may have withered, leaving only one or two carts of tarnished quilted stainless steel. But in Alameda, near the soaring Art Deco concrete filigree of the shuttered Alameda Theater, the **Pampered Pup** is thriving. The skinny beef franks still have soft buns that pucker in the steam table, but (no doubt to appeal to a new clientele) the menu board now lists a dozen Taiwanese-style tapioca drinks.

Catch a headier whiff of weenie history at **Glenn's Hot Dog** in Oakland's Laurel district. Outside the roof flips up like the bill of some well-loved ball cap; inside it's all 1940s knotty pine and boomerang-pattern Formica. The hefty, all-beef Chicago-style dogs have crisp skins, but the real draw is the concentrated grilled-onion-and-fry-oil-scented nostalgia.

The East Bay's most visible thread of wiener nostalgia is tangled up in the contentious history of an Oakland family. In 1939 Armenian immigrant Kasper Koojoolian was North Oakland's weenie king, overseeing a growing realm of hot dog stands. But just as in the opening act of a Shakespeare tragedy, a family disagreement made Koojoolian split his realm in three. From the early 1940s Koojoolian's original Kasper's, a spin-off spelled Casper's, and The Original Kasper's (the name's a brazen play for authenticity, perpetrated by a rogue stepdaughter) all developed along parallel lines.

Closed since 2002 for remodeling, **The Original Kasper's** in Oakland's Temescal neighborhood is a moldering relic of the old-time urban frank. But in the Dimond district the oldest remaining **Kasper's**—the place that traces its lineage directly to Koojoolian—keeps the wiener king's dream alive. The smoky, natural-casing hot dogs are delicious, but the restaurant itself (often filled with cops and seniors) is stunning. It's a little gem of midtwentieth-century design built in 1961, with terrazzo floors, jawbreaker chandeliers, and juicy striped wallpaper; simultaneously elegant and shabby.

The **Casper's** restaurant in Albany has a similarly dented midcentury elegance. A big sign with '60s-style graphic icons (including a gracefully curving frank) dominates its little parking lot; inside, the place is a time warp of brown tile and vinyl stools in multicolored Froot Loops pastels. Pale, tender, and fine-grained, a Casper's dog contains beef mixed with a little pork—a taste as nostalgic as the surroundings.

—*John Birdsall*

Pampered Pup
1401 Park Street
Alameda
(510) 521-2321

Glenn's Hot Dog
3506 MacArthur Boulevard
Oakland
(510) 530-9890

The Original Kasper's (currently closed for repairs)
4521 Telegraph Avenue
Oakland
(510) 655-3215

Kasper's Hot Dogs
eleven East Bay locations, including 2551 MacArthur Boulevard,
   Oakland; (510) 530-2308

Casper's Hot Dogs
eleven East Bay locations, including 545 San Pablo Avenue,
   Albany; (510) 527-6611

PIZZA

A16
See Italian, page 89.

The Cheese Board Pizza Collective
1512 Shattuck Avenue
Berkeley   EAST BAY
(510) 549-3055
Closed Sunday and Monday
$$

This is a place that could have started only in Berkeley. Where else would you find an owner-operated collective that closes for International Workers' Day? An extension of the venerable Cheese Board next door, the Pizza Collective is as interested in the flavor of its pizza as it is in the right-eousness of its politics. By 6:00 P.M. the line that forms at the counter spills out the front door and onto the sidewalk, just across the street from Chez Panisse. Local jazz ensembles play here in the evening, crammed in next to the small tables in the storefront. Many customers order their pizzas to go and take them outside to eat on the sidewalk. In good weather some people even sit in the grassy median on Shattuck Avenue, picnic style.

The pizzas come out of the oven one after the other, and the line moves quickly, as there aren't many choices. Only one kind of pizza is served a day. It's a variation on a theme: a sourdough or yeasted crust, mozzarella, seasonal vegetables, cheese topping (they take advantage of the best selection in Northern California), a brush of olive oil, and a garnish, most often of fresh herbs. You can order a single slice or a whole pie, fully or half baked. Each order, whether a single piece or a whole pie, is generously accompanied by a half-slice on the house—a gesture that never fails to feel benevolent.

Chez Panisse Café
See California, page 25.

Dopo
See Italian, page 92.

Gioia Pizzeria
1586 Hopkins Street, at Monterey Avenue
Berkeley   EAST BAY
(510) 528-4692
Closed Sunday
$

In a tiny space with nothing more than a few barstools, a countertop, and, of course, an oven, Brooklyn native Will Gioia makes all kinds of New York–style pizzas. The slices are oversized and floppy, some with classic toppings like pepperoni and mushroom, and others with zucchini and sausage from The Fatted Calf (see Meat & Fish Markets, page 291). The flavors and smells that waft out of the oven are heavenly. For confirmation, you need only to look to the throngs of local schoolchildren who pile in for an after-school slice, or to the people en route to Monterey Market or Monterey Fish next door. The swinging screen door at Gioia's has barely rested on its hinges since it opened.

Will Gioia is a firm believer that small businesses, local produce, and organic ingredients are essential elements of a strong community. As in the neighborhood of his childhood, this community begins and ends at the table. His only challenge lies in creating a sense of home that lasts: The pizzas are so good most people polish them off in a matter of seconds.

Pauline's Pizza
Mission

260 Valencia Street, between Duboce and 14th Streets
(415) 552-2050
Closed Sunday and Monday
$$

On a still-funky stretch of Valencia Street next door to the picturesque 1906 Levi Strauss Factory sits Pauline's Pizza, a wonderfully San Franciscan pizzeria. Kid-friendly, with its juice glasses filled with crayons and with butcher paper tabletops, yet stylish and fun enough for a date, Pauline's Pizza has been near and dear to our hearts since it opened in 1995.

Part of the Pauline's Pizza magic is in the process—100 to 175 pounds of dough are made fresh daily by hand (no industrial Hobart to ease the task here!), a method they consider critical for their trademark crust; it's not thick, but not wafer-thin either, and has a little crunch from what I suspect to be a hint of cornmeal. Many regulars wouldn't dream of ordering anything other than the signature pesto pizza, but specials like a pie with red mustard greens, sage, rosemary, garlic, and fontina can cause people to stray. Desserts (they always have an ice cream sundae) are homey and delicious.

Another part of Pauline's successful formula is the ingredients they use—all high-quality and mostly organic, with many of the vegetables coming from the owners' garden in Berkeley or their ranch in Calaveras County. The great ingredients in the chefs' skilled hands make Pauline's pizzas stand out.

Some of the wine served here is homegrown too. The owners have an organic vineyard, and they currently offer Pauline's Pizza Wine in various varietals. The Syrah is the current favorite, but there is also a tasty zinfandel.

Pizza Antica
334 Santana Row, at Winchester and Stevens Creek Boulevards
San Jose *SOUTH BAY*
(408) 557-8373
$$

It's all about the crust: thin, crispy, and just the faintest bit yeasty and chewy. The crusts on Pizza Antica's Neapolitan-style pies are the stuff of doughy dreams. The Calvin Klein of pizzas, these stylish, minimalist, rectangular creations prove that less is often so much more. With spare and distinct toppings, each flavorful bite is the perfect balance of just enough foundation and just enough adornment. A large, sixteen-inch oval heirloom potato pizza with caramelized onions and truffle oil is enough to feed two.

Executive Chef Gordon Drysdale, formerly of Gordon's House of Fine Eats in San Francisco, has teamed with Tim Stannard, owner of the Village Pub in Woodside, and Brannin Beal of Postino in Lafayette to create this comfortable spot that uses top-notch ingredients. This is not your run-of-the-mill pizzeria; the first sign of that is the house-made Blood-Orange Limeade, and tangerine and sour cherry sodas made with D'Arbo syrups from Austria. Panini and pasta round out the menu, but it's the pizza that steals the show. End the meal on a perky note: *affogato,* hot Illy espresso poured over a scoop of vanilla gelato.

After shopping at such nearby chic boutiques as Gucci and Burberry, this is the perfect place to unwind—without putting another big dent in your wallet.

Other Location
3600 Mount Diablo Boulevard, Lafayette (East Bay);
(925) 299-0500

Pizzaiolo
5008 Telegraph Avenue
Oakland *EAST BAY*
(510) 652-4888
Open for dinner only; closed Sunday and Monday
$$

Chez Panisse expatriates are responsible for some of the best restaurants around the Bay Area. Charlie Hallowell's Pizzaiolo continues this tradition with a keen eye for details, from the light fixtures made by a friend to the parade of hot pizzas that emerge from the wood-fired oven at a dizzying pace. The interior, a renovated hardware store, feels comfortably broken in, despite having only opened in June 2005.

With high ceilings, wooden booths, and an oversized family table in the back, Pizzaiolo's decor is a fine match for its unfussy but well-crafted food. As you might expect from a veteran of Chez Panisse, the ingredients are pristine. For starters try the *arencini* (fried risotto balls), roasted Monterey Bay squid with chickpeas and aioli, and a green salad with lettuces from TD Wiley Farm. But, as its name implies, pizza is the main feature here.

Hallowell spent many months perfecting his recipe for the dough, including a visit with famed pizza maker Chris Bianco in Phoenix. This hard work paid off, and the result is a bubbly, flavorful crust. Pizzas change regularly, and it's best to order a few for the table. The Salt Cod with Tomato Sauce and the Margherita with Fresh Mozzarella are two to try. Pizzaiolo's wine list is similarly balanced and reasonably priced, and Italian wines like Piedmontese Dolcetto, Nebbiolo, and Barbera are well represented. Make sure you finish the meal with an espresso. Blue Bottle Coffee is right next door, and the roasted beans are delivered warm.

Pizzeria Delfina
Mission

3611 18th Street, between Dolores and Guerrero Streets
(415) 437-6800
$$

It was no surprise when Delfina's pizza place recently opened. Neighbors had been anxiously spying on the progress for months. The place is minute, and the lion's share of the real estate is dedicated to the centerpiece oven. There's room for eight at the bar, and fifteen or so at the tables inside and out, so if you're dining during prime-time hours be prepared for a wait. But it's a pleasant one. Sign your name at the chalkboard by the door, grab a glass of wine (many of them from Campania and further south in Italy), and hang around outside, enjoying the often warm and sunny weather of the Mission.

Five or so thin-crust pizzas are offered here, plus daily specials: a fine Margherita, the Napoletana with anchovies and capers, the Salsiccia that sports the house-made fennel sausage, and a clam pie. And the salads are truly sublime. The greens feel like they have just been plucked from the garden, and for the *tricolore*, a mix of arugula, radicchio and endive, we watched them squeeze the lemon juice and slice the Grana Padana to order. Be sure to get one.

You will wish that the space was twice as big so you could more easily get a table, but once seated, sipping a glass of Greco di Tufo, you'll be glad that it is just the way it is.

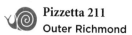

Pizzetta 211
Outer Richmond

211 23rd Avenue, at California Street
(415) 379-9880
Closed Monday
Cash only
$–$$

Ria Ramsey of Pizzetta has hit upon a great concept: Develop a stand-up pizza dough, make up a bunch of it every day, and close when you run out. To supplement the pizza, offer a superfresh salad of local mixed greens, a seasonal vegetable plate, an artisanal cheese course, a delicious flourless chocolate cake or other daily baked special, and terrific, reasonably priced bottles of wine and you will cultivate a happy and devoted customer base.

There are usually five pizzas to choose from. The classic Margherita is always available, as is the Egg Pizza, a pie with two eggs cracked on top before it's slid into the oven. My favorite combination is the egg with prosciutto and arugula, but anything else the staff comes up with is just fine. All the toppings reflect what's at the farmers' market, coupled with the proprietor's whim.

Pizzetta 211 takes no reservations, and there is only room for four at the bar and about sixteen at the tables, so be prepared to wait. Seating at Moroccan café tables outside is an option, or at the wooden bench that circumnavigates the base of the tree in front, but remember, you are deep in Outer Richmond and it can get cold, even under the heat lamps, so dress appropriately. If you have to wait, you can always enjoy a glass of wine outside, and some evenings it can get very social.

Parking is tough, though it is a common practice to spend an entire evening double-parked in front. On Valentine's Day, a special prix fixe menu is offered.

Small Shed Flatbreads
17 Madrona Street
Mill Valley   *MARIN*
(415) 383-4200
$–$$

Small Shed Flatbreads is the ideal place to drop in after fulfilling your physical and spiritual needs hiking on nearby Mount Tamalpais. In addition to using only organic vegetables and grains, Small Shed devotes a place on the menu to produce from Star Route Farms, cheeses like Humboldt Fog from Cypress Hill, and meats from Prather Ranch. The pizzalike flat breads are the stars here, made with great care in a spacious wood-burning oven. They vary in complexity from the austere Virigi's with local fresh mozzarella, Asiago, and Parmesan cheeses and herbs, to the complex Mad River (named for a Vermont waterway) with maple-fennel sausage, oven-dried tomatoes, caramelized onions, crimini mushrooms, cheese, and herbs. Daily specials, salads, and soups are also offered. Desserts include a seasonal fruit crisp with vanilla bean gelato. The well-chosen, reasonably priced wine list is a perfect match for the food.

Tommaso's Ristorante Italiano
North Beach
1042 Kearny Street, at Broadway
(415) 398-9696
Closed Sunday and Monday
$$-$$$$

Tommaso's is home to the first brick oven to be built west of the Mississippi, circa 1935, and is the great-grandfather of Neapolitan-style pizza in the Bay Area. Although their crust is crunchier and the pizza bigger than that of its Neopolitan relatives, you wouldn't expect an exact rendition, as the current owners, who have been there since 1972, are from the Valtellina region of northern Italy. (The specialty there is lasagna, and it is rendered perfectly at Tommaso's—tender and cheesy, much the way Mamma would make it.)

The place is generally packed and guests sit either in old wooden booths or at a long table in the center of the room and dine with others family style. When Augustino, the owner, lumbers over to take your order, he will offer you an array of house wines that are made specially for the restaurant, including the Tommaso Syrah from Monterey and Tommaso Zinfandel from Dry Creek Valley. Tommaso's also boasts a lemony Caesar salad and an array of good antipasti and pastas. For an old school, soulful experience, head to Tommaso's. Before he owned his own pizzeria across the street, Francis Ford Coppola could be found here making pies.

 **Zuni Café**
See California, page 32.

NOTABLE

Café Niebaum Coppola
North Beach
916 Kearny Street, at Columbus Avenue
(415) 291-1700
Closed Monday
$-$$

A small café and bar in the spectacular Sentinel flatiron building, this casual café serves excellent pizza with a lovely selection of wines, including the house wine produced by the director Francis Ford Coppola himself. The decor makes you feel as if you are in a small Southern Italian town with marble tables, great drinking options, and friendly service. And al fresco dining is an option at almost any time during the year, as radiant heating has been installed under the sidewalk.

Other Location
473 University Avenue, Palo Alto (South Bay); (650) 752-0350

Club Deluxe and Pizzetta
Upper Haight
1509-11 Haight Street, at Ashbury Street
(415) 552-6949
Open for pizza Wednesday, Thursday, Friday,
    and Sunday 7:00 to 11:00 P.M.
$$

"Once you understand the life cycle of the yeast," says Jason Pearce, describing early problems he had with dough consistency, "then there's no problem." Pearce makes twelve-inch thin-crust pizzas four nights a week at Club Deluxe, a beautifully preserved '40s-style bar and jazz club in the Upper Haight. He makes his pizza from scratch—he doesn't use a commercial yeast for his starter; rather he cultivates it out of thin (and often foggy) San Francisco air. He uses organic, unbleached flour for his pies and seasonal, often organic toppings. He usually makes four pizzas: three regulars—tomato with fresh basil, sausage and mushroom, and pepperoni—and one nightly special. Settle in at the comfy booth at the end of the bar and tuck into one of these pizzas. Come on a Sunday to hear J. Johnson's bossa nova combo playing.

Little Star Pizza
Western Addition
846 Divisadero
(415) 441-1118
Dinner 5:00 to 10:00 P.M.; happy hour 5:00 to 6:30 P.M.
   and 10:00 to 11:30 P.M.
$$

This stretch of Divisadero in Western Addition is quickly becoming the new Valencia Street, and since taking up digs, Little Star has become a favorite of the hipsters in the neighborhood. It was at the video store across the street, though, where I first tried Little Star pizza. The clerks had ordered a deep-dish pie for dinner, and they proudly shared slices of it with several of us customers.

But don't just order the pizza to go. The dining room is small, candlelit, crowded, and noisy with conversation and music from the jukebox (which lists a few cool bands from college days). Little Star has a thin-crust pizza, but the thick, deep-dish cornmeal crust pizza is the way to go. The restaurant features a compact selection of wine, mostly from the south of France (and even Corsica) and mostly from Kermit Lynch (see Wine Retailers, page 295). A look around the room, though, and you'll find most patrons drink assorted microbeers and even the odd can of PBR. A nice salad of organic greens completes the experience.

Zante Pizza and Indian Cuisine
Bernal Heights
3489 Mission Street, near Cortland Street
(415) 821-3949
$$–$$$

The story goes that about thirty years ago, an Indian family bought a neighborhood pizzeria and started offering typical tandoori fare out of the pizza oven. Regulars convinced them to combine the two, and the famed Indian pizza was born. Though similar to naan, the dough here is actual pizza dough, but the real draws are the toppings and funky ambience. You'll find a curried onion chutney, spinach, cilantro, mozzarella, and cauliflower pie and a version that comes with chopped bits of tandoori meats. The restaurant, like their special pizza, is dressed up with Indian flourishes. Pitchers of Bud Light are offered alongside Taj Mahal and Kingfisher—and it is not uncommon to have several while waiting for your pizza to arrive.

SEAFOOD

Aqua
See French, page 63.

Café Maritime Seafood and Spirits
Marina
2417 Lombard Street, at Scott Street
(415) 885-2530
Dinner only; open daily until 1:00 A.M.
$$

If New York is the city that never sleeps, San Francisco is the city that falls into a deep slumber by sundown. East Coasters are often surprised to find that 5:30 P.M., considered a late lunch at home, is the time when many Californians pull up to the table for dinner. The Maritime Café is the exception to this San Francisco tradition. It keeps its sidewalk seating in place and doors open seven days a week until 1:00 A.M.—a good thing, since the food is delicious, the parking is easy, and the service is delightful.

Chef Mike Selvera has kept the food simple. In fact, his place was conceived as a West Coast version of those venerable New England seafood joints: He uses only the freshest ingredients and allows them to do the talking rather than complicate them with a cacophony of sauces and ingredients.

One of the stellar dishes we tasted was a perfectly assembled and seasoned lobster roll: picture a hauntingly sweet, deliciously crunchy, light-as-air bun filled with chunks of lobster meat, wafer-thin slices of celery, and a creamy tarragon dressing. Other treats included Pacific Coast mainstays like local wild king salmon, grilled and served with a tangerine vinaigrette; whole Dungeness crab, served chilled; and Monterey Bay sardines with white beans and salsa verde.

Designer John Lum, who also designed the interiors of AsiaSF and Hayes & Vine Wine Bar, is responsible for the intimate forty-five-seat restaurant, with its large, curvaceous banquette, evocative of a curling wave, as the main focus of the restaurant. A boat-shaped bar welcomes patrons as they arrive, and a sea-themed mural decorates the wall.

Fish
350 Harbor Drive
Sausalito   *MARIN*
(415) 331 3474
Closed Monday and Tuesday
Cash only
$$

After eleven years at the legendary Masa's, including several as chef, Chad Callahan jumped ship from fine dining and opened Fish in a former bait and tackle shop on Sausalito's waterfront. The linens are gone; diners line up at the counter to order and then sit at picnic tables and benches inside or on the deck overlooking Clipper Yacht Harbor, but the quality of the food and the talent of the chef are still top-drawer.

Fish features all sustainably caught fish and shellfish and local organic produce. It even has its own fishing boat, purchased by Callahan so that he and his kitchen staff could experience firsthand the pleasures and hardships of the independent fisherman. The Portuguese Red Seafood Chowder with fresh Moniz linguiça, clams, Madeira, smoked paprika, cilantro, and watercress is delicious, as is the traditional New England variety. Both are available by the cup, bowl, or quart. The crab roll is sublime, and the fish and chips and crab Louie are local favorites.

Callahan's dedication to independent producers extends throughout the menu, including a hamburger from Prather Ranch Meat Company beef and a peanut butter and jelly sandwich made on *pain de mie* with natural peanut butter and organic jelly. The selection of local oysters changes daily, and there's a good wine list that features both local and international vintages.

While not cheap, Fish's prices are entirely reasonable given the quality of the food. It's cash only, so stop by the ATM first and take out enough to also purchase pristine fish from their fish market to take home.

 Hayes Street Grill
Hayes Valley
320 Hayes Street, at Franklin Street
(415) 863-5545
No lunch on Saturday and Sunday
$$$

Back in 1979, when Hayes Street Grill first opened its doors, Davies Symphony Hall had just gone up around the corner and this was the lone outpost for hungry opera- or symphony-goers seeking a satisfying pre-performance meal. And it has anchored the neighborhood ever since.

Although you can order a handsome Niman Ranch grilled steak, and St. Patrick's Day is religiously celebrated with tender slabs of corned beef and braised cabbage, at Hayes Street seafood is really the thing. Choose from a selection of fish grilled and served with a side sauce of your choosing, such as beurre blanc or homemade tartar, and Hayes Street's legendary French fries. (The late *San Francisco Chronicle* columnist Herb Caen regularly rhapsodized about them.) Some patrons never veer from the grilled, line-caught swordfish served with a pot of spicy Szechuan peanut sauce. But if you're smart, you'll keep an eye out for local sand dabs or petrale sole sautéed with brown butter, capers, and lemon. If it's in season, get the cracked Dungeness crab. And you can be sure that the first-of-the-season Chesapeake Bay soft-shell crab, Connecticut River shad roe, or wild Pacific king salmon will be on the menu. A full bar, sensible wine list, and stand-up starter salads like the Chopped Salad with Beets, Walnuts, and Blue Cheese guarantee satisfaction. For dessert the crème brûlée is a must-have.

You don't have to worry about the provenance of the ingredients: Co-Owner Patricia Unterman, a San Francisco culinary icon, works closely with fishmongers like Monterey Fish to find the freshest, most delicious, and most responsibly harvested fish available. She can also be seen at the Ferry Plaza on every market day, loading up her convertible with local, organic bounty.

Hayes Street, with its wood finishes and brass accents, has the warm feeling of a Paris brasserie. The walls are lined with signed headshots of performing arts glitterati—look for the photo of a very young Mark Morris near the door—a testimony that Hayes Street's hospitality extends to those onstage as well. A word to the wise: Unless you are attending a performance, it's best to avoid the pre-performance crush.

Hog Island Oyster Bar
Embarcadero

Ferry Building Marketplace
One Ferry Building, Shop 11-1
Embarcadero, at Market Street
(415) 391-7117
$$$

Hog Island Oyster Company, just a short drive from Point Reyes Station in the Tomales Bay Marine Sanctuary in Marin County, has long been a destination for Bay Area oyster lovers. Pull into the parking lot by Tomales Bay, claim a picnic table, pick up a couple dozen Sweetwater, Atlantic, French Hog, or the perennial favorite, Kumamoto, from the oyster shack, and settle down to a beautiful do-it-yourself Sunday lunch.

For those of you who don't feel like driving to Tomales Bay—or who aren't skilled in the art of oyster shucking—Hog Island recently opened an oyster bar at the Ferry Building Marketplace in San Francisco. Perched on the edge of the water, this venue offers a stunning view of the Bay Bridge and Treasure Island. The oyster bar serves all of their five species, harvested each morning from Tomales Bay. Eat them raw, or enjoy traditional oysters Rockefeller, oysters casino, or oyster stew with a glass of Sancerre.

Pesce
Russian Hill
2227 Polk Street, between Green and Vallejo Streets
(415) 928-8025
$$

The ambience of this Polk Street seafood restaurant mirrors the simple elegance of its food: The narrow space is made warm by polished wood wainscoting, a long zinc bar, and a smattering of a few small tables. Italian-born Chef-Owner Ruggero Gadaldi treats seafood simply. A sauce of butter, lemon, and capers brings out the delicate nuances of petrale sole. A bubbling *cioppino* is served over polenta. The salmon bruschetta, studded with capers and enriched with horseradish cream, is a delectable treat. The smoked fish plates are a must. Behind the restaurant, racks of fresh fish are smoked daily. A succinct wine list pairs wonderfully with the menu. Before indulging in desserts, make sure to cleanse your palate with a *scroppino*—a slushy combination of Prosecco and lemon sorbet.

Swan Oyster Depot
Nob Hill
1517 Polk Street, between Sacramento and California Streets
(415) 673-1101
Closed Sunday
Cash only
$$

You would have to search long and hard to find a spot more typical of old San Francisco than this family-owned seafood and oyster bar. Locals, chefs, and an array of enthusiastic eaters patiently wait their turn for one of twenty wobbly stools at an ancient marble counter. The food is straightforward and beyond fresh, offering glistening seafood salads with Louie dressing, shrimp cocktails, a wide selection of regional oysters and clams on the half-shell, and assorted smoked fish. The creamy clam chowder is unbeatable. Service is cheery and savvy.

The main attraction at Swan, however, is Dungeness crab—a couple hundred pounds a day are consumed here in season (from mid-November to mid-June), as crab cocktails with red sauce, in crab Louie on top of shredded iceberg lettuce, and cracked in the shell. If you are overly stimulated and hungry when you arrive (and let's assume you will be), take a seat at the oyster bar and order a double crab cocktail, piled high, with sweet ivory legs peeking over the edge of an old-fashioned ice cream sundae glass. Have it with a dish of mayonnaise on the side, along with cracked pepper, house-made horseradish, and a squeeze of lemon juice. And wash it down with a glass of wine or local beer.

Once initiated to Swan, food lovers return for the exquisite food, all of which is raw except for sautéed soft-shell crabs, when available, but they also come back for the extraordinary goodwill and humor of the six handsome proprietors, the Sancimino brothers (their only sister practices law). The brothers remember names and special requests; a habit they picked up from their late father, Sal, who, with great élan, ran this San Francisco institution from 1946 until his retirement.

NOTABLE

Farallon
Union Square
450 Post Street, between Powell and Mason Streets, adjoining the
Kensington Park Hotel
(415) 956-6969
$$$$

The Little Mermaid would be hard-pressed to find a place in which she
would feel more at home than at Farallon. Co-Owner Pat Kuleto's design
is a multimillion-dollar underwater fantasia of hand-blown jellyfish
lamps, glass clamshells, sea-urchin light fixtures, a sea-life mosaic floor,
and a tentacle-encircled bar. Following the restaurant's now trademark
"coastal cuisine" theme, Executive Chef and Co-Owner Mark Franz's cre-
atively upscale dishes are as consistently decorous as the surroundings.

Farallon's menu changes daily and seasonally and features many shellfish and regional dishes from across the country and the Canadian
Maritimes: Malpeque oysters from Prince Edward Island, roasted
Hawaiian ono, Chesapeake Bay soft-shell crabs, and seared Louisiana Gulf
prawns. The extensive wine list (more than four hundred offerings by the
bottle and thirty by the glass) is definitely geared toward the serious
oenophile.

Yankee Pier
286 Magnolia Avenue
Larkspur   *MARIN*
(415) 924-7676
$$

Located in a century-old house—just down the road from where Co-
Owner Bradley Ogden's restaurant empire began at Lark Creek Inn—
Yankee Pier is a great little American fish shack serving classic
preparations of the freshest seafood available. In addition to the expected
raw bar, there's a classic New England clam chowder, fried Ipswich clam
strips, grilled or roasted market-fresh fish served with your choice of sides,
a Maine lobster roll, a Dungeness crab roll, and beer-battered fish and
chips that have become a Bay Area favorite. Desserts are homey, like lemon
meringue pie and chocolate brownie sundae.

STEAK HOUSES

Acme Chophouse
See American, page 11.

Alfred's Steak House
Financial District
659 Merchant Street, alley off Kearny between Clay and
  Washington Streets
(415) 781-7058
Closed Monday
$$$-$$$$

Alfred's is intensely red and gold: deep red walls and upholstered booths, red-and-gold carpet, crystal chandeliers, and mirrors to reflect all this back on itself endlessly. Since its founding in 1928, Alfred's has been a San Francisco institution. Although there are plenty of Italian-American dishes on the menu, the thing to order here is steak: corn-fed beef that is dry aged, mesquite grilled, and perfectly cooked. Indeed the porterhouse steak is offered in three versions: the Prince weighs in at 20 ounces, the King is 32 ounces, and the Kingdom is 60 ounces and requires an hour to prepare. Clearly this is a place to enjoy some serious red meat, albeit meat from a serious feedlot background, which is the only drawback of an evening out at Alfred's.

C&L Steakhouse
Nob Hill
1250 Jones Street, at Clay Street
(415) 771-5400
$$$$

When I think of C&L I think plush. It's in a gorgeous room on Nob Hill and was meant to house a steak house. Put on your low-cut dress and heels and slip into one of the tables at C&L and order a martini. I couldn't keep my eye off of a stately matron sipping hers from across the elegant, candlelit room, where diners speak in hushed tones. Or settle in at the bar. The only thing that complicates the experience is the menu, arranged like a spreadsheet, with classic American steak towns listed horizontally and what the typical appetizers, salads, and starters would be in that city listed vertically. The idea might be to order by city—I don't know. All you simply need to do is look for the salad and side you want, find which city has the rib-eye (Denver), and you're done. The meal starts with a tasty Yorkshire pudding, here a puffy, savory briochelike dish. The meat is from Painted Hills Natural Beef (antibiotic-free, no-added-hormone natural beef from Oregon, fed a diet of alfalfa, corn, and barley). Service is professional.

El Raigon
North Beach
510 Union Street, at Grant Street
(415) 291-0927
Closed Sunday
$$$$

An American who happens to own a ranch in Argentina and a wine importer who happens to hail from Argentina joined forces to open El Raigon, an Argentine-style steak house in North Beach. While beef from Argentina is not allowed to be imported into the United States at the moment, the wines are, and El Raigon offers a diverse selection of Malbec. Examples of Argentine cabernet sauvignon, merlot, pinot noir, and Syrah are also included on the list, as are a few whites and even a sparkling wine.

Until the import ban is lifted, the closest thing the owners could find to 100 percent grass-fed Argentine beef is a lean Piedmontese beef from Montana (grass-fed but grain-finished, no added antibiotics or hormones). While the cuts of steak listed on the menu might sound familiar, they are done Argentine style. The rib-eye, for example, came to the table as a very thick square block, like no rib-eye I had ever seen. The short ribs, which are usually braised, are grilled here. (Get them; they're delicious.) Another good bet is the *bife de chorizo*, which is the "classic" Argentine cut, according to the menu, and similar to the New York strip. The beef is grilled over a wood-and-charcoal fire. Overcooking is always a risk with lean beef, so to be on the safe side order your beef rare. *Chimichurri*, a simple parsley sauce made with garlic, vinegar, oregano, and olive oil, accompanies the ribs.

El Raigon is a casual place, and the interior, with its wood surfaces, cowhide accents, and gaucho memorabilia, makes you feel you're eating at the ranch house that's been spiffed up for a special occasion. Service is genuine and warm.

VEGETARIAN

 **Café Gratitude**
Mission

2400 Harrison Street, at 20th Street
(415) 824-4652
$

When I think of Café Gratitude I can't help but think of Jon Carroll's August 10, 2004, column in the *San Francisco Chronicle*. An excerpt follows:

> "I am flourishing," I said to the waitress.
>
> "Good choice ," she said.
>
> "Also, I am effervescent." She wrote it down.
>
> [My friend] said, "I am fulfilled. No, wait, I am plenty. No, I am fulfilled. And maybe a side of I am generous." She closed her menu. "You'll like this," she said. "It's a great place."

I Am Flourishing are almond-and-sesame-seed falafels served with hummus, cucumber *tzatziki,* and greens. I Am Fulfilled is a big salad loaded with beets, carrots, cukes, avocado, and tomato and served with flax crackers. I Am Plenty is a fruit salad topped with cashew crème frâiche, though it can be made nut-free. I Am Effervescent is a fizzy ginger drink. Ordering here is fun once you get over your own self-consciousness. Everything is raw and organic, even down to the beer and wine—which is mostly European—and some of the wine is vegan, whatever that entails. Fun even for the carnivores. Check out the rest of Carroll's column and check out Café Gratitiude. It deserves an I AM A SNAIL.

 **Geranium**
Bernal Heights

615 Cortland Avenue
(415) 647-0118
Closed Monday
$$

Geranium, located on hip Cortland Avenue in Bernal Heights, hits all the right neighborhood bistro notes: good food, subdued atmosphere, attentive service, and a great wine list. The only thing missing is the steak *frites,* but you won't be disappointed. Ironically housed in a former butcher shop, you can still find a few remnants of its former life. A meat scale dominates one end of the counter, and the rail on which slabs of beef once hung is now a footrest for bar customers. The menu changes frequently and is inspired by seasonal, mostly organic produce and artisan-made food products. Tasty vegetarian comfort food options include won tons

filled with sweet potato and ginger, an Eat Loaf made of beans and nuts, and organic orecchiette ("little ears") pasta tossed with dandelion greens. A well-thought-out wine menu, with selections available by the glass or bottle, complements the food perfectly. Some of you might be happy to know that there is a vegetarian kid's menu for epicureans with little ones in tow.

Greens
See California, page 29.

Millennium
Tenderloin
In the Savoy Hotel
580 Geary Street, at James Street
(415) 345-3900
Dinner only
$$

Millennium restaurant is a dreamy destination not only for vegans but for anyone seeking a unique night out. Chef Eric Tucker cooks without any dairy products and uses organic ingredients whenever possible. The menu changes nightly, spotlighting seasonal fresh produce and taking inspiration and flavors from many cuisines. Savory, elegant vegan options include Truffled Flageolet Gratin with garlic chive polenta, savory marinated tempeh, and fennel in a sherried cashew cream; Plum-Miso Grilled Eggplant with jasmine rice, broccoli, sweet peppers, snow peas, and glazed tofu in a coconut–green curry sauce; and house-made Golden Potato Gnocchi with chanterelle and clamshell mushroom confit. Don't miss the romantic Aphrodisiac Dinner, offered every month on the Sunday closest to the full moon. The dinner is a tantalizing five-course affair that is sure to excite more than your palate.

Millennium also proudly boasts the nation's first all-organic wine list—no small feat.

PART THREE

FOOD SHOPS & MARKETS

Acme Bread Company
1601 San Pablo Avenue, at Cedar Street

Berkeley   *EAST BAY*

(510) 524-1327

All Steve Sullivan wanted was to bake a good loaf of bread. As a busboy at Chez Panisse in the late seventies, he started experimenting in his dorm at UC Berkeley with a toaster oven and a copy of Elizabeth David's *English Bread and Yeast Cookery*. When he made a loaf that reminded Alice Waters of the crusty, chewy, flavorful breads of the French countryside, she hired him to bake at the restaurant.

In 1983 Sullivan left Chez Panisse to open his own bakery in Berkeley. It was a phenomenal success and almost single-handedly revolutionized baking on the West Coast. In the decades since, Acme has expanded into several production bakeries throughout the Bay Area.

One of two retail outlets, Acme's original bakery on the corner of Cedar and San Pablo in Berkeley, stands cheek by jowl with its gustatory relatives, Café Fanny and Kermit Lynch Wine Merchant. Here you'll find all of Acme's signature loaves: the *pain au levain,* made with a starter inoculated by wild grape yeasts; sour-and-sweet baguettes; the Upstairs Bread, so named because it used to be served upstairs at Chez Panisse; Italian loaves; New York rye; and the walnut *levain,* which is irresistible when it's served with a lovely cheese. The entire repertoire is available at their only other retail location in the Ferry Building.

All of Acme's breads are made with organic flour and have the rich taste and satisfying crumb that only come from slow proofing and hand shaping. And although the artisanal breads from his brick-lined hearth ovens can be found in dozens of restaurants and markets around the Bay Area, Sullivan's desire to bake a good loaf is as strong as ever.

Other Location
Embarcadero
Ferry Building Marketplace
One Ferry Building, Shop 15
Embarcadero, at Market Street
San Francisco
(415) 288-2978

Arizmendi Bakery
Inner Sunset

1331 Ninth Avenue, between Irving and Judah Streets
(415) 566-3117
Closed Monday

San Francisco does not lack for good bread. Yet many believe this postage stamp–sized neighborhood bakery bakes the city's best. Arizmendi, named after the Basque labor organizer, is a worker-owned cooperative inspired by The Cheese Board in Berkeley. That pride of ownership is evident in the toothsome, chewy breads with a long-fermented flavor. Each day a specialty pizza is offered for eat-in dining or to go in a "light-baked" form, Arizmendi's version of take-and-bake.

Although there isn't anywhere comfortable to sit here, it's worth a trip for the dense cheese rolls alone (affectionately dubbed vegetarian pork chops). And don't miss the unique Cherry-Corn Scones, Asiago-Provolone Bread, or the breadsticks with Parmesan and cornmeal. But you'd better be there when the sticks come out (usually around 4:00 P.M.), or you'll miss them entirely—they go fast.

Bay Bread Boulangerie
Pacific Heights

2325 Pine Street, near Fillmore Street
(415) 440-0356
Closed Monday

A jangling pocketful of change can't take you far in Pacific Heights when it's sustenance you seek. But a glimpse of tiny Bay Bread Boulangerie's French blue storefront in an otherwise nondescript stretch of Pine Street means your pennies might just buy you a ticket to heaven. Pascal Rigo produces reasonably priced breads from organic flour—from dark, flavorful *pain au levain* to elegant, chewy-crisp baguettes. When the heady scent of freshly baked bread beckons, sweet-talk your way up to the wee glass display case for a delicate, eggy tart with onions and chunks of flavorful sausage, or a baguette sandwich lined with sweet butter, figs, prosciutto, and shaved Parmesan. Don't forget a couple of the *canales*, small, irresistible cakes from Bordeaux with a custardlike interior and hard caramelized shell.

Bakesale Betty
5098 Telegraph Avenue
Oakland   *EAST BAY*
(510) 985-1213
Closed Sunday and Monday

This new corner bakery in Oakland's renascent Temescal District is a high-quality slice of the 1950s' best sweets. Owners Alison and Michael Camp have been selling their baked goods at Bay Area farmers' markets for the past three years, but their new open-kitchen retail bakery is an inviting space for viewing all they do.

Their specialties are American familiars, with pure flavors, great textures, and no skimping on the sugar. Freshly baked scones, lemon bars, and brownies share the bakery case with fat, tender cookies (chocolate chip, ginger, and pecan, for starters), as well as a moist banana bread and an irresistible date cake (she calls it a pudding, as they might in her native Australia). Another Aussie treat, pavlova, is in the works.

There's lunch, too, with a changing selection of salads, pot pies, and a sandwich of buttermilk-fried chicken and coleslaw.

The Cheese Board Collective
1504 Shattuck Avenue
Berkeley   *EAST BAY*
(510) 549-3183
Closed Sunday

In the early days of this landmark cooperative, the baked goods were conceived as a way of using leftover cheese scraps. The bakery has evolved, and now sells an enormous variety of cheese-free breads, such as their sourdough baguettes and *bâtardes,* unrivaled English muffins, and a wide variety of scones. Although they still sell cheese rolls, the selection of baked goods is vast and changes daily; Tuesday brings a local favorite, the curried Berkeley Buns, and you can find soft, eggy challah on Fridays. Call ahead to reserve your bread. Visit their Web site, http://cheeseboardcollective.coop, for a complete listing. For more about The Cheese Board see Cheese, page 243.

Crixa Cakes

2748 Adeline Street
Berkeley   **EAST BAY**
(510) 548-0421
Closed Monday

Crixa's earth-toned plaster walls and open kitchen with vintage metal scales and hanging copper dessert molds is the perfect setting for Elizabeth Cloian's Old World cakes and pastries.

Taught by her Russian grandmother, Cloian draws inspiration from the taste memory of her childhood. Her grandmother, she says, "was really a nineteenth-century person" who lived in twentieth-century Russia, where little was available for purchase. As a result she made absolutely everything by hand. So when traditional *lekvar* was unavailable from her distributors, Cloian bought an antique grinder to make the poppy seed and fruit filling herself for her delightful *kifli*—a Hungarian turnover made with sour cream pastry. Available only on Tuesday, Wednesday, and Saturday, her *rugelach* is equally delicious. A surprise delight is the *ma mdul,* a soft cookie shaped in a wooden mold with the delicate essence of orange-flower water, filled with minced, sweetened nuts and then generously dusted with powdered sugar.

Customers love the simple apple cake and the more extravagant chocolate cake with whipped cream, caramel, and lofty swirls of chocolate ganache called Carmella. Then there's the lavish Rigo Jancsi, a Hungarian chocolate mousse square named after a nineteenth-century Gypsy musician made famous by his affair with a naughty princess.

Della Fattoria
Embarcadero

Ferry Plaza Farmers Market, 1 Embarcadero, at Market Street
Saturday

To celebrate her fiftieth birthday, Kathleen Weber of Della Fattoria enlisted the help of her husband, Ed, friends, family, and renowned masonry oven builder Alan Scott to build a wood-fired oven at the family's farm in Petaluma. Della Fattoria, which means "from the farm," now produces what is considered by many to be the best bread in the Bay Area. Loaves of rustic, country-style bread in a dozen varieties, such as *levain, ciabatta*, Kalamata olive, seeded wheat, and pumpkin seed, are baked daily. The starter is made from organic flour, springwater, and grapes grown on her farm, and the loaves are made from organic flour, local organic extra-virgin olive oil, and Brittany sea salt. And the secret ingredient? Weber believes Petaluma soil and sea breezes enhance the taste of each loaf.

The Webers have produced a progeny of bread converts. Her son bakes bread on the farm, and her daughter-in-law is pastry chef at their Della Fattoria Downtown café in Petaluma. Their daughter handles the company Web site, and their son-in-law pitches in wherever he's needed. Even grandchildren aren't exempt. All in all, three generations of Webers live on the farm and help.

Della Fattoria's fragrant treasures can be found at several locations around the Bay Area—on the shelf at Whole Foods, at the elegant Fifth Floor restaurant, or in the bread salads at their café. The French Laundry chose Della Fattoria as the house bread before opening their own bakery. But the best way to get your hands on a loaf is to buy it directly from Kathleen and Ed Weber at the Saturday Ferry Plaza Farmers Market. Although the Webers double their production on market day, they almost always sell out.

Other Locations

Della Fattoria Downtown, 141 Petaluma Boulevard North, Petaluma; (707) 763-0161.

Also available at various Whole Foods locations throughout San Francisco.

Fleur de Cocoa

39 North Santa Cruz Avenue
Los Gatos   *SOUTH BAY*
(408) 354-3574
Closed Monday

Fleur de Cocoa is a sweet touch of France in downtown Los Gatos, and this classic pastry shop tantalizes customers with some of the most buttery, flaky, crispy croissants around. Be sure to take home a slice of the *tarte Normande,* a specialty from Owner–Head Baker Pascal Janvier's native Normandy. Big slices of Braeburn apples peek out from under a rich vanilla custard enrobed in a puff pastry shell. Hot chocolate is a specialty, with Ivory Coast cocoa beans giving it a strong, deep flavor that lingers and lingers.

Handmade chocolates include the signature Fleur de Cocoa, made with extra-dark 70 percent chocolate ganache. Other varieties include Earl Grey–Infused Milk Chocolate Ganache, Coffee Praline, Passion Fruit White Chocolate Ganache, and Tahitian Vanilla Bean Caramel. A half-pound box is $27.50. And Fleur de Cocoa will ship via FedEx, except during the hot summer months.

Janvier, who runs the bakery with his wife, Nicola, has been studying pastry since he was a thirteen-year-old apprentice in Normandy. He holds a master's degree in chocolate, pastry, and ice cream from CIFPA, the Centre Internationale Formation Alimentaire Professionale Academie in Paris—a certification held by only 12 percent of French pastry chefs. For years he also competed in pastry competitions, winning several gold medals.

La Farine French Bakery
6323 College Avenue
Berkeley   *EAST BAY*
(510) 654-0338

Although La Farine has been serving locals from its spot on the Berkeley-Oakland border for nearly three decades, it wouldn't look out of place in Paris. Aromas of baking butter, sugar, and flour envelop the charming storefront on College Avenue, and the display cases are arranged with cakes, tarts, breads, cookies, and pastries. If you can manage to lift your eyes, you'll see bakers in the spacious room beyond, quietly rolling, cutting, baking, and frosting.

La Farine's breakfast pastries are made with buttery, flaky croissant dough and puff pastry. Most people's all-time favorite is the morning bun, a spiral of dough, brown sugar, and cinnamon. This is probably the only place where you can find a "Swiss Twinkie"—puff pastry wrapped around a spicy nut mixture. After ordering your pastry and coffee, have a seat at

the big, old-fashioned family table, complete with crocheted tablecloth, and visit with some of the regulars or read the paper.

On the way out, pick up one of the extremely well-made baguettes and something for dessert. If you want a fancy cake, try the classic Reine de Saba, a rum-soaked chocolate-almond torte glazed with bittersweet chocolate, or the provocatively named Jezebel, an almond cake flavored with amaretto, filled with chocolate mousse, and frosted with vanilla buttercream. And La Farine even offers that rare luxury: high-quality frozen puff pastry, sold by the pound.

Lou's Living Donut Museum
387 Delmas Avenue
San Jose   **SOUTH BAY**
(408) 295-5887
Open Monday through Saturday 5:30 A.M. to 2:00 P.M., Sunday
   7:00 A.M. to noon (closing times are relative to sales)
Cash only

A lot of places serve doughnuts. But not many serve fresh, warm doughnuts with their hole reattached, along with a heaping side of history and patriotism. This landmark shop was opened in 1955 by a former B-24 Liberator pilot named Lucius Ades, with the help of a GI loan. When he retired, he sold the shop to brothers Chuck and Rick Chavira, who had worked for him since they were teenagers.

Inside the shop you'll find models of military aircraft and an exhibit that not only tells Lou's story, but also gives a brief history of World War II. And every morning at 6:00 A.M., workers go outside to raise the flag, recite the Pledge of Allegiance, and sing "The Star-Spangled Banner."

The shop sells two hundred dozen doughnuts a day, all hand kneaded. And they almost always sell out by noon. That's not surprising; who could resist fluffy doughnuts made with organic flour, Swiss chocolate, free-range eggs, five types of potatoes, and Ades's original starter? Look for special flavors during the holidays, such as pumpkin doughnuts in October, lemon custard and cherry-filled ones in spring, and even doughnuts shaped like Christmas trees in December. The newest twist? Doughnuts with rose-petal oil swirled into the glaze and decorated with real rose petals. To taste them, though, you'll have to place a special order.

Masse's Pastries
1469 Shattuck Avenue
Berkeley   **EAST BAY**
(510) 649-1004
Closed Tuesday

Whether it's a towering wedding cake for one hundred fifty or a mousse tart for one, served at a café table inside or on the sidewalk, Paul Masse's creations are picture-perfect examples of the art of the classic patisserie. However, unlike some of the famous pastry emporiums of Europe, Masse's neighborhood-cozy small shop at the far end of Berkeley's Gourmet Ghetto (Chez Panisse, César's, and the Cheese Board are neighbors) does not have a set repertoire. Especially for the fruit pastries that figure prominently in his lineup, the classically trained baker lets the seasons and the market guide his work.

Masse has moved from buying from commercial suppliers to doing all his produce shopping in person, relying on Berkeley's two outstanding produce markets, Berkeley Bowl and Monterey Market, where he peruses, smells, and tastes the day's offerings and selects what pleases him. It may be time-consuming, he admits, but as he says, "It's so much better than ordering from a piece of paper." Whenever possible, Masse buys organic fruit, but first it has to pass the taste test.

Masse is equally fussy about the butter he uses. Some butters he has tried had a high moisture content, which can ruin a recipe. And Masse does use a lot of butter—in fact, he has to chill the flour for his scrumptious croissants and brioches overnight so it can incorporate copious amounts of the stuff without melting it.

Miette
Embarcadero
Ferry Building Marketplace
One Ferry Building, Shop 10
Embarcadero, at Market Street
(415) 837-0300
Closed Monday

One can imagine Audrey Tautou in a ruffled apron behind the counter of this whimsical patisserie in the Ferry Building. And in the film version, her love interest would undoubtedly be one of the handsome farmers who sell vegetables in the plaza during the biweekly farmers' market. Miette's cakes, cookies, and tarts star local ingredients like dairy products from Straus Dairy, berries from Ella Bella farm near Santa Cruz, and almonds from Lagier Ranches in the Central Valley.

Perched on pale-green milk-glass cake stands, the cakes look like a Wayne Thiebaut still life, simple yet artful enough for any dinner party. Parisian macaroons are light and chewy, the lemon tart made from organic lemon curd is a perfect balance of sweet and tart, and the ginger cakes and cupcakes have just enough spiciness, perfectly complemented by a generous layer of cream cheese frosting. For those who prefer their cakes light and airy, it is best to steer clear of the yellow cake, which can sometimes be dense. Bite-size scones are a thoughtful offering for those who just want a little something sweet.

Montclair Baking

2220 Mountain Boulevard, Suite 140, between Snake and Scout
  Roads
Oakland   *EAST BAY*
(510) 530-8052

Just about the only complaint Montclair's owner Cheryl Lew ever hears is that an occasional customer would like her fruit cakes to be sweeter. That's not going to happen, because Lew insists on preserving the integrity of the ingredients, so apricots retain a slight edge of acidity and cranberries a delicately bitter bottom note. Lew, an Asian studies graduate of the University of California at Berkeley who fell in love with pastry while working her way through school, does spectacular special-occasion cakes and homey plum *kuchen* with equal attention to detail.

She is close friends with some of the crew at Berkeley's Monterey Market (especially owner Bill Fujimoto and John Amano, who also happens to be Lew's ex-husband), and they provide her with whatever is best, be it strawberries, figs, or pears. But much of it is organic, she says, citing organic apples from the Apple Farm in the Anderson Valley as her favorites for fall desserts. About a quarter of the regular flour she uses is organic, though not the cake flour, and she favors turbinado sugar, which is far less processed than common granulated white sugar.

Stan's Donut Shop

2628 Homestead Road
Santa Clara   *SOUTH BAY*
(408) 296-5982
Cash or checks only

The glazed doughnut is so finger-licking good that it practically has a cult following. Stan's sells about two thousand doughnuts a day, and half those orders are for the glazed. Most doughnut shops start making their pastries at night, letting them sit in the display case until morning. Not Stan's. Employees arrive at 3:30 A.M., and about three hours later the first doughnuts are done. Batches are made throughout the day, which means that no matter what time you go, you're likely to land a warm doughnut. The pastries are rolled out and fried right behind the long counter, where customers plop down on swivel stools to enjoy coffee and a snack, or tuna sandwiches, smoothies, and root beer floats.

Tartine
Mission

600 Guerrero Street, at 18th Street
(415) 487-2600

Tartine began its life as Bay Village Bakery, a tiny outpost in Point Reyes Station where, with flour, water, and sea salt over a blazing wood-burning hearth, Chad Robertson made some of the tastiest *levain* this side of Paris. After a brief stint in Mill Valley and a name change, Robertson and his wife, Elisabeth Prueitt, opened up Tartine on the corner of 18th Street and Guerrero, joining Delfina and Bi-Rite Market on this food-savvy stretch of 18th Street.

The bread is not the only starring attraction at Tartine. Prueitt, a formally trained *pâtissier*, has put together a full line of tarts, cakes, and cookies, as well as assorted pastries both sweet and savory. The *gougère* has a devout following as does the orange-infused morning bun. And the luscious ham-and-Gruyère quiche, at $2.75 a slice, represents one of the best values around. There is almost always a line at Tartine, often extending out the door. And it moves slowly; it seems that after more than a year in business, they are still figuring out the *feng shui* of the checkout stand.

Robertson and Prueitt are very thoughtful about their ingredients and use organic flour, sugar, coffee, dairy, fruit, herbs, and vegetables. On a recent Friday I witnessed the delivery of an armload of fromage blanc fresh from the local Cowgirl Creamery. Eggs are sourced locally too, and most of the meat comes from Niman Ranch. Wines by the glass are all from Italy and France and are chosen to represent biodynamic, organic, or smaller producers.

A couple of caveats: First, if you plan to sit down and eat here, it is best to stake your claim for a table before getting in line. Otherwise you may find yourself sitting outside on the curb with your Hot-Pressed Prosciutto and Provolone Panini. Second, the bread doesn't come out of the ovens until 4:00 P.M.

NOTABLE

Liguria Bakery
North Beach/Telegraph Hill
1700 Stockton Street
(415) 421-3786

If you don't get to Liguria by noon, you're pushing your luck. Liguria makes four items: plain focaccia, onion focaccia, raisin focaccia, and pizza focaccia. And every day they sell out quickly. They open at 8:00 A.M. and close when everything's gone.

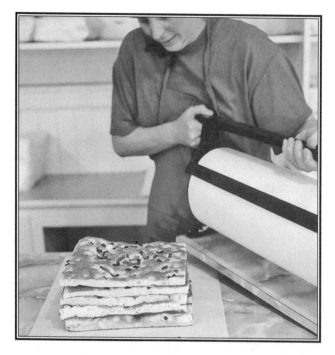

Three brothers from Genoa started the bakery back in 1911, and it is still family run. It's a no-nonsense place; make up your mind before you go in. Once you've placed your order, the rectangular sheets of bread are retrieved from the back, slapped on the counter, wrapped swiftly in crisp white butcher paper, and secured with a double knotting of string. It makes for a beautiful package. The trick is to get wherever you're going without opening it up and eating it all on the way.

Noe Valley Bakery and Bread Company
Noe Valley
4073 24th Street, at Castro Street
(415) 550-1405

Founded in 1995, Noe Valley Bakery is an old-style neighborhood bakery in a part of the city that takes these types of institutions seriously. Pies, cookies, and cupcakes with fluffy white frosting and rainbow sprinkles have a hand-crafted aura about them, while the éclairs and Summer Berry Mousse are a bit more elegant. Although many of Noe Valley's customers look like they live just down the street, fans come here from all over the city for their fig bread, cherry-chocolate bread, and blueberry-pecan scones. Noe Valley products are also sold at the Saturday farmers' market at Ferry Plaza.

Phoenix Pastaficio
1786 Shattuck Avenue
Berkeley   *EAST BAY*
(510) 883-0783

Eric's Olive Bread enjoys a cult following, and the platters of cookies, cakes, and perfect Danish that crowd the counter are fresh and irresistible. Phoenix's olive bread and pastas are also available at their stall at each of the Berkeley Farmers' Market locations (for more about Phoenix Pastaficio, see Ethnic & Specialty Markets, page 252).

Emporio Rulli
464 Magnolia Avenue
Larkspur   *MARIN*
(415) 924-7478

A visit to Emporio Rulli feels like a vacation in Milan, as you sip and nibble against the backdrop of mahogany and marble, sparkling glass cases, and the great draw, a massive mural of a gondola carrying chefs in toques, wearing masks. There is an excellent selection of panini for a light meal, Italian wines by the glass, and seasonal pastries and breads for holidays— now so legendary that huge numbers of people place orders for Colomba Pasquale (Easter Dove) well in advance. Besides the *pasticceria* and café, a third room is an emporium of elegant treats like marmalades, olive oils, dessert wines, chocolates, and coffee beans.

Owners Gary (who trained in Milan and Turin) and Jeannie Rulli have since opened additional locations in San Francisco and at the San Francisco Airport, attesting to the café's appeal. Some Slow Food purists have speculated on what Emporio Rulli might be like if organic ingredients were used. Lingering under the gondola mural, thoughts turn to dreams and everything seems possible.

Other Location
Emporio Rulli Gran Caffè, 2300 Chestnut Street, at Scott Street,
   San Francisco (Marina); (415) 923-6464

Semifreddi's Bakery
372 Colusa Avenue
Berkeley   *EAST BAY*
(510) 596-9935, 596-9930

Founded in 1984, in the midst of the Bay Area bread revolution, Semifreddi's Bakery remains one of the better producers of artisanal breads. The family-owned bakery has grown from its original location in

Kensington and is now distributed far and wide, in groceries from San Jose to Novato. Although it's a behemoth, at least in the world of independent bakeries (it employs thirty bakers), Semifreddi's is still known for the sourdough baguette that was a staple when it first opened. As Co-Owner Mike Rose explains, they "continue to play around with sourdough starters, experimenting with various methods of fermentation." This devotion is reflected in their other well-crafted loaves like the challah, ciabatta, country *levain*, and the sweet *bâtarde*. The white flour they use is ground by a single mill in Idaho, and the whole-wheat and rye flours are organic.

Retail Location at Main Bakery
4242 Hollis Avenue, Emeryville (East Bay); (510) 569-9942

Other Location
3084 Claremont Avenue, Berkeley (East Bay); (510) 596-9942

Stella Pastry
North Beach
446 Columbus Avenue, between Stockton and Vallejo Streets
(415) 986-2914

The famous Sacripantina cake is available only at Stella. The recipe is a closely guarded secret, as is the name. In fact, the bakery had it trademarked: You can see the certificate from the California Secretary of State's office that is displayed proudly on the wall. It reads:

> *Name: Sacripantina.*
>
> *Description: "Cake in the form of a half ball filled with zabaglione cream and sponge cake."*

Certainly this is one of the more interesting trademark applications that ever passed through Sacramento. These days the cake is shaped less like a ball and more like a dome and is basically a layered sponge cake with zabaglione filling. Its sides are covered with a thin crust of toasted sponge-cake crumbs. It is Stella Bakery's biggest seller.

They still make the Sacripantina in the back of the store, and there are usually three sizes available at any given time. It can be made into a wedding cake or a sheet cake—whatever you want. You can also buy an individual square serving to eat in or to go. In addition, assorted cookies and a tiramisu cake are available.

CHEESE

Bi-Rite Market
See Groceries & Produce Markets, page 270.

The Cheese Board Collective
1504 Shattuck Avenue
Berkeley   *EAST BAY*
(510) 549-3183
Closed Monday

For selection, quality, and price, The Cheese Board is the one of the best cheese stores in California. Its broad selection is due partly to nearly forty years of developing relationships with distributors and partly to serving some of the most demanding cheese consumers in the country. What's better today, the Camembert or the Reblochon? What makes a nice cheese course with this Epoisse? Just ask—although the owner who waits on you (there are more than thirty of them at this worker cooperative) will insist that you taste and decide for yourself.

Their stock runs the gamut from inexpensive brick cheddar for kids' sandwiches to raw-milk Camembert extravagances such as highly perishable Brin d'Amour, scarce domestic cheeses like Sally Jackson Sheep's Cheese, and obscure imported delights like Hoch Ybrig. Look at the chalkboards and the cheeses displayed on top of the coolers for rarities and special values. When waiting for your number to come up don't forget to cast a glance at the rack in back, where Bries and other big double- and triple-cream wheels are stacked.

They also carry some of the best olives around: Ask for a sample of the *luques* or *picholines*. A cooler by the register displays fresh dairy products, including Apple Farms quark, butters from Vermont and Europe, house-made cheese spreads and salsas, and precut cheeses you can take right to the cash register if the line's too daunting.

For more on their pizza and bread see Pizza, page 207, and Bakeries, page 231.

Cowgirl Creamery at Tomales Bay Foods
Embarcadero
Ferry Building Marketplace
One Ferry Building, Shop 17
Embarcadero, at Market Street
(415) 362-9354

"Good cheese simply must start with good milk," emphasizes Peggy Smith, co-owner of Cowgirl Creamery. At the heart of Cowgirl's fragrant, subtle, and sometimes pungent cheeses often lies milk from the Straus

Family Creamery in West Marin County, which claims to be the first modern organic dairy west of the Mississippi.

Legend has it that when Smith and partner Sue Conley informed Ellen Straus of their desire to make cheese, she warned them, saying, "It's the Wild West out there, ladies." And so the former Chez Panisse chef and the one-time owner of Bette's Oceanview Diner in Berkeley became cowgirls, forming Tomales Bay Foods, the foundation of Cowgirl Creamery, in Point Reyes Station in 1997.

On-site production still takes place in Point Reyes under the experienced eye of Maureen Cunnie, an alumna of Greens, but the cowgirls moved the focus of their retail operations to the city and opened their flagship shop in San Francisco's Ferry Building.

Whether it's Abbaye de Belloc, a raw sheep's milk cheese made by Benedictine monks in the Western Pyrenees; Shelburne Farms Cheddar, a sharp Brown Swiss cow cheese made by a nonprofit environmental education center in Vermont; or the Cowgirl's Red Hawk, which won best of show at the American Cheese Society competition in 2003, you will be hooked on artisanal *fromage*. The milk they use, the technical expertise, and the careful, well-choreographed aging—all combine to produce cheeses that are worth every bit of their price tags.

You can sample Cowgirl cheeses at either location: the Ferry Building Marketplace or at their Point Reyes facility, where you can also watch cheese being made and then head for a hike along the coast, with a picnic of cheese in tow.

Other Location

80 Fourth Street, Point Reyes Station (Marin); (415) 663-9335; closed Monday and Tuesday; call ahead for cheesemaking schedule.

Cheese Plus
Russian Hill
2001 Polk Street, at Pacific Avenue
(415) 921-2001

When Leonard of Leonard's 2001 decided to hang up his hat after twelve years of purveying cheese and other premium larder goods to the Russian Hill neighborhood, Ray Bair jumped at the chance to take over the space. He left his nineteen-year career and post as West Coast regional director of cheese, wine, and specialty foods at Whole Foods to open something smaller and more personal. The focus is on American artisanal and farmstead cheeses. Currently in the store, in addition to our local favorites like the superfresh chèvre from Harley Farms in Pescadero, is Pleasant Ridge Reserve, a raw-milk Gruyère-style cheese from Uplands Dairy in

Wisconsin, and Schwarz and Weiss, a handmade raw-milk farmstead blue made by the Amish in Iowa. The Neal's Yard stable and other British and European producers are also well represented. Cheese Plus stocks wine, cured meats (like Alps prosciutto from New York), and carries on a Leonard's tradition of offering duck and pork *rillette* from Le Charm Restaurant. Take-out panini from the deli and a nice selection of dry goods put the *plus* in Cheese Plus.

The Pasta Shop
See Ethnic & Specialty Markets, page 251.

St. Benoit Yogurt
www.stbenoit.com

St. Benoit Yogurt is the dreamy yogurt dreamed up in 2003 by *frères* David and Benoît de Korsak. They brought the yogurt culture and style from France and make it from milk of local Jersey cows and local honey and organic fruit. They truly celebrate the idea of local: the milk travels less than two miles from cow to kitchen. And the yogurt is sold in beautiful, returnable, brown ceramic pots. The plain yogurt is delicious, but the Santa Rosa plum reigns supreme to me, even beating out the new honey flavor. St. Benoit has many fans at the Saturday Ferry Plaza Farmers Market. One market day a regular returned over fifteen pots, and restocked with the same number. That's consumption of just over two a day, and it's perfectly understandable.

PRODUCER PROFILE:
STRAUS FAMILY CREAMERY

A small herd of milk cows, grazing quietly on seasonal pasture overlooking the ocean, blissfully unaware that when the rainy season ends there is a stockpile of organic feed to tide them over. Is this a misty memory of how dairy farms used to be many years ago? Perhaps, but it is also the everyday reality at the Straus Family Farm, located where Highway 1 dips and curves along Tomales Bay north of San Francisco.

The Straus family has been dairy farming for more than sixty years on the same piece of land. About ten years ago, Albert Straus converted the dairy to produce organic milk and soon after established the creamery where the family now bottles the milk and produces a number of other products, including yogurt, ice cream, and cheeses.

This family leads the West Coast in sustainable dairy production. The cows never receive antibiotics or growth hormones. The occasional sick cow is treated with aspirin or homeopathic remedies. Heavy, old-fashioned returnable glass bottles are used for all their fluid milk products. The manure from the cows is turned into methane gas to generate electricity for the farm.

But how is the milk? It tastes just how we imagine milk should: fresh, rich, and flavorful. Many of the Bay Area's top restaurants use Straus milk, cream, and butter. Straus milk also goes into award-winning cheeses made by Cowgirl Creamery in Point Reyes. The milk is pasteurized but not homogenized, so remember to shake the bottle before pouring yourself a glass.

—Alan Tangren

ETHNIC & SPECIALTY MARKETS

Boulette's Larder
Embarcadero

Ferry Building Marketplace
One Ferry Building, Shop 48
Embarcadero, at Market Street
(415) 399-1177
www.bouletteslarder.com
For private dining information: (415) 399-1155

As you enter Boulette's Larder, you notice on your left a virtual pharmacy of spices, all housed in glass apothecary jars that occupy an entire wall. A sign above reads NOT FOR CONCEPTUAL USE ALONE.

And while Boulette's Larder is beautifully conceived, and it is a fantastic space—gorgeous open kitchen, a wonderful wood-burning hearth, a large farm table set for eighteen; in fact, it's hard to say where the kitchen ends and the retail space begins. It is first and foremost a working kitchen, and Co-Owners Amaryll Schwertner and Lori Regis want you to join in. "It's our larder and your larder, too," says Amaryll. It is as though they have a secret to share. Their eyes twinkle as they describe green almonds with a rare tenderness. Perhaps they are bathing in sensory memories, maybe of Schwertner's Hungarian grandmother, whose yeasted donuts fried early in the morning in lard and eaten with homemade butter and jam were simply a "normal breakfast."

There are limitless possibilities within the larder's philosophy; you can construct an entire meal from what they have whipped up that day or use the larder to supplement a meal of your own conception. On one counter, there are small terrines of pork and duck rillette, artisanal rices and sea salts, and Niman Ranch lardo. On another, a tall, fat jar of homemade pickles stands brining in a fennel solution. Stocks of every sort and a variety of pastry doughs are available daily, while take-out offerings might include a cassoulet in a terra cotta dish ready to be heated at home, a roasted pork loin, or a Niman Ranch filet mignon roast, which can be accompanied by a variety of vegetable dishes and salads. Pastries are exquisite, and if house-made ice cream is available, don't miss it.

This self-described café and "epicurian studio" is open for breakfast and lunch and available for private dinner parties at night, with the counters rolled back, the hearth lit, and the Bay Bridge twinkling outside. Schwertner and Regis are contemporary hunter-gatherers, serving up braised greens, poached farm eggs, and Hungarian cabbage rolls and extending an invitation to share their kitchen.

La Palma Mexicatessen

Mission

2884 24th Street, at Florida Street

(415) 647-1500

This shop on tree-lined 24th Street is the soul of the neighborhood. In the back, gathered around a huge *camal*, a handful of women expertly pat freshly ground masa into tortillas, *gorditas*, and *sopes*. These are some of the best around, and you can buy them still warm in bags of a dozen. The masa is ground in-house, and La Palma sells it to taquerias throughout the Mission. If you're interested in making tamales at home, stop by for a few pounds of the stuff. And you can pick up banana leaves or corn husks to wrap them in.

You also might want to check out the refrigerated cases against the wall, where they keep quart containers of house-rendered lard, slightly smoky and salty—entirely unlike that uncannily flavorless substance you find in the grocery stores. Or maybe you're looking for a block of *queso fresco* or *cotijo* cheese. Dry goods include bulk beans, chile peppers, rice, and spices, as well as their house-made chips.

There's a kitchen back by the camal, and I always look for the specials, such as the *lengua taquitos*—three tiny corn tortillas filled with tangy stewed beef tongue and topped with fresh spicy salsa. The tamales and *pupusas* (a Salvadoran specialty) are good. At La Palma you can get them filled with cheese, beans, or both, along with some crunchy *chicharrones* (pork cracklings).

La Raccolta
North Beach
521 Columbus Avenue, between Union and Green Streets
(415) 693-0199

La Raccolta is predominately a ceramics shop with painted platters, vases, teapots, and dinnerware from the various regions of Italy, and decorative tiles from the ancient floor-tile factory of Pinto. But walk to the back and you will find a full pantry of jams, honeys, olive oils, antipasti, condiments, sweets, and artisanal, handmade pastas. The foods have been crafted with age-old methods, sometimes by the families that have been making them for generations.

Lucca Delicatessen
Marina
2120 Chestnut Street, between Pierce and Steiner Streets
(415) 921-7873

Lucca is so perfect it could be a Hollywood stage set, possibly for some 1950s Roman sitcom. The narrow shop is bursting with imported ingredients and freshly made foods, including salads, deli meats, fresh pastas, and sauces. All the fixings for a proper picnic, or even a cozy supper with company, are available. The Italian frittata is superb.

Perhaps what makes Lucca so special is its rapport with the community. Many neighborhood homes have Lucca's ravioli, Bolognese sauce, and lasagna stored in their freezers. This is the type of place where the woman behind the counter, who was born only a few blocks away, will greet you with a "Good evening, darling. What can I get you?" And she'll follow your order with a quick recipe suggestion to make it even better.

Lucca Ravioli Company
Mission
1100 Valencia Street, at 22nd Street
(415) 647-5581
Closed Sunday

Lucca Ravioli on Valencia Street has one of the best Italian deli personalities in the Bay Area. *Salumi* hang from the rafters. A rectangular slab of seasoned marble, separating the cheese and meat cases, serves as the checkout counter. Sturdy sandwich rolls are stacked on a wooden shelf behind the counter, waiting for action. The staff—seemingly entirely male—wears white service coats and hats, and from 9:00 A.M. to 6:00 P.M. every day but Sunday they scuttle back and forth behind the counter, cutting and wrapping chunks of *teleme* and dry jack cheese and shearing paper-thin slices of proscuitto and *coppa* at the helm of the mighty stainless steel meat slicer. These guys are pros, and it's fun to watch them in action. They even give good cooking tips. Fresh pasta is made on site, and the pasta-making apparatus, located in a workroom behind the retail shop, is perennially under a snowdrift of flour.

Unless you don't mind a long wait, avoid coming here at lunch hour and on Saturdays, and when you enter, don't forget to take a number.

Mitsuwa Marketplace
675 Saratoga Avenue
San Jose   *SOUTH BAY*
(408) 255-6699

In the big refrigerator case at the front of the store you'll find all manner of maki sushi, bento boxes, *karaage* (fried chicken), cold soba-noodle salads, and even *oden,* the comfort food dish of simmered root vegetables and fish cake. The packaged prepared food (about $6) is made daily. But get there early for the best selection; the food is sold out usually by 6:00 P.M.

Load up at the small stand inside the store that serves big steaming bowls of ramen and udon. Or head to the fresh seafood department for a huge array of sushi-grade and sashimi-grade fish to take home.

Mitsuwa also stocks a large selection of Japanese ceramic plates, bowls, and cups, as well as chopsticks. As you comb the aisles, you'll spot wonderful gadgets such as sushi molds, bamboo mats, and graters that are perfect for using on daikon, ginger, or fresh wasabi root.

New World Market
Richmond
5641 Geary Boulevard, at 21st Avenue
(415) 751-8810

The impressive ethnic diversity of Inner Richmond is part of what makes a city like San Francisco so remarkable. New World Market is one of several dozen Russian and Eastern European delis situated on Geary Boulevard among the many Chinese and Korean shops and restaurants. Inside, this bustling market has the grandeur of those you might encounter along St. Petersburg's Nevsky Prospect, with high ceilings, ornate moldings, and maternal women in blue smocks behind the counter. Granted, New World is a much-updated version, though it still sells all the staples and delicacies that Russians depend on. The market's primary attraction is its deli case, bulging with house-cured and -smoked meats and fish. A glimmering whole smoked mackerel sits beside a tray of delicate cured sardines. The sausages and salamis range from the enormous knockwurst to the long and skinny *kabanisyt*. There are other, more exotic cured meats, like the jellied veal-tongue loaf set in aspic, or the *basturma* (dried beef). Along with rows of pickles and krauts imported from Eastern Europe, New World Market also sells tubs of their own pickled tomatoes, cucumbers, onions, and carrots and prepared foods like *pelmeni* and *piroshki*.

Nijiya Market
143 East El Camino Real
Mountain View   *SOUTH BAY*
(650) 691-1600

This is the place to pick up fixings for your next sushi party, satisfy your craving for *mochi,* or stop off for a bento box. A full-service market, Nijiya has just about everything in the way of Japanese ingredients.

There are six shelves in the refrigerator case alone stacked with different types of miso. Another couple of shelves are piled high with different varieties of rice. The large refrigerator case immediately to the left of the entrance holds fresh, prepackaged sushi, bento boxes of teriyaki chicken, grilled eel and *tonkatsu,* and an assortment of packaged pickled vegetables. There's even Spam *musub*—yes, Spam sushi, a favorite of Japanese Hawaiians—made fresh daily in big, palm-sized portions.

The produce aisle has everything from fresh *mitsuba* leaves and *enoki* mushrooms to *kabocha* squash and *gobo* (burdock root). And the meat/fish case offers precut pork loin for *shabu shabu,* as well as rectangles of *tamago* (egg omelette), plus portions of fresh broiled eel and trimmed fresh tuna, all ready for making sushi.

Nijiya has a whole aisle with every rice cracker imaginable, fresh udon noodles in the freezer case, and even Japanese magazines to brush up on your language skills.

Other Location
737 Post Street, San Francisco (Japantown); (415) 563-1901

The Pasta Shop
1786 Fourth Street, between Virginia Street and Hearst Avenue
Berkeley   *EAST BAY*
(510) 528-1786

The Pasta Shop is in many ways the quintessential gourmet and specialty food store. The deli case is well stocked with freshly rolled pasta, as well as house-made ravioli and tortellini. And they carry a wide selection of imported dry pastas. *Rusticella* is sold in bulk from cardboard bins in favorite varieties such as *strozzapreti, mangiango,* and *garganelli.*

There is a first-rate cheese counter featuring more than two hundred varieties of cheeses, primarily European varieties, but also a handful of locally made farmstead cheeses. The shop also has a wide variety of vinegars and olive oils. The latter are sold in individual bottles and in bulk from impressive steel canisters. Valrhona, Scharffen Berger, and Guittard chocolate, both in massive blocks and in shaved and chip form, are part of the inventory. Other baking supplies range from the very basic multi-colored sprinkles to the exotic and slightly mystifying gold-flaked cake strips. Are you in the mood for hot chocolate? Apparently someone is: there is an entire rack filled with charmingly packaged Swiss, French, Belgian, and Aztec cocoa mixtures. Teas from the famed Mariage Freres in Paris are sold in bulk, and they also offer jams and preserves, nut butters, tiny tins of cured fish, canned Italian tomato sauces, jars of cornichons and pearl onions, salts from every corner of the world, and dozens of beautiful candies. Every inch of this store is laden with these lovingly packaged and immodestly priced items.

Phoenix Pastaficio
1786 Shattuck Avenue
Berkeley   *EAST BAY*
(510) 883-0783

Phoenix Pastaficio is one of those special places that, when you first walk in, makes you feel like you have been a regular for years. The house-made pastas and breads are good solid fare, and Owner Eric Sartenaer and his staff seem to live to serve you as they shake their stuff to the '70s funk music that plays at a brave volume in the background.

Phoenix supplies many of the Bay Area's best restaurants with fresh pasta, while also managing to turn out baked goods, simple pasta lunches, and a satisfying espresso. The floor of the Shattuck Avenue storefront pasta factory is slippery with organic semolina flour. Huge, gleaming machines produce *bucatini* and spaghetti, cut pastas like linguine and tagliatelle, and ravioli with seasonally changing fillings. Sartenaer 's olive bread enjoys a cult following, and the platters of cookies, cakes, and perfect Danish that crowd the counter are fresh and irresistible. There are fine homemade sauces for sale, as well as a small selection of cheeses, olive oils, and vinegars.

At Phoenix you can stop in for an afternoon coffee and something sweet and leave with the makings for an extraordinary dinner. Phoenix's olive bread and pastas are also available at the Phoenix stall at each of the Berkeley Farmers' Markets locations (see Farmers' Markets, page 263).

Ranch 99

3288 Pierce Street, in the Pacific East Mall
Richmond   *EAST BAY*
(510) 769-8899

Ranch 99 is a taste of home for millions of Asian immigrants and Asian Americans. The chain started in 1984 outside Los Angeles. The store's owner, Roger Chen, saw the potential in the market and expanded his operation, which now includes more than twenty stores in California.

Fresh produce from California and around the world is for sale at reasonable prices, and the variety is stunning: bok choy and a plethora of Asian greens, bitter melons, radishes, persimmons, plums, durian, taro root, and so forth. Almost every Asian country is represented in the mix, and the store maintains departments for live seafood, freshly butchered meats, baked goods, dry goods, frozen foods, and even Asian cooking equipment.

If the sheer mass of items for sale overwhelms you, you can always take a break at the in-store snack bar and order something you've never tried before.

Samirami's

Mission
2990 Mission Street, at 26th Street
(415) 824-6555

Whether you are in need of sumac, couscous, or a new hookah, Samirami's is the place to go. For thirty-two years, owner Samir has held forth at the corner of Mission and 26th Street, providing a taste of the Middle Eastern bazaar. Choose between the Palestinian, Syrian, or

Lebanese *zather*. Find couscous in bulk, bags of lentils in several different colors, and just about any other dried legume you could think of (as well as many that you haven't). You'll see lots of bottled syrups; on a recent visit I counted five different brands of rose syrup. The roster of foodstuffs circles the Mediterranean, from Persian-style yogurt to sheep cheese from Greece and Turkey. There's a good selection of coffee and tea implements, plus Arabic-language newspapers, glossy gossip magazines, and a huge inventory of videos.

The Spanish Table
1814 San Pablo Avenue
Berkeley   *EAST BAY*
(510) 548-1383

Walking into this shop, you're met with a flood of sensations that will make you nostalgic for Spain, even if you've never been there before. The glint of sun reflecting off copper clam steamers, the smell of olive-wood utensils, the sound of Spanish guitar in the background—all these combine to create an almost reverential experience. The first Spanish Table store opened in 1995 by retired customs agent Steve Winston in Seattle. Winston's desire was to provide the ingredients necessary to recreate dishes from some of his memorable trips to Spain.

There are terra cotta *cazuelas,* the all-purpose cookware of Spain, and Portuguese chorizo roasters. The shelves are stocked with everything to fill your Spanish larder, like a dozen varieties of paprika (smoked and sun-dried, sweet, hot, and bitter), sherry vinegars, olive oils, heirloom dried beans, Valencia and Bomba rice, preserved vegetables in olive oil or brine, and countless cans of smoked and cured fish and shellfish.

The back of the store is devoted to wine, pans, and dishes. There are racks of sherry, port, Madeira, and table wines from across the Iberian Peninsula. Dozens of paella pans, ranging from single-serving pounded copper pans to five-foot-diameter stainless steel skillets for parties of three hundred or more, hang on the back wall.

Sunset Super
Outer Sunset
2425 Irving Street, between 25th and 26th Avenues
(415) 682-3738

The streets of Outer Sunset can sometimes seem a bit empty. It might be the fog, or it may be that all the action is inside Sunset Super. This market is always packed with merchandise and with people. It's a one-stop shopping place for Asian foodstuffs. In between the produce section and the fresh fish and meat markets, the aisles are chockablock with preserved foods of every variety, some identified only by Chinese characters. You'll find pickled kimchee in bulk, many different kinds of noodles, and jars of preserved tofu in a whole range of treatments. In fact, there are so many salted, pickled, dried, canned, and preserved items that despite being surrounded by such plenty, one can't help but reflect on the primal human instinct to put up food during times of harvest. Western items like ketchup and olive oil do appear here, and it is a great place to pick up spices on the cheap.

Zand's
See Middle Eastern, page 138.

NOTABLE

Eugene Market (Gateway Food Inc.)
900 Market Street, Suite B
Oakland   *EAST BAY*
(510) 208-3260

The Eugene Market (often called the New Eugene Market) addresses the relative dearth of produce and vegetables in this predominantly African-American neighborhood. In addition to standard household items, there is also a unique selection of Asian (particularly Korean) goods and prepared foods, such as various kimchees; sweet potato noodles with beef and vegetables *(jap chae);* and fish coated in flour, dipped in egg, and pan-fried *(jun).* A local traveler to Japan once complained that he could not find his favorite Japanese beverage upon returning stateside; after months of frustrated searching, he found it at the Eugene Market.

European Food Store
Richmond
3038 Clement Street, between 31st and 32nd Avenues
(415) 750-0504

This unassuming store in San Francisco's Richmond district is well stocked with Russian and Eastern European standards like bratwurst, frozen *pelmeni,* and *piroshki* (dumplings). An enormous kitchen in back churns out industrial-sized batches of stuffed cabbage rolls, beet salad, lamb stew, and Russian-style potato salad. Predictably there are rows of vodkas and tiny tins of caviar, but other, less expected items are the packages of "Putinskaya" sausages (with cutouts of the Russian president's head floating across the label) and minikegs of Baltica, a favorite Russian beer.

Guerra Meats and Deli
Forest Hills
490 Taraval Street, at 15th Avenue
(415) 564-0585

On a clear day you can see the ocean from this old-school Italian deli and meat market. Guerra's is owned by John Guerra and his two cousins, Paul and Robert Guerra, whose fathers started the business back in 1952. In addition to the deli and a tightly edited dry goods section emphasizing Italian standards such as tinned fish, capers, pasta, olive oil, and wine, Guerra's boasts a full-service butcher shop. You can easily pick up the mainstays for a multicourse dinner with a quick spin around Guerra's. Wild, in-season salmon or Alaskan halibut? Chicken from Fulton Valley Farms or lamb from Superior Farms in Dixon, and would you like that lamb legged, chopped, or fricasseed? Or what about some of their homemade sausages (we especially like the chicken apple)? If you're feeling a bit peckish, the homemade minestrone, navy bean, or other soup of the day will hit the spot.

Halal Food Market

1964 San Pablo Avenue
Berkeley *EAST BAY*
(510) 845-2000

Dried figs from Turkey, pickled thyme from Lebanon, and powdered sumac from Iran fill the shelves at this tidy and well-stocked Middle Eastern market on San Pablo Avenue. But the real treasures here are local. The butcher case at the back of the store contains organic chicken from Petaluma, and lamb and goat arrives twice a week from Sonoma and Stockton. The animals arrive whole, so look for the usually impossible-to-find lamb kidneys and liver. Proprietor Naiem Ayyad, who learned butchery from his grandfather in Palestine (and who is teaching his young son the trade), makes his own highly spiced *merguez* lamb sausage from a family recipe. All the meat, of course, is halal—slaughtered by hand according to Koranic laws. Ayyad's wife fries falafel several times a day and sells her own tabbouleh and hummus.

The Milk Pail

2585 California Street
Mountain View *SOUTH BAY*
(650) 941-2505

This is a European-style market with great selection and prices on cheeses, produce, and specialty items like croissants, empanadas, and freshly ground peanut butter. Some items are handmade by local producers. You'll find unhomogenized milk in glass bottles, Acme breads from Berkeley, and grains for sale in bulk. You will probably hear lots of different languages being spoken, especially Russian, which only adds to the cosmopolitan shopping experience.

 ## Mistral Rotisserie Provencale
Embarcadero

Ferry Building Marketplace
One Ferry Building, Shop 41
Embarcadero, at Market Street
(415) 399-9751

A small shop in the Ferry Building, Mistral is dominated by an immense rotisserie and a spectacular view of the bay, but the real attraction here is the simple but beautifully crafted food of Fabrice and Betty Marcon. It is a favorite place to stock up for a low-maintenance weekend: meltingly tender and roasted organic chickens, small Niman Ranch pork rib roasts, white beans, ratatouille, and hearty soups. Best of all is the potato confit, cooked slowly with garlic and onions at the bottom of the rotisserie. A changing selection of box lunches and drinks are available to take away or eat outside by the bay.

Molinari's Delicatessen
North Beach
373 Columbus Avenue, at Vallejo Street
(415) 421-2337
Closed Sunday

A little bit of old North Beach lives on at Molinari's, where you can find Italian cheeses, pastas, fresh ravioli, their own brand of *salumi,* and huge sandwiches. They also carry a wide array of Italian specialty foods, olive oils, and wines.

Parkside Farmers Market
Forest Hills
555 Taraval Street, at 16th Avenue
(415) 681 5563
Closed Sunday

Parkside stocks many Middle Eastern and Eastern European specialty food items, including many with labels that have no English description on them at all. They offer a wide selection of bulk olives at very good prices and some delicious but lesser-known olive oils, including one from Croatia. They don't carry much organic produce, but they do have unusual items like fava bean greens and fresh olives for curing at home.

Stonehouse Olive Oil
Embarcadero
Ferry Building Marketplace
One Ferry Building, Shop 28
Embarcadero, at Market Street
(415) 765-0405

Best known for their Olio Santo brand of cold-pressed olive oil, Stonehouse Olive Oil crushes olives from their orchards in Oroville. Both locations offer a full tasting bar featuring their award-winning oils.

Other Location
1717 Fourth Street, Berkeley (East Bay); (510) 524-1400

PRODUCER PROFILE:
JUNE TAYLOR COMPANY

While working as a baker for Oliveto, Paul Bertolli's legendary restaurant, June Taylor began experimenting with preserves. She started to sell her marmalades in the early nineties, produced exclusively from organic, sustainably grown fruits (with the exception of bergamot), mostly sourced from her fellow stall holders at the Ferry Building Farmers Market. What she can't find in the market she gets from organic farms and distributors in Southern California. Her preserves go well beyond the ordinary, with rare citrus like Buddha's Hand and the addition of various flower and herbs. The flavor combinations, such as Pluot and Lavender, are sometimes unexpected, but never gratuitous or muddled.

Taylor adds only the minimal amount of sugar that is required to best showcase the fruits' flavors. She and her assistant produce twenty thousand jars a year, in small batches of eight to ten jars, cooked the old-fashioned way in a stovetop kettle. Everything is done by hand, from chopping the fruit to jarring the hot preserves. Even the pectin she adds to the marmalades is handmade from citrus seeds and membranes.

Taylor makes everything from fruits poached in syrup to fruit butters and cheeses, but the clear standouts are the dozen marmalades, including a divine Bergamot and a zingy Silver Lime and Ginger. Her current favorite is the Seville Orange, which she suggests adding to mincemeat pies. The syrups, such as Boysenberry and Rose Geranium, make a lovely aperitif when added to a flute of Champagne or Prosecco.

You can find June Taylor and her marmalades at the Ferry Plaza Saturday market and at various stores around the Bay Area. For a list of stores that carry the preserves go to www.junetaylorjams.com. Or you can order by phone at (510) 548-2236.

—*Sarah Weiner*

BERKELEY'S INDIAN MARKETS

For many years, the Bazaar of India was Berkeley's one and only Indian grocery. Yet today, with the rapidly growing South Asian population drawn to the Bay Area for education, business, and employment, University Avenue and its cross streets now seem to be a magnet for shoppers from India, Pakistan, Bangladesh, and Sri Lanka.

San Francisco itself has nothing like this, so whenever I need to do serious shopping for Indian goods, it means a trip to the East Bay. Stock is always subject to the vagaries of export and import, so I go to all the groceries—Milan, Vik's, Bombay Spice House (formerly Bombay Bazaar), Bazaar of India, and the halal markets like Indus Market on San Pablo Avenue—until I find what I'm looking for.

All the groceries have a variety of basmati rice ranging from good to superlative; some offer regional favorites from Gujarat, such as *Surti kolam, ponni* from South India, Sri Lankan samba rice, or occasionally rice from Bangladesh. These stores offer good to excellent Indian and Sri Lankan brands of tea, and all of them sell spices, legumes, grains, and other necessities for South Asian domestic life, including devotional articles, cooking utensils, toiletries, and Ayurvedic medicines, plus books and videos, in some instances.

Milan has the advantage of staples in bulk: rice, wheat, other grains, legumes (like the various *dals*), and a wide range of spices (clove, cinnamon, chile powder, dried red chile, mustard seed, cumin, coriander, and so forth). Buying supplies in prepackaged units is fine as long as you know you can use them in a reasonable amount of time.

Once so hard to find, fresh curry leaves have become a standard offering. Other popular perishable items sought by South Asian cooks include bottle gourd, ivy gourd (*tendli* or *tindola*), bitter melon, guar beans, hot green chiles, fresh turmeric rhizomes, ginger, coconut, and yams. Milan, Vik's, and Bombay Spice House are all good resources for such items. If you see mangoes for sale—ripe for eating as is, or hard and green for pickles and relishes—you can be sure they've been vetted by critical buyers.

Look at the kitchen utensil section for well-priced, traditional handmade kitchen tools like granite mortars and pestles, wooden rolling pins and boards, iron griddles, or useful industrially produced stainless steel or copper ware in traditional shapes: trays *(thalis)*, containers, and cooking pots. Like rice, tea, and saffron and other spices, these things find a place in any kitchen or household, not just South Asian ones.

The owners and their assistants are usually happy to help the uninitiated, and prices are always reasonable.

—*Niloufer Ichaporia King*

FRESHLY MADE TOFU

These days most tofu sold is mass produced, vacuum packed, and woefully nondescript in texture and taste. But the tofu produced at the tiny San Jose Tofu Company is so rich and smooth, it's almost like custard. It's been made this way, all by hand, since 1946, when the Nozaki family first opened for business. Regulars have been coming here for years, as have tourists from Taiwan and Japan. Devotees swear that once you've had tofu this fresh, you'll never go back to the grocery-store variety again.

The yellow soybeans are soaked overnight in old soy sauce cans, then ground, boiled, and strained. The resulting liquid is mixed with a coagulant before being poured into wooden molds. It takes twenty hours to make one batch.

San Jose Tofu Company
175 Jackson Street
San Jose   *SOUTH BAY*
(408) 292-7026
Closed Sunday; cash and checks only

FARMERS' MARKETS

Alemany Farmers' Market
Bernal Heights

100 Alemany Boulevard .
(415) 647-9423
Saturday 6:00 A.M. to 5:00 P.M.

Alemany Farmers' Market was founded in 1943 as a wartime measure, providing an outlet for surplus crops from the farms of surrounding areas. In 1945 the voters of San Francisco overwhelmingly decided to make it permanent, and it continues to be an invaluable outlet for more than one hundred small farmers and producers and an incredibly diverse crowd of shoppers.

The variety here is astounding. Eggplants, cucumbers, and herbs in an untold number of varieties from Hmong, Chinese, and Vietnamese farmers; chile peppers still on the bush; and bounteous quantities of whatever is in season, whether it be daikon, cabbage, or stone fruit from the family-run Bellaviva Orchards, one of the founding vendors of the market. This is community-supported agriculture, and though the emphasis is not on organic, there are a handful of certified organic vendors scattered throughout. If you're lucky, you might even cross paths with the fisherman from down the coast who comes with a barrel of seawater and live Santa Barbara spot prawns to sell from the back of his truck.

Every Sunday a flea market is held here.

Berkeley Farmers' Market
Berkeley   *EAST BAY*

(510) 548-3333
www.ecologycenter.org
Tuesday 2:00 P.M. to 7:00 P.M., Derby Street at Martin Luther King Jr. Way
Saturday 10:00 A.M. to 3:00 P.M., Center Street at Martin Luther King Jr. Way
Thursday 3:00 P.M. to 7:00 P.M., Shattuck Avenue at Rose Street

Shoppers at the Berkeley market are notoriously demanding about quality and price, and buyers from San Francisco's better restaurants often cross the bridge to shop at this market. In fact, the market is often so full of chefs that you may feel like a co-conspirator in the California food revolution.

But don't buy the first thing you see: Make at least one pass through the market, then start devising a dinner plan. The tomatoes looked good at Full Belly Farm, but did you sample the Costoluto Genovese variety at the Riverdog stand? Or the Sungolds at Tip Top? You might have to buy all of them. Didar at Guru Ram Das Orchards has apricots that look a shade green, but they are selling fast. Did that sign say $9 a pound for almonds? That can't be right! On the other hand, what is the crunchiest, sweetest

almond on earth worth to you? Not everything is so expensive—during the height of the season most of the produce is abundant and cheap. Often, toward the end of the day, you can work out some amazing bargains. Come to the market regularly and you will begin to wonder why any restaurant would consider serving out-of-season, nonorganic produce.

If you want to fit in at the Berkeley market scene, bring your Mexican shopping bag (save the French basket for the Ferry Plaza), plenty of used plastic bags for small items, some dollar bills for the guy singing old Clash songs, and a pen to sign petitions. And be aware. Read the charts posted at each stand to make sure what you buy was grown with principles you stand behind. Not all the farms are organic, with the exception of those at the smaller Thursday summer market on Shattuck.

Ferry Plaza Farmers Market
Embarcadero

Located along the Embarcadero, at the end of Market Street
(415) 291-3276
www.cuesa.org
Tuesday 10:00 A.M. to 2:00 P.M. (year-round); Thursday 4:00 to 8:00 P.M.; Saturday 8:00 A.M. to 2:00 P.M. (year-round); Sunday 10:00 A.M. to 2:00 P.M.

The highest-profile, most exquisite, and most controversial farmers' market in the Bay Area takes places every Saturday at the beautifully restored Ferry Building on San Francisco Bay. This is San Francisco's piazza; it's a place where friends meet weekly and make their way through the best selection of prime local organic produce, flowers, grass-fed beef, and artisanal cheeses the area has to offer.

This is the market that makes European visitors and New Yorkers swoon. It is where Alice Waters can be found most Saturday mornings, along with other noted chefs. Here you will find locally famous farmers, selling their breathtaking produce in person. And one of the city's great pleasures is eating a Mexican breakfast or an oyster po'boy at picnic tables right on the bay, with a view of the Bay Bridge. If you don't find everything you need, the Ferry Building Marketplace, with it's collection of food shops, will provide the rest.

But why the controversy? Along with the carefully regulated quality—both in terms of taste and sustainability—and the unsurpassed traceability of products sold here, the prices are undeniably high. But this food is grown by farmers who care for the land and provide greenbelts for the urban Bay Area. There is no one we'd rather give our money to.

Smaller versions of this market take place on Tuesdays, Thursdays, and Sundays. For seasonal schedules visit www.cuesa.org.

Grand Lake Farmers' Market

Grand Avenue and Lakepark Way, across from the Grand
Lake Theater

Oakland   *EAST BAY*

(415) 456-3276

Saturday 9:00 A.M. to 2:00 P.M.

Situated between the restored Grand Lake Theater and Lake Merritt, this
is one of the most vibrant farmers' markets in the East Bay. Among the
fifty or so vendors, along with the usual kettle corn, you'll find a good
number of organic farmers. Search out Tip Top's organic Lipstick Sweet
peppers or Sungold cherry tomatoes picked when perfectly ripe. Live Oak
farm, based in the fertile Capay Valley, grows beautiful salad greens, and in

the fall they pick and bag walnuts for sale. Suzane Fish Company, run by a fifth-generation fisherman from Bodega Bay, sells Dungeness crab November through March and wild king and Chinook salmon from May to October—both caught in the waters right off the coast.

Heart of the City Farmers' Market
Tenderloin

United Nations Plaza, corner of Market and 7th Streets
(415) 558-9455
Wednesday 7:00 A.M. to 5:30 P.M.; Sunday 7:00 A.M. to 5:00 P.M.

The bustling Heart of the City market, on United Nations Plaza just down from City Hall, stretches along the walking street from the new main public library to Market Street. In the middle of Tenderloin grit, this market is a celebration of the glorious diversity of the city. Live chickens, fresh fish, mountains of produce, Asian varietals that are rarely spotted in grocery stores, and hordes of serious shoppers make this a highly charged experience. There are a handful of organic growers, but most are conventional and prices tend to be low.

Mandela Farmers' Market
7th Street and Mandela Parkway
Oakland   *EAST BAY*
www.mobetterfood.com
Saturday 10:00 A.M. to 4:00 P.M.

It's no surprise that the area's poorest sections also have the least access to real food. Similar in concept to the People's Grocery (see page 253), the Mandela Farmers' Market aims for food justice: to make high-quality, locally grown organic food available to the people who have the least access to it. Mandela Farmers' Market does a beautiful job of this by connecting black farmers like Mr. Musgrave and Mr. Robinson with neighborhood shoppers.

Old Oakland Farmers' Market
9th Street, between Broadway and Clay Street
Oakland   *EAST BAY*
(510) 745-7100
Friday 8:00 A.M. to 2:00 P.M.

This is a classic certified farmers' market. The products are seasonal, but not necessarily organic. The proximity to Chinatown translates into long beans, a half-dozen varieties of eggplant, pea greens, bitter melons, bok choy, and a huge collection of herbs.

Marin Farmers' Market
Marin County Civic Center
Civic Center Drive
San Rafael   *MARIN*
(415) 456-3276
www.marincountyfarmersmarkets.org
Open year-round, Thursday and Sunday 8:00 A.M. to 1:00 P.M.

In the shadow of the space-age Marin Civic Center, one of Frank Lloyd Wright's last buildings, the Marin Farmers' Market rivals the Ferry Plaza market for the selection and quality of its produce. A county with a deep agricultural heritage, Marin is home to many of the Bay Area's organic farmers. You'll find them here selling pristine produce, alongside grass-fed-beef ranchers, honey producers, flower vendors, and seafood purveyors from the area. Many of the farmers who sell here can also be found at the Berkeley and the San Francisco farmers' markets.

LOCAL PRODUCERS

The farmers in the Bay Area are the basis for so many groundbreaking restaurants. Here are some of our favorite producers:

Andante Dairy: handmade cheeses

Avalos Farm: fava beans, cilantro, and jalapeño peppers

B 'n' B: eggs

Basic Soy: organic tofu

Blue Bottle: organic coffee (see Coffee Shops & Teahouses, page 173)

Blue Heron: tiny scallions, Little Gem lettuce, and carrots

Cocina Primavera: tortillas and tamales (see Mexican, page 118)

Dirty Girl Farm: little green beans, radishes, and dry-farmed
  Early Girl tomatoes

Ella Bella: raspberries, blackberries, and strawberries

Fairview Gardens: Charentais melon, asparagus, and haricots vert

Fatted Calf: charcuterie, including *rillettes* and *salumi*
  (see Meat & Fish Markets, page 271)

Four Sisters Farm: kiwifruit, watercress, and roses

Frog Hollow: peaches and nectarines

Full Belly Farm: Bintje new potatoes, eggplant, any winter squash

Guru Ram Das Orchards: white peaches, apricots, and almonds

Happy Boy Farm: garden cress, and arugula

Kaki Farms: persimmons and walnuts

Kashiwase Farm: Flavor King pluots and Emerald Beaut plums

Kennedy Farm: cherries and blueberries

Knoll Farms: arugula, figs, and green garlic

Lagier Ranches: cherries, berries, Bronx grapes, and almonds

La Tercera: shelling beans and winter squash

Lucero Farm: Costata Romanesco zucchini and strawberries

Mariquita: Erbette chard, Broccoli di Cicco, basil, and tomatoes

Riverdog Farm: shelling peas, asparagus, tomatoes, and
  Cavolo Nero (Tuscan kale)

Sebastopol Berry Farm: berries

Star Route Farms: shelling beans, escarole, and frisée

Swanton Berry Farm: strawberries

Terra Firma Farm: garlic, tomatoes, corn, and grapefruit

Tierra Vegetables: smoked chiles

Tip Top Farm: okra, ground cherries, garlic scapes, and soybeans

Tunitas Creek Apiaries: honey

Twin Girls: nectarines and pluots

White Crane: beautiful flowers and greens

Woodleaf Produce: peaches and nectarines

GROCERIES & PRODUCE MARKETS

Berkeley Bowl
2020 Oregon Street, at Adeline Street
Berkeley   *EAST BAY*
(510) 843-6929

Loyal shoppers from all over the Bay Area make their way to the Berkeley Bowl supermarket, crowding the always chaotic parking lot and jostling for cart space in the aisles inside. Nearly everyone considers this market their own—black, white, Indian, Mexican, Chinese, the prosperous and the poor all shop side by side, and it's easy to see why.

The Bowl's produce section is reputedly the largest in Northern California. Depending on the season you might find *gai lan* and sweet pea shoots, green chickpeas still on the branch, Persian cucumbers, freshwater chestnuts, one or two dozen varieties of citrus, galangal, matsutake mushrooms, jackfruit, and juneberries. And although locally grown organic produce makes a respectable showing, some rightfully protest that local farms could be better represented.

The bulk section sells everything from organic flours and sea salt to French lentils and Thai black rice. The crush of shoppers ensures the bins are replenished often, making this an affordable way to stock up on fresh staples and fragrant spices.

Behind the enormous meat counter, the staff butchers will gladly bisect a Niman Ranch pork shoulder for you on the band saw, or slice local Western Grasslands grass-fed beef thin enough for sukiyaki. Likewise, you can watch as the fishmongers fillet whole salmon or halibut behind the seafood counter.

The third-generation Japanese owners keep a well-stocked Asian-food section with locally made *mochi*, a half-dozen varieties of tofu, local Japanese pickles, and freshly made Chinese noodles. The Bowl carries bread from Bay Area bakeries and dairy from local creameries like Straus (whose organic milk comes in beautiful, old-fashioned glass bottles; see page 246).

Bi-Rite Market
Mission
3639 18th Street, between Guerrero and Dolores Streets
(415) 241-9760

Bi-Rite has been serving the needs of its neighborhood since 1940, but never with such aplomb as when Sam Mogannam and his brother Raphael took it over in 1998. They revamped the space, adding a kitchen and an expanded deli counter that offers not only prepared foods, but fresh,

thoughtfully chosen meats and seafood. Expect to find first-of-the-season wild local halibut and Pacific King salmon (and flash-frozen wild salmon in the off-season) alongside various cuts of Niman Ranch beef and pork. Sausages and the smoked salmon are made in-house, as are the cakes and cookies by Anne Walker, Mogannam's wife.

Bi-Rite boasts a fine selection of artisanal cheeses, many locally made like Red Hawk and St. Pat's from Cowgirl Creamery, as well as a wide assortment of affordably priced wine. Much of the produce is organically grown, and the Mogannams' parents provide the store with apples, figs, and kiwi from their farm in Placerville.

Monterey Foods
1550 Hopkins Street
Berkeley   *EAST BAY*
(510) 526-6042

Home to everything from Buddha's Hand citron to Oregon white truffles, fresh lychee nuts, organic Bing cherries, and *nopales* (cactus pads), Monterey Market is the region's largest produce market.

Go during the rainy fall and winter for wild porcini and chanterelles. In the spring you will find the sweetest cherries and tropical mangoes and pineapples. Summer brings tomatoes in countless colors, at least half a dozen varieties of eggplant, and enough melons, figs, and berries to make your head spin. Each week in the fall a new variety of mandarin orange or grapefruit seems to show up.

The Fujimoto family has had a market in this neighborhood for more than forty years, and today the guiding force is Bill Fujimoto, the son of the founders. Fujimoto loves to buy produce that is difficult to find elsewhere— he says that if it exists, someone will want it. But more importantly, Bill values his role as a link between the farmer and consumer. He's constantly on the phone with farmers from all over California. He knows what each one grows particularly well, which varieties they have, and how they take care of their crops and the land.

Looking across the parking lot, a sharp-eyed shopper might spy Bill chatting with local farmer Al Courchesne about his peaches from Frog Hollow Farm in Brentwood, Tim Bates about Sierra Beauty apples from the Apple Farm in Mendocino, or Ignacio Sanchez about pluots and satusma mandarins from Twin Girls Farm in the San Joaquin Valley.

People's Grocery
West Oakland BART Station
3625 Market Street
Oakland   *EAST BAY*
Saturday 10:00 A.M. to 2:00 P.M.

West Oakland is home to twenty-five-thousand people and a single grocery store. Riding the border between downtown Oakland and its enormous shipping port, this low-income neighborhood of beautiful rambling Victorian homes tempts gentrification. In stark contrast to neighboring Berkeley's wealth of organic and natural grocers, farmers' markets, and specialty purveyors, this community is compelled to shop at heavily gated liquor stores, where staples like milk and bread are overshadowed by cigarettes and long-distance phone cards.

Enter the booming orange-and-purple People's Grocery truck—this biodiesel delivery vehicle makes stops all over the neighborhood, selling everything from organic snacks to the after-school crowd to rice and greens for family meals. Staffed by youth from the neighborhood and furnished with beautiful handmade wooden market boxes filled with local oranges, walnuts, and lettuce, this truck also thumps! When asked about the sound system on a recent visit, People's Grocery member Aswad proudly stepped away from arranging the neat rows of produce to turn the solar-powered stereo way up.

Emphatically local in outlook, the grassroots People's Grocery works for food justice—good food for local people, grown and produced by the same, regardless of economics. Founded three years ago by residents Brahm Amadi and Malaika Edwards, the organization sells fresh fruits and vegetables from local school and community gardens, bulk grains, and fresh bread at prices subsidized to compete with the corner store. Not only are the foods locally grown, but the People's Grocery is grounded in the cultures of West Oakland. Hip-hop music and graffiti style; the legacy of the Black Panther party; industrial artists working in the area's warehouse studios; and generations of Asian, African, and Latino families are all reflected in both the foods and flavor of this deliciously just program.

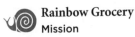

Rainbow Grocery
Mission

1745 Folsom Street, at 13th Street

(415) 863-0620

If your first impression of the thirty-thousand-square-foot store at the fringe of the Mission is that it's a bit funky, relax. Once inside, the vast selection of organic foods and housewares will strike you as nothing short of fabulous. The worker-owned cooperative is known for astute buying and fair prices, particularly for bulk foods.

Handcrafted treasures abound: wood-fire-roasted organic sesame tahini from Turkey; preserved lemons and roasted artichokes sold in bulk; aged, organic Carnaroli rice for risotto; sheep's-milk yogurt; artisanal honeys. There's a giant selection of great teas and coffees, herbs, and locally made breads and treats. In fact, the store seems to sell everything except meat and fish.

NOTABLE

Berkeley Natural Grocery
1336 Gilman Street

Berkeley   *EAST BAY*

(510) 526-2456

Open Monday through Wednesday 9:00 A.M. to 8:00 P.M.

Berkeley Natural is what in another era would have been called a health food store. It is a small, privately owned, user-friendly store in North Berkeley and a great alternative to the craziness of Berkeley Bowl and the corporate feel of Whole Foods. It also has the advantage of having exclusively organic produce—much of it from the same farmers who sell at the Berkeley Farmers' Market. There is a good-sized bulk-foods section for dry goods, a daily delivery from Acme Bread, and a range of dairy products from Straus Family Creamery.

Other Location

El Cerrito Natural Grocery (Berkeley Natural's sister store), 10367 San Pablo Avenue, El Cerrito (East Bay); (510) 526-1155

Good Earth Natural Foods
1966 Sir Francis Drake Boulevard

Fairfax   *MARIN*

(415) 454-0123

Home to some of the some of the best organic produce to be found at retail in the Bay Area, Good Earth has been serving the small and progressive town of Fairfax since 1969. Each day the wood-fired oven turns out rustic pizzas, whole-grain breads, and top-shelf pastries (fresh fruit tarts, sweet rice cookies, and so forth). After a visit to the juice bar, you'll feel like you had a transfusion, not a drink. Throughout the store there are gems—heirloom grains, fabulously fresh fish, and delectable provisions for a picnic if you're heading out to the coast for the day.

Good Life Grocery
Potrero Hill
1524 20th Street
(415) 282-9204

Good Life Grocery is an extraordinary neighborhood grocery store offering many organic products, including Rosie's chickens and Niman Ranch meats. It also seems to serve as the neighborhood community center, especially in Bernal Heights.

Other Location
448 Cortland Avenue, San Francisco (Bernal Heights);
   (415) 648-3221

Speedy's New Union Grocery
Embarcadero/Telegraph Hill
301 Union Street, at Montgomery Street
(415) 781-6168

Speedy's has a little bit of everything—grass-fed beef, organic chicken, a gourmet deli, nice produce, unique regional products and juices, old charm, and great classical music. The young, personable owners are clearly connected with local producers and farmers. One of the owners makes homemade desserts, preserves, and pickles, adding a warm, personal touch to the place. They have a good wine and cheese selection for a small store. Prices are a little higher, due to location and quality, but it's great to have a corner store that carries organic eggs and heirloom tomatoes.

Star Grocery
3068 Claremont Avenue
Berkeley   *EAST BAY*
(510) 652-2490

Owner Nick Pappas cares about his customers, community, vendors, and the planet. In return Star's customers have an unusually strong commitment to the store. After the Oakland Hills firestorm destroyed the homes of many of Star's customers, one resident said, "Losing our neighborhood was bad, but if we lost Star . . . that would have been horrible."

On a May morning, a handwritten sign on the front door informed passersby that the first Frog Hollow peaches were expected that afternoon. You'll also find local produce from such growers as Full Belly Farm, Blue Heron Farm, and T&D Willey Farms. Beyond local produce, Star offers almost anything the average family would buy at a large supermarket. Among this standard fare, you still might come across some surprises. The store's extensive selection of chocolates includes smaller brands without major distribution outside Berkeley, like Lisa Lerner's gorgeous chocolate-covered tuile wafers or Carnival Chocolates, made in Oakland. Also look for jars of June Taylor jams and preserves (see page 259).

Valencia Whole Foods
Mission

999 Valencia Street, at 21st Street
(415) 285-0231

With no relation to the national chain, Valencia Whole Foods stocks organics—from produce to groceries—at their best. There is a delicious fresh salad bar at one end, and both staples and specialty items take up the rest of the store. Everyone who works here is so warm and friendly that you'll end up feeling like family in no time and will come back again and again.

Village Market
Richmond

4555 California Street, at 8th Avenue
(415) 221-0445

Village Market is a corner store with just the right mix of dry goods, organic produce, and nicely priced, interesting wines. There's even a café where you can enjoy an espresso or a cup of tea.

Other Location

Ferry Building Marketplace, One Ferry Building, Shop 29,
   Embarcadero at Market Street, San Francisco (Embarcadero);
   (415) 989-9200

ICE CREAM, CHOCOLATE & CONFECTIONERY

ICE CREAM

 Fairfax Scoop
63 Broadway Boulevard

Fairfax   *MARIN*
(415) 453-3130

The tiny Fairfax Scoop serves up all-organic, handmade ice cream and fruit sorbets. They start with organic dairy products from the local Straus Family Creamery and incorporate locally grown fruits and nuts into their seasonal flavors. Although their vanilla and chocolate are compelling, honest flavors, try one of the imaginative specials, like Honey Lavender. Everything is made in small batches, including the cones. They even offer frozen soy treats for vegans. You'll feel like a kid again as you wait in the long line that often stretches out the door and down the street.

Mitchell's Ice Cream
Bernal Heights
688 San Jose Avenue, at 29th Street
(415) 648-2300

Though located on that awkward, hard-to-find strip of San Jose Avenue where Mission and Valencia merge, neighborhood kids and adults alike know exactly where Mitchell's is. They've been coming to Mitchell's for ice cream since 1953. Its old-fashioned menu board lists which of the dozens of flavors are available that day. The shop offers standards like strawberry, coffee, and rum raisin (made with Bacardi rum) and tropical flavors too, like cantaloupe and mango. They even have an avocado ice cream. While it's disappointing to see that gum, corn sweetener, and some mono- and diglycerides have sneaked into the base recipe alongside the cream, milk, eggs, and sugar (though these substances make up less than 0.3 of 1.0 percent by volume), Mitchell's ice cream is still worth a trip. The ice creams are available by the cup or by the cone in both standard or waffle format. Mitchell's milk shakes are also recommended.

 ## Sketch
1809A Fourth Street, at Hearse Street
Berkeley   *EAST BAY*
(510) 665-5650
Cash only

It is immediately clear on walking into this diminutive storefront on Fourth Street in Berkeley that this shop is the product of many carefully made decisions. The owners of Sketch—Eric Shelton and Ruthie Planas, who met in the pastry kitchen at Aqua—are earnest in their undertaking, and their passion is inspiring. The ice cream case displays more than a dozen options, some conventional, like vanilla bean and chocolate, and some surprising, like the plain yogurt flavor, with a tanginess that is uncommon in most ice creams. There are other uncommon flavors too, like basil, Earl Grey, or lemon verbena granita. They use organic Straus Family Creamery milk, as well as local organic fruit and organic coffee.

Folks with a more intense ice cream appetite might consider topping a freshly made waffle with their favorite flavor or, for that matter, have it sandwiched between two cookies, also freshly made. For the sweet tooth on the run, there are packaged confections like meringues, cookies, and caramels—all made right here.

Sketch's prices are noticeably higher than those at run-of-the-mill ice cream parlors, but considering the ingenuity, care, and attention that the two young proprietors put into their products and the constantly changing menu, you should consider it money well spent. This is a chance to broaden your ice cream horizons.

Swensen's
Russian Hill
1999 Hyde Street, at Union Street
(415) 775-6818
Closed Monday; cash only

This tiny corner ice cream shop on the top of Russian Hill is the birthplace of Swensen's Ice Cream. In 1982 when Earle Swensen sold the rights to his name and recipes as a franchise, he requested that this flagship store not be included in the corporate holdings. Lucky us! They still make all the ice cream here, right in the front window. Not that you need to see just how much cream and eggs are used in each gallon.

San Franciscans and tourists alike make a pilgrimage to the top of Russian Hill for old-fashioned flavors such as lemon custard, strawberry, and mocha fudge swirl. Seasonal offerings include pumpkin and spumoni. The Walk Away sundae, a large waffle cone piled high with whipped cream, nuts, and a cherry, is an especially nice treat after traversing hills and riding cable cars.

CHOCOLATE & CONFECTIONERY

Benkyo-do
Japantown
1747 Buchanan Street, at Sutter Street
(415) 922-1244
Closed Sunday

You may be distracted by the smells of coffee and hot dogs in this small Japantown shop, but the real reason to go to Benkyo-do is for their *okashi*, traditional Japanese sweets. Brothers Ricky and Bobby Okamura make the *mochi*-and-adzuki bean delicacies by hand every morning from family recipes passed down since the shop's original opening ninety-nine years ago. They are perfect with green tea, as Japanese tea ceremony teachers and practitioners will attest, but the velvety, mildly sweet morsels are delicious anytime.

Fleur de Cocoa
See Bakeries, page 233.

Joseph Schmidt Confections
Castro
3489 16th Street, at Sanchez Street
(415) 861-8682

Joseph Schmidt defined the modern American truffle, and his trademark egg-shaped confections are available at his tiny flagship store on the quiet corner of 16th and Sanchez Streets. While the assorted truffles, almond bark, and chocolate bars are beautiful, the ornate seasonal chocolate sculptures are truly impressive. Some days huge vases of chocolate tulips sit behind the counter; others find paper-thin faux-wooden bowls filled with faux fruit. On Valentine's Day and Easter the store is positively rococo in cocoa.

Michel Richart
Union Square
393 Sutter Street, at Stockton Street
(415) 291-9600

When Michel Richart first opened on Sutter Street, next door to Wilkes Bashford, I nearly walked right past it. I thought it was a jewelry store. What looked like carats in the window were actually tiny cubes of chocolate from Richart's recent collection, "Spirit of Originality." Each chocolate square was intricately decorated with patterns ranging from subdued to positively phantasmagorical. They are infused with essences from seven flavor families: balsamic, roasted, fruity, citrus, herbal, floral, and spiced. Richart loves to pair chocolate in the same way you would match wine with food, and each flavor family offers seven different combinations.

Richart, who is the original chocolate designer, comes from the French chocolate hub of Lyon. He's a purist and insists that his chocolate have single-bean varietal origins. For most of his confections he uses a 73 percent Venezuelan chocolate because, as he says, "it is strong but not aggressive." His original collection, though, is beautifully restrained: thin squares of chocolate, each simply embossed with the cacao's region of origin and percentage of concentration.

Recchiuti Confections
Embarcadero
Ferry Building Marketplace
One Ferry Building, Shop 30
Embarcadero, at Market Street
(415) 834-9494

Michael and Jacky Recchiuti's shop in the Ferry Building is, for many, the chocolate epicenter of San Francisco. Confectionery visionaries, their penchant for fine taste is evident in everything they touch, from their sweets and packaging to their handsome little shop.

Recchiuti's palate includes fresh herbs from local farmers, delicate infusions from tea and flowers, and the world's best chocolate, including single-origin varietal chocolates. S'mores, brownies, and caramels—usually low on the hierarchy of treats—are reinvented and displayed side by side with the classic, unexpected, and always beautiful boxed chocolates. Don't miss the Fleur de Sel Caramels.

Richard Donnelly Chocolates

1509 Mission Street, at Trescony Street
Santa Cruz   *SOUTH BAY*
(888) 685-1871
Closed Monday

Richard Donnelly dropped out of law school to follow his culinary passion at La Varenne in Paris. He later apprenticed with Robert Linxe, who developed Valrhona chocolate, and moved to Santa Cruz, where he opened his eponymous shop. His chocolates will make you swoon. They're all hand-made, hand-dipped, and hand-wrapped. Candy bars are a best-seller and come in such flavors as Dark Chocolate Ginger, Milk Chocolate Cappuccino, and Pure Dark Chocolate. And don't forget the Liquor Bombs: fine dark chocolate balls filled with Germain Robin brandy, Patrón anejo tequila, Cointreau, wine, rum, or mixed drinks. They all come wrapped in gorgeous rice paper or in glassine bags made in France.

Scharffen Berger

914 Heinz Avenue, at 7th Street
Berkeley   *EAST BAY*
(510) 981-4050
www.scharffenberger.com

These days, it seems like Scharffen Berger chocolate is everywhere: on dessert menus across the country, at upscale markets, even at newsstands. Recently it was even spotted on the menu of the trendy Milanese restaurant Lovenfood.

Scharffen Berger specializes in dark chocolate, offering bars with a variety of cocoa-solid levels, from the 62 percent semisweet to the 82 percent extradark. A new addition to the factory's offerings is a 41 percent milk chocolate bar, and a standby favorite is the Nibby bar, which is the 62 percent semisweet bar with bits of cocoa nibs mixed in for an intense crunch.

A visit to the modern factory in Berkeley's warehouse district is a perfect way to spend a lazy Sunday, followed perhaps by a little snack at the adjacent Café Cacao. There are free guided tours of the factory, and reservations can be made easily through the Web site. There is also a retail out-let at the San Francisco Ferry Building. In 2005 Sharffen Berger was aquired by Hershey's. We hope they don't change a winning formula.

Shuei-Do Manju Shop

217 East Jackson Street, between 5th and 6th Streets
San Jose   *SOUTH BAY*
(408) 294-4148
Closed Monday; cash only

When this Japanese confectionery store opened in 1951, it was the only shop of its kind between San Francisco and Los Angeles. Even now it remains a rarity, one of only three *manju* shops in Northern California. The amount of work required to create these handmade, hand-shaped pastries is largely the reason why.

The *manju* made at this shop are elaborately decorated, steamed *mochi* confections. They are filled with a custard of either red adzuki beans or baby lima beans and are an integral part of Japanese holidays, weddings, funerals, and other special occasions. Owners Tom and Judy Kumamaru make all fourteen different varieties of *manju* themselves—eight hundred to two thousand pieces a day. One batch can take ten hours from start to finish.

PRODUCER PROFILE:
THE BAY AREA'S LONGTIME
LOVE AFFAIR WITH CHOCOLATE

In the mid-1800s, under the spell of the Gold Rush, two small chocolate companies, Ghirardelli Chocolate and Guittard, set up businesses in the new city of San Francisco. With a temperate climate and an international port, the area was a smart choice for chocolate makers. A century and a half later, while Ghirardelli has been sold to the multinational Lindt Company, Guittard is still family owned and still producing chocolate in San Francisco.

Etienne Guittard had already studied chocolate making with his uncle outside Lyon, France, when at age twenty-two he was drawn by stories of the Gold Rush and boarded a ship for California in 1860. He brought some of his uncle's chocolates to trade for supplies. Three years later he gave up on finding gold in the Sierra and, at the urging of newly wealthy miners in San Francisco, he decided to open a shop on Sansome Street in 1868. Today Guittard is the oldest family-owned chocolate company in America and is well known as a supplier of chocolate to many large and small customers. In 2001 Gary Guittard, the company's fourth-generation president, launched his E. Guittard artisan line to honor Etienne. The E. Guittard collection includes both cooking and eating chocolates and is distinguished for its rare, single-origin varietal chocolates from around the world. Visit www.eguittard.com or call (800) 468-2462 for more information.

XOX Truffles
North Beach
754 Columbus Avenue, between Greenwich and Filbert Streets
(415) 421-4814

You'll have no trouble exceeding the recommended daily allowance of health-promoting chocolate flavonoids at XOX. These perfectly proportioned truffles, a tad bigger than a marble, make it much too easy to rationalize eating more than you should at any one sitting. The hazelnut, rum, and simple dark chocolate truffles remain my favorites, but there are more than twenty types to choose from. These bedeviling confections are all produced by Jean-Marc Gorce at his small shop on lower Columbus Avenue. Gorce hails from Valence, deep in the heart of French chocolate country. "Traditionally," he says, "we make these truffles for after Christmas dinner. You serve them with the coffee and then you play cards." A charming tradition, to be sure, but why wait for Christmas?

MEAT & FISH MARKETS

 Berkeley Bowl
See *Groceries & Produce Markets, page 270.*

 Bi-Rite Market
See *Groceries & Produce Markets, page 270.*

 Café Rouge Butcher Shop
1782 Fourth Street, at Virginia Street
Berkeley   *EAST BAY*
(510) 525-1440

Marsha McBride's celebrated butcher shop is surprisingly small considering the range of meat she sells. In the case against the back wall of the
restaurant you'll find collected in one place the best-tasting sustainably
produced meats in the Bay Area. The hard-to-find Hoffman chickens from
Manteca are famously flavorful. Much of the beef is from Niman Ranch,
and McBride sells the cuts she loves: the uncommon onglet (hanger
steak), flatiron, and bavette (sirloin flap), as well as fillet, T-bone, New
York strip, and rib-eye, which is dry-aged in house. The squab comes from
Paine Farm and the duck from Liberty Ranch, both in Sonoma. You might
find lamb from Don Watson in Napa or from her cousin's McCormack
ranch in Rio Vista; and the pork, while shipped from far-off Iowa, is raised
on small family farms by the likes of Paul Willis of Niman Ranch Pork.

A veteran *charcutière* from Zuni Café, McBride also stocks a first-rate
selection of house-made cured meats. She's particularly proud of her bre-
saola, pancetta, and *boudin noir* and is widely praised for her parslied ham
and mortadella. The staff is knowledgeable, and if you stop in for, say, hog
casings or *crépinette,* they'll happily offer advice on the best way to stuff a
sausage or the very barest amount of pink salt you'll need to mix into your
pork terrine. While at the cash register, pick up a house-made pepperoni
stick or a piece of beef jerky (grass-fed during the season) to satisfy your
hunger on the way home to the kitchen.

Dittmer's Gourmet Meats & Wurst Haus
400 San Antonio Road
Mountain View   *SOUTH BAY*
(650) 941-3800
www.dittmers.com
Closed Sunday

Upon opening the door to Dittmer's you will enjoy the pleasant and
slightly exotic aroma of a butcher shop in, say, Dusseldorf or Bremen.
Founded by German-born Dittmer Bubert in 1978, today Dittmer's sells

more than forty types of house-made sausages, pâtés, smoked meats, and salamis, as well as a large selection of imported candies, jams, and soups.

Here you'll find everything from the not-so-prosaic frankfurter (made with lightly smoked veal and pork) to the esoteric and otherwise impossible-to-find-west-of-Milwaukee sausages such as *grutzwurst* (a blood sausage made with pork and cracked oats). The long display of assorted wursts tempts shoppers with the likes of ring bologna, *landjaeger,* head cheese, Thuringer-style bratwurst, spicy lamb *merguez* sausages, and *boreswores,* a South African sausage seasoned with coriander and allspice. Poland, Ukraine, Denmark, Sweden, Italy, Nouveau California (Chicken Portobello Mushroom), Cajun, and of course Germany are all represented in spades.

In addition to its virtual sausage smorgasbord, Dittmer's customer favorites include house-cured bacon, first cured in a salt-and-sugar brine, then smoked; *leberkase* (veal loaf); and house-smoked turkey and ham. Sandwiches made from the store's sausages, salamis, ham, and turkey are available to go or to eat at outdoor tables. Dittmer's also offers an interesting assortment of imported specialty items that will make a visit to this traditional delicatessen and meat market enjoyable even for the vegetarians in the family.

Drewes Brothers Meat Market
Noe Valley

1706 Church Street, at 29th Street
(415) 821-0515

The original Drewes brothers opened a meat market on this very spot back in 1889. Two sets of owners later, brothers Isaac and Josh Epple are carrying on the tradition. Drewes' is a full-service butcher shop, some-

thing of a rarity in our age of big boxed meat. Half a dozen lambs are broken down each week, and hamburger is ground fresh daily. Fish arrives six out of every seven days, and veal and rabbit are available on short notice. The Epples keep the place stocked in accordance with the neighborhood's rhythms. "We order on a day-to-day basis," says Isaac. And the provenance of the inventory is key. "Our mission," he says, "is to be as natural and organic as possible, while staying competitive." Niman Ranch meats and Rosie's organic chickens are always on hand. And during the holidays you can even place an order for pumpkin pies.

 ### Golden Gate Meat Company

Retail outlet
Embarcadero
Ferry Building Marketplace
One Ferry Building, Shop 13
Embarcadero, at Market Street

Original Location
SOMA
550 7th Street, between Bryant and Brannan Streets
(415) 983-7800

Golden Gate Meat Company is a family-run affair and was a wholesale operation until opening a retail outlet in the Ferry Building. They offer a wide selection of meats that are either natural—no antibiotics, no hormones—or organic. Golden Gate Meats contracts with ranchers in Northern California to provide their natural beef, and the organic cuts come from Organic Valley in Wisconsin. They have their own line of pancetta and prosciutto, and the full-service butcher shop can accommodate your special orders.

Guerra Meats and Deli
See Ethnic & Specialty Markets, page 256.

Halal Food Market
1964 San Pablo Avenue
Berkeley   *EAST BAY*
(510) 845-2000

A good place for whole lamb or goat, slaughtered according to Koranic law, of course. For more on Halal Food Market see Ethnic & Specialty Markets, page 257.

Little City Market Selected Meats
North Beach
1400 Stockton Street, at Vallejo Street
(415) 986-2601
Closed Sunday

Little City Market, now owned by the third generation of the Spinali family, has been serving the North Beach community since 1951. One of the most popular items is their Sicilian sausage, made from an old family recipe, but there is also a rotation of links with names like Green Street and Café Puccini, as well as Easter and Christmas specials.

Little City also sells eggs, chicken, numerous cuts of pork and beef, rabbit, their own demi-glace, Nana Connie's meatloaf (ready to bake at home), a shelfful of spices, and their own line of special condiments.

The Spinalis also regularly offer suggestions for the preparation of your cuts, and you might even leave with a printed recipe. Concerned that the younger generations are not cooking at home enough, the Spinalis want to do everything they can to make your cooking successful.

Mission Market Fish & Poultry
Mission
2590 Mission Street, at 22nd Street
(415) 282-3331
Closed Sunday

Take the back steps down to Mission Market off Bartlett Street, and it's as if you have entered another time and place. Serving its customers since the 1930s, the market's polite and knowledgeable fishmongers are happy to tell you which fish is wild or locally caught and which one *they* would take home to fix for dinner tonight.

You're likely to hear Italian and Spanish spoken here. The counter offers something for everyone, from fish heads to baby octopus to local rock cod. They also sell Rosie's organic chickens.

Nijiya Market
See Ethnic & Specialty Markets, page 251.

 **Monterey Fish Market**
1582 Hopkins Street
Berkeley   *EAST BAY*
(510) 525-5600
Closed Sunday and Monday

This small, cheerful store ("If you don't like our tuna, try us for the halibut!") began twenty-five years ago, selling fish from the back of a pickup truck to Chez Panisse. They now sell to two hundred restaurants daily out of Pier 33 along the San Francisco waterfront and still maintain a retail presence across the bay "as a thanks to our customers." The emphasis here is on fresh, sustainably caught fish and shellfish that they buy directly from small-scale independent fishermen who use environmentally safe methods. Here you will find harpoon-caught West Coast swordfish, hook-and-line-caught local halibut, or even Sacramento River Chinook. Dozens of varieties of fish are available Tuesday through Friday (fewer on Saturday), as well as oysters and clams from Hog Island Oyster Company, mussels, and live Maine lobsters. Look for incomparable sardines and squid straight from the Monterey Bay. If they don't have what you want, you can order it (as little as half a pound), and they'll have it for you the next day.

 ### Prather Ranch Meat Company
Embarcadero

Ferry Building Marketplace
One Ferry Building, Shop 32
Embarcadero, at Market Street
(415) 378-2917
Closed Monday

Prather Ranch Meat Company features certified organic, dry-aged beef from the family-owned Prather Ranch—a pristine, fifteen-thousand-acre spread located near Mount Shasta. This retail space in the Ferry Building is one-stop shopping for all your quality meat needs: they carry Berkshire pork raised on pasture and leftover organic fruits from Capay Organics in the Capay Valley, grass-fed lamb and bison from Oregon, free-range veal, sausages, hot dogs, and beef jerky.

Ralph's Smokehouse

885 Delmas Avenue
San Jose   *SOUTH BAY*
(408) 279-4009
Closed Sunday

Ralph's Smokehouse is the place to go if you're lucky enough to get your hands on a freshly shot wild boar, black-tailed deer, or blue teal. Ralph's will butcher and smoke the game and produce fillets, steaks, sausages, or any cut you choose. Billed as the last of it's kind in the San Jose area (and one would guess in the entire Bay Area), Ralph's is currently run by the aptly named Montana Hutton.

While some products and gift boxes are available, most of the retail operation has been taken up by Willows Smokehouse Deli, an establishment opened expressly to sell the meats (sorry, no game) that have been processed and smoked at Ralph's. Here you'll find fifteen types of sausages, five types of jerky, smoked fish, ham, marinated tri-tip, and much more. They also offer cold and hot deli sandwiches and complete barbecue dinners that are sold either as takeout or dine-in.

Tokyo Fish Market

1220 San Pablo Avenue
Berkeley   *EAST BAY*
(510) 524-7243

This family-owned market is a favorite of the considerable Japanese expatriate community in Berkeley. One of the few places with true sashimi-grade fish, the helpful people behind the counter will happily cut a quarter-pound piece of top-quality tuna for a weekday dinner; or you might try yellowtail, snapper, or local clams for a more elaborate dinner. You'll also find Japanese pickles; hard, crunchy rice crackers; *konbu* (stock kelp); *katsuoboshi* (dried, shaved bonito); locally made tofu; miso; and of course, a dozen varieties of Japanese rice—especially the Koda variety Kokoho Rose, grown in the Central Valley. The small produce section is usually stocked with *mitsuba, shungiku* (edible chrysanthemum leaves), *gobo,* Japanese green peppers, and other difficult-to-find vegetables. There is also a small but useful collection of cooking gadgets (like the extraordinarily handy Benriner mandoline), rice and soup bowls, and various plates and serving dishes.

Yum Yum Fish Market

See Japanese, page 107.

Amidst the smoked tofu dip, wild salmon sausage, and medicinal plant extracts at the Saturday Berkeley Farmers' Market you can find The Fatted Calf, an unassuming stall with Old World Italian- and French-style charcuterie. Owned by a young couple, Taylor Boetticher and his wife, Toponia, this newly founded business operates out of a kitchen in San Francisco and uses top-quality meat and poultry, often organic, from producers such as Niman Ranch and Liberty Farm Ducks, together with herbs bought from their fellow market vendors. Taylor trained at Café Rouge in Berkeley and briefly with legendary salumiere Dario Cecchini outside Florence. The couple's philosophy is to "try not to be stuffy or take ourselves too seriously." It must be working, based on the crowd that lines up every Saturday.

This is the place to buy authentic sausages and ingredients for traditional European recipes. Half a dozen different sausages are offered for around $7 a pound. They range from the Toulouse, a fresh sausage for pan frying or grilling and made of coarsely minced pork to Cotechino, a soft Italian sausage made with pig skin and lean meat, for boiling and pairing with lentils or in a grand Piedmontese *bollito misto*.

They also sell a variety of pâtés and mousses for around $13 a pound. The duck pâté is nice, mildly spiced and wrapped in bacon with finely ground meat and savory specks of liver. Salamis, broths, and demi-glace fill out the offerings, and a few changing weekly specials can be thrown on the grill for a simple dinner. Among the specials, the *crépinettes* always sell out early. Taylor is continually tweaking his recipes and adding new ones to The Fatted Calf repertoire.

Sold at the Berkeley Farmers' Market and the Ferry Plaza Farmers Market in San Francisco; visit www.fattedcalf.com for more information.

—*Sarah Weiner*

The Fatted Calf
Berkeley Farmers' Market
Center Street, between Martin Luther King Jr. Way and Milvia
   Street
Berkeley   *EAST BAY*
(510) 653-4327
Saturday only

▬▬ PRODUCER PROFILE: NIMAN RANCH ▬▬

To call Bill Niman a pioneer isn't quite right. The hormone-free, natural beef he introduced more than three decades ago actually signaled a return to tradition, not an innovation. And though he says he began simply wanting to make "great-tasting meat in a sound way," today Niman's goal is to "influence the rural landscape and make family farms viable again." To that groundbreaking end, his Oakland-based Niman Ranch has expanded well beyond that first herd of cows that grazed in Bolinas on the pastures overlooking the Pacific Ocean. The current product line includes natural pork that's helping to revitalize Iowa farm communities devastated by agricultural industrialization and pasture-raised veal that not only wins accolades from chefs around the country, but also helps Wisconsin dairy farmers keep their businesses profitable and sustainable.

Sold at the Berkeley Bowl, Bi-Rite Market, Café Rouge, and restaurants around the Bay Area.

—Jan Newberry

▬▬ PRODUCER PROFILE: HOBBS BACON ▬▬

Hobbs Shore never intended to run a smokehouse. In fact, if you had suggested the idea to him early in his life, he would have told you that you were nuts. Shore first started making bacon and hams when he was a kid working on his grandfather's farm in New York's Hudson River Valley. "I had visions of spending my summers swimming and fishing, but my grandfather insisted that I work in his smokehouse," recalls the eighty-two-year-old Shore. "I would haul a wagon through the barn, with tears from the smoke running down my cheeks. I hated it and swore once I got out of there I'd never go near a smokehouse again." But after retiring from his career as an economist, Shore crafted a smoker from an old refrigerator and started smoking again, this time as a hobby. That hobby status changed when Bradley Ogden, the owner of Lark Creek Inn in Larkspur, tasted Shore's bacon at a dinner party and placed an order for his restaurant.

Today Shore oversees production of about eight core products at his Richmond-based smokehouse, using pork from a former employee who raises hogs in Canada according to Shore's specs. "He doesn't want to bother with the paperwork to become certified organic," says Shore, "but he does all the right things." When asked what his grandfather might think of his bacon, Shore just laughs. "He'd tell me it's not good enough. That's just the kind of guy he was."

Available at Golden Gate Meat Company (see page 287).

—Jan Newberry

WINE RETAILERS

D&M Wine and Liquor Co.
Pacific Heights
2200 Fillmore Street
(415) 346-1325, (800) 637-0292
www.dandm.com

When most people think of D&M they think of the bubbly, but according to manager Mark Mitchell, "On any given day we probably have the largest selection of vintage Armagnac of anyone in the world." You can't miss it either; the bottles are stacked up the wall right behind the cash register, along with the Calvados, the brandies, and the single-malt scotch. That and the magnums of Champagne perched all around the room, and you can't help but wonder what D&M's earthquake readiness plan could possibly be.

In the wine category the spotlight is on California. With its long history in the trade—opened in 1935, owned by the same family since 1959—and its track record of championing California wines, D&M has garnered privileged allotments of many of those hard-to-get labels. Not blinded by hype, D&M's welcoming and knowledgeable staff sniffs out values in all price points both here and abroad. "We blind-taste everything that comes in the door," says Mitchell, "and we try not to have anything we don't like."

Ferry Plaza Wine Merchant
Embarcadero
Ferry Building Marketplace
One Ferry Building, Shop 23
Embarcadero, at Market Street
(415) 391-9400

Located in between many of the best foods shops in San Francisco, the Ferry Plaza Wine Merchant is both a store and a tasting bar. You are welcomed, in fact encouraged, to pick up provisions from any of the nearby food stalls and picnic in their tasting area. One gentlemen, just about every Saturday during the farmers' market hours, takes the same prime-time table that looks out over the market action and puts out an elaborate spread of the local bounty. You can get a bottle or something by the glass, and the staff will gladly help you find a match for your repast, however elaborate or modest. We like the strength of their inventory of wines from Austria, yet there is something for everyone, with every major world wine region well represented—as one would expect from owners Debbie Zachareas and Peter Granoff. Zachareas gained notoriety selecting wines at Ashbury Market, then at EOS and at Bacar, and Granoff is a Master Sommelier.

K&L Wine Merchants
SOMA

638 Fourth Street, at Brannan Street

(415) 896-1734

At K&L each wine-producing region has been assigned its own expert buyer, and because some of the store's inventory is bought at auction, the shop has a wider and more comprehensive selection than most.

The wines are organized by country, and there are also displays with staff picks, Rhône bargains, and the top *Wine Spectator* selections, with some good organic and biodynamic wines mixed throughout. Both store locations host wine tastings, and there is a lengthy monthly newsletter. Prices are reasonable, with plenty to choose from on the lower end of the price range. Although a serious wine shop for serious enthusiasts, it's also a great place to stop in for a fantastic $15 bottle of red to go with your *osso buco.*

Other Location

3005 El Camino Real, Redwood City (South Bay);
   (650) 364-8544

Kermit Lynch Wine Merchant

1605 San Pablo Avenue, at Cedar Street

Berkeley   *EAST BAY*

(510) 524-1524

Kermit Lynch was something of a bad boy in his younger days. He opened his shop on proletarian San Pablo Avenue in 1972, and rather than stock the famous châteaus you'd find at the other important shops, he celebrated smaller, relatively unknown vintners like Gerald Chave and Lucien Peyraud. For years, he's campaigned against modern winemaking techniques that flatten the character of a wine in favor of traditional methods passed from generation to generation. Lynch has impressed upon his producers the importance of using live, unfiltered juice—an ancient practice that, in part due to his efforts, is coming back into vogue. And he insists that his wines be shipped from Europe in refrigerated containers. His efforts show, and you can taste the difference in the cuvées that Lynch brings into Berkeley against the same wines imported under less stringent oversight to the East Coast. When you pour the first glass of, say, Domaine Tempier Bandol Rouge, the juice explodes with the aromas of *terroir,* not just the oft-stated concept sold nowadays.

Lynch spends part of every year in Provence near Bandol, visiting wineries and sniffing out new vintages. Back in his store, you can find almost everything he imports, and the staff is knowledgeable and equally

helpful navigating the plush hallways of grand Burgundies or the over-grown paths of *vin de pays*. You'll also find a large rack of reserve wines and a smaller but growing selection of Italian producers.

If you are willing to explore some of the unknown corners of France, you'll discover a lot of interesting bottles for less than $20. When you browse the cool aisles yourself, imagine, if you will, California's wine selection in the early seventies and the chasm Kermit Lynch has helped to bridge. Just don't search for Californian wines here. For that you will have to look elsewhere.

Paul Marcus Wines
5655 College Avenue, at Keith Avenue
Oakland   *EAST BAY*
(510) 420-1005

Marcus's philosophy is simple: wine is food. While the inventory appeals to collectors, the shop's ideal customer is the person who stops in every day after work to pick up a bottle for dinner. And the excellent wine need not break the bank. Boxes of wine are organized into sections based on price; in the $11 and under bins, one can find dozens of outstanding French and Italian bottles. Mixed cases of wine—easily assembled from the boxes at the front of the store—can be bought at a 10 percent discount.

The selections change frequently, as Paul Marcus and his staff constantly search for high-quality wines in all price ranges. The staff relays their opinions in a forthright system. Throughout the store, in each price area hang placards marked in red: OUTSTANDING, HIGHEST RECOMMENDATION, EXCELLENT. And the staff is always eager to provide more descriptive detail.

Although the store sells some Californian wine, the majority is European. Small-scale, family-run vineyards produce many of the store's imports, particularly the Champagnes.

PlumpJack Wine Store
Marina
3201 Fillmore Street
(415) 346-9870

Second Location
Noe Valley
4011 24th Street
(415) 282-3841

When PlumpJack Wines, part of the larger PlumpJack restaurant empire founded in part by San Francisco Mayor Gavin Newsom and other well-heeled Pacific Heights folks, annexed the beloved 24th Street wine shop Caruso's several years ago, there was enormous potential for neighborhood pushback. Noe Valley is on the other side of town. But the changes amounted to expanding the interesting inventory. And they built up a fantastic selection of wines around $10, which quickly endeared PlumpJack to everyone. The flagship Fillmore Street shop features a large selection of Italian and cult California wines, and both shops have a good stock of spirits and Belgian beers.

Vin Vino Wine
437 California Avenue
Palo Alto   *SOUTH BAY*
(650) 324-4903
Closed Sunday and Monday

One of the best wine shops in the Bay Area, Vin Vino is heaven for serious wine lovers, particularly those with a penchant for Burgundies and the reds of Piedmont. Check out their Web site for the schedule of their amazing daily tastings, which center around a theme, like the Best of the Languedoc, or a particular producer. It's a wonderful opportunity to educate your palate, and the staff is extremely knowledgeable and helpful, as are some of the regular customers, who like to hang out and lend advice to newer buyers. The prices are reasonable.

NOTABLE

Arlequin Wine Merchant
Hayes Valley
384 Hayes Street
(415) 863-1104

This small, well-designed store is owned by the same people who own Absinthe Brasserie next door, and the luxurious feel of the restaurant carries through to the shop. They have an eclectic selection focused on lesser-known bottles from around the world. On a recent quest for Sardinian wine, the staff quickly ferreted out a delicious red from Issolus. Prices can be slightly high, but it's worth it to be so ably taken care of. The garden in the back is a good place to ponder your purchase before stepping back out into the world.

Arlington Wine & Spirits
295 Arlington Avenue
Kensington   *EAST BAY*
(510) 524-0841

Nestled in the East Bay Hills in the town of Kensington, this shop has a good selection of small-producer country wines from around the world, as well as some big-name Bordeaux, Burgundy, and California producers. A good town shop that doesn't try to be everything to everyone, it also has an excellent selection of spirits.

Beltramos
1540 El Camino Real
Menlo Park   *SOUTH BAY*
(650) 325-2806

A very large store offering everything from cheap commercial wine to vintage Bordeaux. They have the largest selection of Southern Italian wines on the Peninsula, and a good selection of spirits. They've had some problems with corked bottles, so take note. More staff members would be beneficial. Prices are fair.

Berkeley Bowl

2020 Oregon Street
Berkeley   *EAST BAY*
(510) 843-6929

Keenly choosing from all lands and importers, the Berkeley Bowl's buyer, Simon Ball, has fashioned a great wine island just east of the chips and north of the deli.

Many of the wines have handwritten blurbs, and inevitably there's a great bottle of Macon or California zinfandel at half the price it goes for elsewhere. Ball does carry a small case of hard-to-find wines, but his main focus is on mirroring the wealth of produce around you in the store with interesting, flavorful wines that will leave you enough change in your wallet to buy one of those cheeses across the aisle.

The French Cellar

32 East Main Street
Los Gatos   *SOUTH BAY*
(408) 354-0993
Closed Monday

Run by admitted Francophiles Sallie and Jay Druian, this is more than a wine shop. The selection of top-notch, boutique wines from France is impeccable, with good selections of smaller, eclectic producers as well as the big names. Mixed in with the wines is an intriguing selection of French antiques, crystal, artwork, and chocolate. Here the French table is king.

The Jug Shop

Russian Hill
1567 Pacific Avenue, at Polk Street
(415) 885-2922

This is a large, bare-bones liquor store that also boasts a great selection of wines, especially Italian vintages. A neighborhood institution since 1959, it is across the street from Cheese Plus, which makes for terrific one-stop shopping. The people who work here are true wine aficionados —they really know their stuff and are happy to help. Their wine buyer is particularly knowledgeable.

North Berkeley Wine

601 Martin Luther King Jr. Way, at Cedar Street
Berkeley   *EAST BAY*
(510) 848-8910
Closed Sunday

For many years North Berkeley Wine was one of the quieter denizens of the Gourmet Ghetto. However, in the mid-nineties, it moved to its present location and changed its face, starting to bring in its own cuvées and producers. The store now carries some notable producers, like Cotat and Verget, and follows the same model as neighboring Kermit Lynch— although North Berkeley often has more cask selection and oak-driven cuvées. Look for a great selection of Californian bottles, with a range of vintages to choose from.

Oddlots

1025 San Pablo Avenue
Albany   *EAST BAY*
(510) 526-0522

Oddlots has such a low profile that many people are still unaware of Morgan Miller and his thoughtful selection of wines. A graduate of Kermit Lynch Wine Merchant, his approach to choosing wines is similar to that of Lynch—he stocks distinctive, little-known European wines from smaller wineries. Miller imports from a broader range of countries than Lynch and has a deeper selection of inexpensive, interesting bottles.

Premier Cru

5890 Christie Avenue
Emeryville   *EAST BAY*
(510) 655-6691

You can find everything from cult Californian wines such as Bryant Family and Turly Zins to a 1976 Clos Vougeot, Arnoux, and 1985 Krug Champagne at some of the lowest prices anywhere in the United States. The store is more of a warehouse, but the staff is friendly and knowledgeable.

Roberts of Woodside

3015 Woodside Road

Woodside   *SOUTH BAY*

(650) 851-1511

This historic grocery store located in beautiful Woodside receives large quantities of hard-to-find wines from around the world. The Burgundy selection is of note here, as wine manager John Akeley is especially knowledgeable in this area. Don't think that he only sells expensive wines, though; his selection is very deep in small, country wines from California and Europe.

Ruby Wine Shop

Potrero Hill

1419 18th Street

(415) 401-7708

The compact Ruby Wine Shop, located a few doors down from Chez Papa on 18th Street in Potrero Hill, offers amazing bang for the per-square-foot buck. Proprietor Joel Bleskacek, a longtime resident of Potrero Hill, has hand-picked everyday wines in the $8 to $10 range, as well as many interesting and affordable second labels from fancy California producers. "We buy what we like and what the neighborhood likes" is the motto here. Ruby also stocks a nicely edited assortment of dry goods—tuna, capers, pasta, olive oil, and so forth—almost everything you need to build a meal around. There are even bags of charcoal. And Crepe & Brioche bread is delivered twice daily.

Solano Cellars

1580 Solano Avenue

Berkeley   *EAST BAY*

(510) 525-9463

Located on bustling Solano Avenue in North Berkeley, this is a fine neighborhood shop that turns into a bistro in the evenings. Many selections are open to try at the bar, and organized tastings take place on Saturday afternoons.

The Spanish Table

1814 San Pablo Avenue

Berkeley   *EAST BAY*

(510) 548-1383

The largest collection of Madeira, port, and Spanish and Portuguese wines in the Bay Area, with a knowledgeable and helpful staff and a lot of great stemware. For more on The Spanish Table see Ethnic & Specialty Markets, page 254.

Vino Locale

431 Kipling Street, between University and Lytton Avenues
Palo Alto   *SOUTH BAY*
(650) 328-0450

Vino Locale specializes in local wine and food made or produced in and around the Bay Area in places such as Santa Clara, Santa Cruz, San Mateo, Alameda, and Livermore counties. Located in a historic Victorian house in downtown Palo Alto that has a lovely courtyard, Vino Locale is also an excellent choice for private parties and events.

Weimax Wines & Spirits

1178 Broadway
Burlingame   *SOUTH BAY*
(650) 343-0182
Closed Sunday

Well regarded for their selection of German wines, one of Weimax's strengths is buying lesser-known wines from small producers all over the globe. With a very friendly and knowledgeable staff, this is one of the best wine shops on the Peninsula. Prices are fair.

William Cross Wine Merchants
Russian Hill
2253 Polk Street, at Vallejo Street
(415) 346-1314

This small shop on Polk Street is run by the energetic Steven Sherman. He's got a good selection of both lesser- and well-known wines, and he tastes everything before bringing it in and makes no compromises. Very strong in small-producer Californian and European selections, he invites winemakers and importers to present their wares at a bustling tasting every Wednesday evening.

The Wine House
Portrero Hill
129 Carolina Street, between 16th and 17th Streets
(415) 355-9463
Closed Sunday

The Wine House is a gem of a store on Potrero Hill. The staff specializes in French wines, particularly Burgundies and Alsatians, and they import some of their own labels. A good selection of hard-to-find and highly allocated California producers can be found here. They have a monthly wine buying program called the "dirty dozen," which provides a case of wine for about $100—a fun and inexpensive way to learn about French wine. Finally, it is a great place to look for a special older bottle of wine, such as a fully aged Burgundy or Bordeaux. The staff is helpful and friendly, and their prices are very fair.

The Wine Club
SOMA
953 Harrison Street
(415) 512-9086

The Wine Club is a warehouse-style store and is open to everyone, contrary to its name. The bare space allows them to carry an extremely large selection of wines, particularly Bordeaux and Californian. However, you will also find wines from Australia, Spain, the Rhône, Italy, and just about everywhere that grows grapes in smaller amounts. Prices here tend to be the lowest in the area, and the staff is generally knowledgeable and helpful.

Other Location
1200 Coleman Avenue, Santa Clara (South Bay); (408) 567-0900

PART FOUR

OUTLYING AREAS

In and around the 75,000-acre Point Reyes National Seashore, you'll find many of the Bay Area's most beautiful sustainable farms and ranches and some of the region's most delicious handmade foods. Just about an hour from San Francisco, this area is blessed with dramatic ocean beaches, a calm bay, miles of hiking trails, Tule elk, and other wonders. When The Prince of Wales (an outspoken advocate of small-scale organic farming) came to the United States recently on a state visit, along with the requisite dinner with the President of the United States, he spent a day in West Marin, touring farms and visiting restaurants.

Cowgirl Creamery at Tomales Bay Foods
80 Fourth Street
Point Reyes Station
(415) 663-9335
Wednesday through Sunday, 10:00 A.M. to 6:00 P.M.

Visit the barn in Point Reyes Station where Sue Conley and Peggy Smith make their cheeses with milk from neighboring Straus Family Dairy. See Cheese, p. xxx.

Hog Island Oyster Company
20215 Highway 1
Marshall
(415) 663-9218
$

The oyster farm on Tomales Bay provides outdoor tables and grills for an ideal Sunday afternoon picnic with a view of the bay. See Seafood, p. xxx.

Drake's Beach Café
At Drake's Beach, just off the road to the lighthouse
Point Reyes National Seashore
(415) 669-1297
$

Head due west and, just about where you fall off the edge of the continent, you'll find Drake's Beach Café. Located in the Point Reyes National Seashore, overlooking the crescent-moon-shaped shoreline known as Drake's Beach (named because of speculation that Sir Francis Drake took shelter here back in 1579), National Park Service concessionaire Jonne LeMieux has been modeling the local, sustainable ethos for nearly a quarter century at her beachfront snack bar. Line up at the counter and order her Fried Oyster Burger, made with oysters from nearby Drake's Estero or from Tomales Bay. The hamburger is 100 percent grass-fed beef from

Marin Sun Farms; the produce is nearly all organic: the organic apples in the house-made apple pie are from Sebastopol. The bagel with cream cheese sports wild salmon that was locally caught and smoked by a local resident. You might even consider celebrating the opening of the local Dungeness crab season here: Jonne serves it simply with a little drawn butter. The place is modest—plank wood floors and wooden tables with a vase holding a fresh nasturtium or two. Prices are drop-dead reasonable and the view is drop-dead gorgeous.

Jonne keeps limited hours in the wintertime and weekends can be crowded, especially when the weather is good. Call ahead to confirm hours of operation. If you'd like wine or beer, bring your own. Jonne will provide glasses.

 ## Manka's Inverness Lodge
30 Callender Way
Inverness
(415) 669-1034
$$$

While only an hour and a half north of San Francisco, an evening at Manka's Inverness Lodge is sure to put you in another time zone and time frame altogether. Manka's is the very personal vision of owner/innkeeper Margaret Grade, and from the minute you turn off of Sir Francis Drake Boulevard and start winding your way up Argyle Road through the redwoods you sense adventure. When you pull into Manka's, nestled among the foggy mist and trees, it will come as no surprise that it was once a hunting lodge. And Grade pays her respects to that tradition by serving lots of game, wild fish, and foraged mushrooms and berries. She takes pride in the fact that most of what she serves comes from within walking distance. Well, maybe not quite, but certainly within *bicycling* distance. You'll find lettuces, greens, and root vegetables from Bolinas, local duck eggs and grass-fed beef, and wild halibut and salmon caught in the nearby Pacific by Grade's fisherman friends. Just a quick read of the menu gives you the sense that a visit to Manka's offers more than a meal—it's a window into the community of West Marin. After you announce your arrival, you can take refuge in the darkened receiving room, where you can settle in by the fire with your preferred libation while your table is being readied. You will most likely get a hint of what is to come, as generally one the chefs will be grilling something from the prix fixe menu over the flames. Then you will be led into the open dining room, lined with windows that afford a view of the forest outside. The courses are nicely paced, with an interesting list of wines to accompany the meal. You may want to end your repast with a stay over in one of the handful of elegant yet rustic rooms or cabins on the property.

 Marin Sun Farms
10905 Highway 1
Point Reyes Station
(415) 663-8997
www.marinsunfarms.com
$

Dave Evans, a fourth-generation rancher in West Marin County, bucked family feedlot tradition and has become one of our leading local advocates and suppliers of grass-fed beef. He formed Marin Sun Farms in 1999 and to date has several thousand acres of pasture under certified organic production. You will find Marin Sun Farm beef on menus around town, including at Zuni Café and Acme Chophouse. And if you're up in West Marin you might very well spot some of the MSF cattle happily grazing. You don't have to hurry back to the city to try some; simply head over to the newly opened Marin Sun Farm Butcher Shop and Eatery just south of Point Reyes Station on Highway 1 for a bite to eat and to take home a rib-eye (or two) and a dozen of his pasture-raised eggs.

HALF MOON BAY
& SANTA CRUZ

Al Dente Restaurant
415 Seabright Avenue
Santa Cruz
(831) 466-0649
Dinner only; closed Sunday and Monday

The menu at Al Dente features both grilled meats and pastas in tomato or cream sauces. Owner Lucio Fanni's *fettuccini alfredo* is simple and wonderful; even better is the special version with fresh tuna. The seafood he serves here is the freshest possible, and all the meats are all excellent quality as well. This restaurant may look like a neighborhood pizza joint, its exterior clad in aluminum and Arizona flagstone. But you should never judge a book by its cover. Inside, the scene is energetic and crowded, with loud rock music playing and Fanni himself working the stoves behind the counter.

Cetrella Bistro & Café
845 Main Street
Half Moon Bay
(650) 726-4090

This restaurant is much too grand for the name "Bistro & Café," although it does offer a select menu of California cuisine. Cetrella supports a Saturday farmers' market in its parking lot and cultivates relationships with local produce farmers.

Gayle's Bakery & Rosticceria
504 Bay Avenue
Capitola
(831) 462-1200

Gayle's is a neighborhood restaurant with a national reputation, based in part on Joe Ortiz's celebrated book, *The Village Baker*, and Gayle Ortiz's book on cakes and pastries, *The Village Baker's Wife* (no kidding!). Gayle's offers a bright, delightful, and very, very busy site for café dining, but a lot of its trade is take-out cakes and pastries, roast meats, pasta, and elaborate sandwiches (on Joe's bread). Somehow the word *sandwich* is inadequate to describe these elegant creations.

Oswald Restaurant
1547 Pacific Avenue
Santa Cruz
(831) 423-7427
Dinner only; closed Monday

Many locals believe Oswald is Santa Cruz's best restaurant, and it does indeed feature excellent cuisine, served in a small, comfortable space. Oswald serves a French-inspired California cuisine, with touches of modern Spanish cooking and other eclectic, subtle influences. The menu includes a few classic entrées, including a duck leg confit, roasted marrow bones, and sweetbreads. The less adventuresome will find skirt steak with (real) French fries, roasted Monterey Bay salmon, and other delicacies.

Pasta Moon Ristorante
315 Main Street
Half Moon Bay
(650) 726-5125

Pasta Moon Ristorante has a long and deep connection to the local environment—both natural and agricultural—of this coastal region that lies south of San Francisco. Kim Levin, who has owned Pasta Moon for seventeen years, works with local farmers who grow much of the food used in the restaurant, such as Monterey sardines and Pacific salmon from Half Moon Bay, as well as locally grown red and yellow beets, summer squash, basil, English peas and fava beans, radishes, lettuce, arugula, and strawberries.

Ristorante Avanti
1711 Mission Street
Santa Cruz
(831) 427-0135

Behind an unprepossessing exterior of drawn blinds is one of Santa Cruz's most delightful culinary finds. If you weren't looking for it, you could drive right past it, and that would be a shame. Avanti's cuisine is Italian-inspired Californian, with a strong emphasis on local, seasonal, sustainably raised ingredients. For instance, they serve only shrimp harvested from Monterey Bay, which are frequently unavailable, but wonderful when they are in season.

The wine list at Avanti is lengthy and impressive, with many refined and interesting vintages to choose from that have been carefully selected and reasonably priced.

Bistro Jeanty
6510 Washington Street
Yountville
(707) 944-0103

There is something extremely cozy about Chef Phillipe Jeanty's restaurant, Bistro Jeanty, in Yountville. Whether it's the low ceilings, the casual yet professional style of the waitstaff, the décor, or the incredible bistro-style French comfort food that this Champagne region native offers at Jeanty, the feeling you will leave with is one of culinary warmth.

Cindy's Backstreet Kitchen
1327 Railroad Avenue
St. Helena
(707) 963-1200

Cindy Pawlcyn is best known for her work at Mustard's Grill in Oakville, one of Napa Valley's most recognizable dining venues, but she recently opened Cindy's Backstreet Kitchen, which has quickly become a favorite for locals and for tourists willing to venture off of Route 29 (Main Street) in St. Helena. Cindy's specializes in foods inspired by the bounty of California agriculture. Her cooking is classic California cuisine, yet the atmosphere belies this in its casual and hip tonality. A premeal mojito (a Cuban mint and rum cocktail) is a tradition among locals.

Cole's Chop House
1122 Main Street
Napa
(707) 224-6328

So what does a Napa Valley cult Cabernet Sauvignon scream for as a food accompaniment? That's right, a big, fat, juicy, fresh-grilled steak. The place in Napa Valley for just such a meal is Chef Greg Cole's Chop House. Here twenty-one-day aged prime cuts are served just how you like them with a variety of à la carte side dishes.

The Culinary Institute of America at Greystone and Wine Spectator Restaurant
2555 Main Street
St. Helena
(707) 967-1100

One could spend a full day at this premier culinary institute, which is built on a slight rise that looks across the St. Helena portion of Napa Valley. An affiliate of the CIA in Hyde Park, New York, the CIA at Greystone specializes in pastry arts and continuing education for the professional chef, though the opportunities to learn for the day visitor in any of the culinary arts are immense. Call ahead for a cooking demonstration schedule in one of several auditorium kitchens. Visit the campus bookstore and marketplace for probably the best collection of books devoted to the culinary arts in the Bay Area. Take a tour of what was one of the very first wineries in Napa Valley, built in 1887–89, that now houses the CIA and its adjoining gardens. And finish off with a spectacular meal at the Wine Spectator Greystone Restaurant.

The restaurant not only serves the fare you would expect from this well-respected venue, but it does so in an interactive way. The dining area actually surrounds the kitchen, and the chefs are almost always open to discussing what they are doing in the preparation of that evening's meal. This is a school that specializes in dessert, so be sure to order an appropriately decadent finale to your meal.

French Laundry
6640 Washington Street
Yountville
(707) 944-2380
Prix fixe

Located in a building that housed a French steam laundry back in the 1890s, Chef Thomas Keller's five-star restaurant represents the pinnacle of dining experiences, not only in Napa Valley but arguably in the whole United States. Typically the prix fixe menu, chef's or vegetarian, consists of approximately eight courses, though most times it is bumped up to twelve courses by virtue of several *amuse bouche.*

The service here is extraordinary, each table overseen by a team of people who are hardly noticed as they swoop in and out with a myriad of cutlery and crockery; your needs are recognized before you have even given thought to them. A jacket is required for gentlemen, and there's a $50 corkage fee if you bring your own wine.

Genova Delicatessen
1550 Trancas Street
Napa
(707) 253-8686

One of the most popular local delis in the Napa Valley resides amidst and actually in one of the strip malls stationed on this street. Typically overlooked by most tourists, Genova Delicatessen offers a wide selection of imported and domestic cheeses and meats, salads, and much more behind the counter. You can have sandwiches made to order or choose from their menu options.

La Luna Market
1153 Rutherford Road
Rutherford
(707) 963-3211
Takeout only

Are you craving barbecued pork or beef tongue tacos, maybe served with a hearty helping of rice milk? Then make your way to La Luna Market. It's a real Mexican *mercado,* hidden away in the heart of Napa Valley. You can find a variety of Mexican spices, cheeses, peppers, and uncommon cuts of meat for sale here, but the real draw is the takeout counter in the back, which is usually crowded at midday with vineyard workers ordering their lunch to go.

Don't expect to be able to taste the nuances of a fine cabernet for several hours after eating here; instead, buy a six-pack of Corona and a *cesos* (beef brain) burrito and live it up.

Napa Valley Coffee Roasting
1400 Oak Avenue, Suite A
St. Helena
(707) 963-4491

Do you need the freshest-roasted cup of coffee the Napa Valley has to offer? Then you ought to be going to the place that provides many of the Napa Valley restaurants with their coffee.

Other Location
948 Main Street, Napa; (707) 224-2233

Napa Valley Olive Oil Mfg. Co
835 Charter Oak Avenue
St. Helena
(707) 963-4173

For excellent olive oil and a full array of Italian foods visit the Napa Valley Olive Oil Mfg. Co. This is also the perfect place to stop for picnic food if you'd like to enjoy Napa Valley without the hustle and overcrowded atmosphere some of the region's markets provide.

Pancha's
6764 Washington Street
Yountville
(707) 944-2125

Don't bring a credit card or an attitude to Pancha's: they don't accept either at this bar. This is a truly local hangout, catering to everyone.

Tourists, cattle ranchers, winemakers, restaurant folk, politicians, and Napa's upper crust all make it to Pancha's for a game of pool, a chat with the bartender, or a quiet drink. Open till 2:00 A.M., the place picks up after 10:00 P.M. when restaurant staffs start getting off work. Be aware that this is one of the few establishments in California in which people are still allowed to smoke.

Pilar
807 Main Street
Napa
(707) 252-4474

Pilar's menu is a combination of California cuisine and French haute cuisine that stresses fresh farmers' market produce, off-the-boat seafood, and freshly slaughtered meats. The atmosphere in the small, tastefully decorated dining room makes any meal here a wonderfully cozy, yet sophisticated dining experience. And an eclectic wine list exemplifies and enhances their similarly eclectic menu.

Silverado Brewing Company
3020 North St. Helena Highway
St. Helena
(707) 967-9876

The saying in Napa goes, "It takes a lot of beer to make really great wine." The Silverado Brewery is a testament to that saying, a place where one can enjoy hearty American cooking and superb, freshly brewed beers. Pot roast from Napa Valley Grass Fed meats; house-cured olives, garlic, peppers and pickles; as well as the "spent-grain" rye bread and stout cake are not to be missed. Try an organic blond ale or an India pale ale, and make sure to have a glass of one of the seasonal brews—our favorites being the Belgian Trappist ale and the *Hefeweizen*—all made with the utmost care and quality by master brewer Ken Mee.

Tra Vigne and Cantinetta Tra Vigne
1050 Charter Oak Street
St. Helena
(707) 963-4444

Tra Vigne (the name means "between the vines") is the legendary Napa Valley restaurant begun by Chef Michael Chiarello and his general manager/partner Kevin Cronin. The kitchen is now overseen by Chef Michael Reardon. Classics of the Tra Vigne menu are items such as the braised rabbit and wild mushroom ragu with organic house-made *papparadelle* pasta. If the Dungeness crab is in season, be sure to try it, or opt for the braised short ribs served on a bed of garlic polenta. There's a well-balanced wine list featuring notables from both Italy and California.

Wappo Bar and Bistro
1226 Washington Street
Calistoga
(707) 942-4712

One of the restaurants that exemplifies Calistoga's feel is Wappo. Serving California fusion food taken to a new extreme, Wappo combines a vast array of flavors, aromas, and textures in an ever-changing menu that will tantalize your palate.

Café La Haye
140 East Napa Street
Sonoma
(707) 935-5994
Dinner only; closed Sunday and Monday

Café La Haye serves truly local food, only a few steps away from the Slow Food Garden in downtown Sonoma where Chef John McReynolds literally picks organic vegetables, then serves them within minutes of harvest. The café also features Hog Island Oysters and a cheese plate from the CheeseMaker's Daughter, which is located thirty steps away from the restaurant. With few tables and a great wine selection, Café La Haye is definitely the place to be in town.

Farmhouse Inn
7600 River Road
Forestville
(707) 887-3300

Once a real farmhouse, then a funky hangout, the Farmhouse is now a favorite restaurant of local foodies.

Each exquisitely prepared dish reflects Sonoma County's diversity of agriculture and artisan producers; its rich heritage of Italian, French, and Mexican immigrants; and a consistent focus on organic and sustainably farmed fruits and vegetables.

John Ash & Company
4330 Barnes Road
Santa Rosa
(707) 527-7687

John Ash & Company is one of the Wine Country's oldest and most successful restaurants. Jeff Madura has continued the tradition of creating flavorful recipes from the freshest of local ingredients He now draws from a two-acre garden for the herbs and fresh produce that are the foundation of his cuisine. All the meats are humanely and sustainably raised. John Ash & Company remains an ever-evolving Wine Country tradition. It is the perfect place for a special occasion or just for a casual bite and a glass of wine at the bar.

K & L Bistro
119 South Main Street
Sebastopol
(707) 823-6614

Chef-Owners Karen and Lucas Martin moved to Sebastopol from San Francisco in search of a place to raise their family and work their magic in the kitchen, and K&L Bistro is the result. Situated in an old brick building on Main Street, the room is warm and intimate with soft lighting illuminating beautiful paintings of Paris set against the brick walls. The bistro food is fresh, organic, and delicious.

Lucy's Bakery and Café
6948 Sebastopol Avenue
Sebastopol
(707) 829-9713

Jonathan Beard, who co-owns Lucy's with his wife Chloe, worked in kitchens in France and at BayWolf restaurant and Acme Bread Company in Berkeley before moving to Sebastopol. The dining room and open kitchen at Lucy's are dominated by wood-fired brick ovens in which bread is baked daily and spectacular pizzas and oven-roasted dishes are baked nightly. Beautiful breads and other baked goods are also sold at the Sunday farmers' market in Sebastopol, right outside the door on the town plaza.

Manzanita
336 Healdsburg Avenue
Healdsburg
(707) 433-8111
Dinner only; closed Monday and Tuesday

Manzanita is a half-block stroll from the square along Healdsburg Avenue, the town's main drag. Established in 2001 by Mike and Carol Hale, Manzanita has quickly become part of the growing Healdsburg dining scene. The décor is best described as industrial-trendy, with polished concrete floors and exposed whitewashed wooden rafters. The centerpiece of the dining room is a wood-fired oven and steel chimney. The wood-burning oven is used to produce delicious baked mussels, cassoulets and stews, and flat breads featuring ingredients that change with the seasons. Grilled items, such as rabbit stuffed with polenta, various cuts of beef, and local poultry, are handled expertly.

Mirepoix
275 Windsor River Road
Windsor
(707) 838-0162
Dinner only; closed Sunday and Monday

Mirepoix's kitchen is headed by Matthew Bousquet, who insists on using fresh, seasonal ingredients. Bousquet has worked for more than twenty years at a number of restaurants in the Bay Area and throughout the United States. Almost everything is made from scratch here, including the breads and desserts.

The menu, containing five or six appetizers and entrées, changes daily and uses the best available ingredients. Fresh fish, including wild salmon, is brought in from Bodega Bay, only thirty miles away; suppliers also provide locally grown lamb, pork, and beef.

MIXX
135 Fourth Street
Santa Rosa
(707) 573-1344

Dan and Kathleen Berman started MIXX in 1989 in Santa Rosa's historic Railroad Square, with the idea of making people feel comfortable mixing up several small plates instead of the usual appetizer, salad, main course, and dessert (hence the name MIXX). It proved an instant hit.

The menu changes seasonally, yet there are still classic favorites that have been there from day one such as Guajillo chile and roasted tomato soup. The daily pasta special is invariably superb—a great choice for those wanting something light or quick.

Ravenous
420 Center Street
Healdsburg
(707) 431-1320
Closed Monday and Tuesday

Ravenous is one of the most popular and beloved dining spots in Wine Country. Its new location, a block and a half off Healdsburg's plaza in a former bungalow residence, is secluded from a lot of the town's casual traffic, yet accessible for tourists and locals alike. Chef-Owners John and Joyanne Pezzolo have maintained a steady standard of quality, creativity, and value that is rare in the restaurant industry in any location. The seasonally inspired menu has standard fare, such as a Caesar salad; eclectic combinations, such as smoked salmon with corn cakes; semi-ethnic dishes, such as assorted quesadillas; and comfort foods, such as fruit crisps with ice cream for dessert.

The Red Grape
529 First Street East
Sonoma
(707) 996-4103

Sam and Carol Morphy moved away to Connecticut for a few years, but are we ever glad they've come back! Their delicious thin-crust pizza is perfect, no matter which toppings you choose. The place is family-friendly and has a nice outdoor patio for dining al fresco in the summer months.

Santi
21047 Geyserville Avenue
Geyserville
(707) 857-1790
Closed Monday

Santi has raised Italian cuisine to levels that would make this area's early Italian settlers proud. Chefs Thomas Oden and Franco Dunn have succeeded in forming bonds with produce growers, livestock producers, cheese makers, and, of course, wineries to "follow the seasons" in offering a rich and varied menu. The interior of the classic 1902 stone building has been comfortably renovated, and the service is attentive and knowledgeable. This is truly a classic Italian-style country restaurant, where the food is carefully and lovingly prepared.

Sonoma Saveurs
487 First Street West
Sonoma
(707) 996-7007
Closed Monday

The charming atmosphere and European-inspired menu at this casual bistro will transport you to the intimate cafés of France. The produce and meat come from local farmers, and staples consist of a classic French onion soup, rotisserie chicken, and grilled duck breast. Start your culinary adventure with the house charcuterie plate, followed by a grilled fish sandwich or popular duck burger with Gruyère, and ending with the classic gateau Basque.

Syrah Bistro
205 5th Street
Santa Rosa
(707) 568-4002
Closed Sunday and Monday

Conviviality, great cooking, and one of the best wine lists in Sonoma County make Syrah a must if you are traveling to California wine country. Josh Silvers and his team provide an experience, not just food. The menu is disciplined, usually ten small plates and eight mains. It might include lamb, beef, chicken, or fish caught off the Sonoma coast, or perhaps some locally raised duck. The cheese menu has thirteen different offerings, many made by local producers. And the chef's tasting menu (four or seven courses) allows Silvers to showcase his considerable talent.

Underwood Bar & Bistro
9113 Graton Road
Graton
(707) 823-7023

Willow Wood Market Cafe
9020 Graton Road
Graton
(707) 823-0233

If you find yourself in the West County village of Graton, you need not be concerned about getting a decent meal. Chef Matthew Greenbaum and partner Sally Spittles have created two establishments that provide you with an abundance of choices.

The newer of the two establishments, Underwood Bar & Bistro, has an extensive wine and cocktail selection and a delicious tapas menu. Across the street, the more casual Willow Wood Market Café serves breakfast, lunch, and dinner most days. This decade-old cafe offers hearty Mediterranean sandwiches and polenta dishes, and you will always find a selection of seasonal daily specials.

Willi's Seafood and Raw Bar
403 Healdsburg Avenue
Healdsburg
(707) 433-9191
Closed Tuesday

The middle child of Mark and Terri Stark's three-restaurant mini-conglomerate, Willi's Seafood and Raw Bar is not your typical Wine Country restaurant, with pages and pages of wines from small local producers and menus featuring artisan producers. Instead, along with a nice selection of wines, Willi's features a full bar with potent cocktails like mojitos and martinis. The menu may seem a bit incongruous in the heart of Sonoma County, but it recalls Mark Stark's Chesapeake Bay roots. Impeccably fresh seafood is presented in a number of ways, including a daily ceviche. With its dark walls and pressed tin ceilings, its secluded booths and multilevel dining area, Willi's interior is reminiscent of a New Orleans chowder house. The place has become a bit of a local social center, and patrons often spill out onto the open-air patio in the front.

Zazu

3535 Guerneville Road, at Willowside Road
Santa Rosa
(707) 523-4814

Located in a cozy, funky little cottage at the corner of Guerneville and Willowside roads, Zazu is eclectically decorated with copper-topped tables, antique mirrors on the walls, and a long counter where you can peek into the kitchen as you dine on the exceptional and creative food served up by Chef-Owners John Stewart and Duskie Edwards. In addition to sourcing from local providers, they use the eggs from their own chickens and cure all their own meats in-house. There is a large selection of small plates to choose from, as well as the beautifully prepared and presented big plates.

NEIGHBORHOOD & CITY INDEX

SAN FRANCISCO

EAST BAY

HALF MOON BAY & SANTA CRUZ

MARIN COUNTY

SOUTH BAY

ALPHABETICAL INDEX

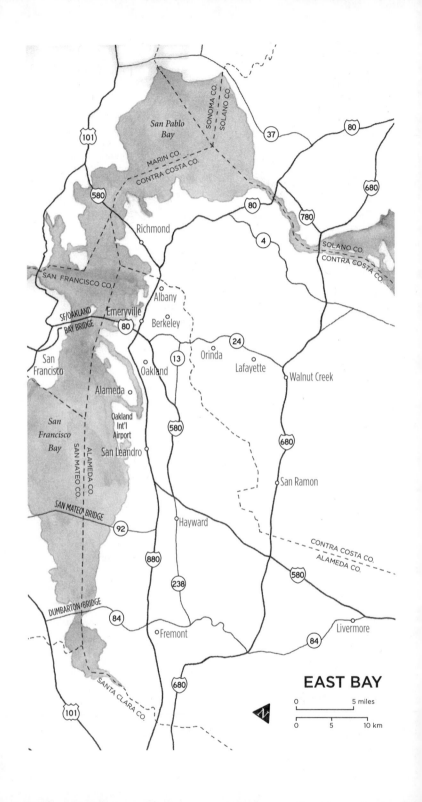

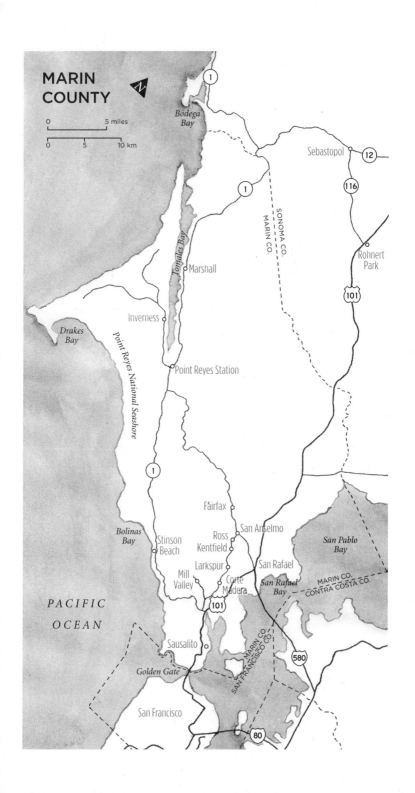

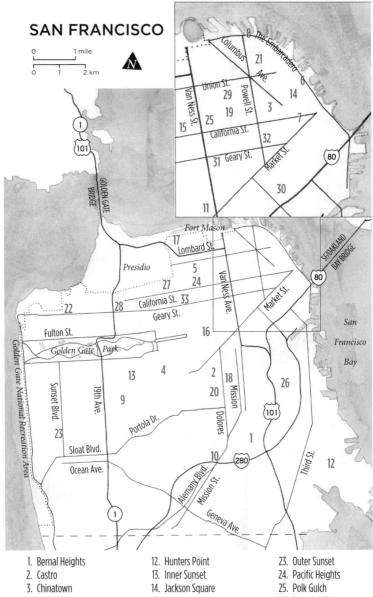

SAN FRANCISCO

0   1 mile

0   1   2 km

N

1. Bernal Heights
2. Castro
3. Chinatown
4. Cole Valley
5. Cow Hollow
6. Embarcadero
7. Financial District
8. Fisherman's Wharf
9. Forest Hills
10. Glen Park
11. Hayes Valley
12. Hunters Point
13. Inner Sunset
14. Jackson Square
15. Japantown
16. Lower Haight
17. Marina
18. Mission
19. Nob Hill
20. Noe Valley
21. North Beach
22. Outer Richmond
23. Outer Sunset
24. Pacific Heights
25. Polk Gulch
26. Potrero Hill
27. Presidio Heights
28. Richmond
29. Russian Hill
30. South of Market (SOMA)
31. Tenderloin
32. Union Square
33. Western Addition

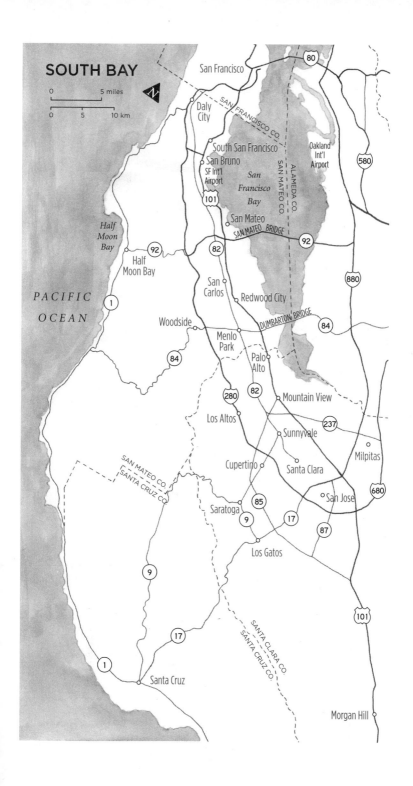

SOUTH BAY

0 —— 5 miles
0 —— 5 —— 10 km

San Francisco

Daly City

San Francisco Co.

South San Francisco
San Bruno
SF Int'l Airport

Oakland Int'l Airport

Alameda Co.

San Mateo Co.

San Francisco Bay

San Mateo
SAN MATEO BRIDGE

Half Moon Bay

Half Moon Bay

San Carlos
Redwood City

Woodside

DUMBARTON BRIDGE

PACIFIC OCEAN

Menlo Park

Palo Alto

Mountain View

Los Altos

Sunnyvale

Cupertino
Santa Clara

Milpitas

San Mateo Co.
Santa Cruz Co.

Saratoga

San Jose

Los Gatos

Santa Clara Co.
Santa Cruz Co.

Santa Cruz

Morgan Hill

CHELSEA GREEN
PUBLISHING

the politics and practice of sustainable living

SUSTAINABLE LIVING has
many facets. Chelsea Green's
celebration of the sustainable
arts has led us to publish
trend-setting books about
innovative building tech-
niques, regenerative forestry,
organic gardening and agriculture, solar electricity and
renewable energy, local and
bioregional democracy, and
whole foods and Slow food.

For more information about
Chelsea Green, publishing
partner of Slow Food U.S.A.,
visit our Web site at
www.chelseagreen.com and
find more than 200 books on
the politics and practice of
sustainable living.

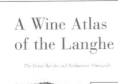

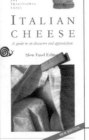